'Let me recommend [this] hilarious new book . . . All of [the names] make you happy to belong to a people who believe it is their patriotic duty not to take themselves too seriously . . . It really is laugh-out-loud funny.'
Allison Pearson, *Daily Mail*

'I can see no possible justification for a puerile and tasteless compendium that panders to the lowest barrel-scraping grade of British bodily-functions "humour" – apart from the fact that it may well make you laugh like a hyena.'
Boyd Tonkin, *Independent*

'Hours of fun.' James Doorne, *Bizarre* magazine

'Amazingly, this is the first ever complete collection of unlikely-but-true British names. Handily assembled in appropriately-titled chapters such as Private Functions and Nature or Torture, the list includes everyone from Dick Brain to Hugh Fatty to Jemima Panties.'
Henry Sutton, *Daily Mirror*

'This compendium of amusing British names is as smutty as its title promises.'
Sameer Rahim, *Daily Telegraph*

'It goes without saying that, as a *Sunday Times* reader, you have highbrow tastes in comic writing. You enjoy a bit of Aristophanes now and again, and can't get enough of the satires of Juvenal. So I hesitate to mention a title called *Potty, Fartwell & Knob*. The best jokes come at you unexpectedly, and so it is with this list of real people with extraordinary names . . . I defy you not to laugh. Some names are rather rude and would require lavish use of the asterisk, but I think I can mention Fanny Tickler (born 1816) and Nancy Boys (born 1842). And wouldn't you like to know more about Mr William Tippen Useless, not to mention Thigh McKay, Herbert Sherbert and Mary Fairy?'
Roland White, *Sunday Times*

Potty, Fartwell & Knob

Extraordinary BUT TRUE NAMES of British People

Russell Ash

headline

First published in 2007
by HEADLINE PUBLISHING GROUP

First published in paperback in 2008
by HEADLINE PUBLISHING GROUP

3

Cataloguing in Publication Data is available from the British Library

ISBN 978 0 7553 1655 7

Designed by Bernard Higton

Printed and bound in Great Britain by
Clays Ltd, St Ives plc

Headline's policy is to use papers that are natural, renewable and recyclable
products and made from wood grown in sustainable forests. The logging and
manufacturing processes are expected to conform to the environmental
regulations of the country of origin.

HEADLINE PUBLISHING GROUP
An Hachette Livre UK Company
338 Euston Road
London NW1 3BH

www.headline.co.uk
www.hachettelivre.co.uk

pottyfartwellandknob@headline.co.uk
www.pottyfartwellandknob.co.uk

To anyone who has ever had a strange name

Contents

Nutty Haddock

Introduction

Pottier, Fartier & Knobier

The book in your hands could be regarded as the literary equivalent of the 'director's cut'. Authors are rarely granted the privilege of re-visiting their books, but in this instance I have been given the opportunity to revise, expand and enhance the text of the hardback, originally published in 2007, adding several new sections and hundreds more names. It is, in fact, Pottier[1], Fartier[2] and Knobier[3].

Censored!

Following the publication of the original book, I undertook a number of radio interviews – although some interviewers were concerned about which names I could and could not say on air pre-watershed, which, on a couple of occasions, extended to the title of the book. One interview for a national newspaper was tragically spiked when its delivery unfortunately coincided with an editorial clampdown on a perceived tide of 'smut', and thus appeared a deliberate act of rebellion on the part of the journalist. (It reminded me of the incident in Evelyn Waugh's *Vile Bodies*, when gossip columnist Adam Fenwick-Symes' editor tells him under no circumstances to mention Count Cincinnati, Espinosa's or green bowler hats, subcontracts to someone who reports that

---

[1] *Sabrina Pottier, born c.1838; died Hackney, London, 1891*
[2] *Samuel Fartier, died Lambeth London, 1838*
[3] *John Knobier, born Norfolk, c.1839 (Catton, Norfolk, 1841 census)*

Count Cincinnati has been seen going into Espinosa's in a green bowler hat – and is promptly sacked.)

People who bought this . . .

Like many authors, I became obsessed with my rankings on Amazon, especially when it hit No. 1 in obvious categories, such as History and Personal Names, but was also bizarrely identified as No. 1 in the category Humour: Fiction (even though it isn't) and Crime, Thrillers and Mystery (outranking Rankin, as it were). Amazon's 'people who bought this also bought that' items are usually other books by the same author, or at least in the same genre, but this is not the case with *Potty, Fartwell & Knob*, whose readers are a much more eclectic lot. People who bought it apparently also bought an oven thermometer, a 500 gigabyte hard drive, an Amy Winehouse CD, cowboy boots, flip-flops, disco lights, slimming tablets, false nails, a laundry hamper, a branding iron (for barbecues, I think), a Cliff Richard calendar and a set of Nigella Lawson measuring spoons (very useful, if you need to measure a Nigella Lawson, although a measuring jug might be better). What this tells us about purchasers of the book – people like you, in fact – is frankly unfathomable.

Naming and shaming

As well as such new sections as dyslexic names and anagrams, palindromes and ananyms (reverse spellings, such as Trebor for Robert) – which diverge somewhat from the 'accidental' humour of most of the names, but are more common than might be supposed – I have added more strangely apt married couples, more modern names (without sources – I don't want kids being bullied at school, whereas adults can fend for themselves), and some choice new discoveries throughout. This expansion has been enabled in part by my ongoing quest for ever-sillier names – the research has been so much fun that it can hardly be considered work – but also through the generous submissions of readers who sent in innumerable entries: people were happy to give me names dredged from their own family history researches, but equally delighted to shop their friends and relatives, work and school colleagues; there were even instances of teachers betraying their pupils. Among those with a silly name to share, there is clearly not a shred of honour.

To begin at the beginning

Let's back-pedal a bit. In 2005, Renée Jackaman, an archivist then at the Cornwall Record Office (now at the Devon Record Office), produced a 'Silly Names List' (see page 336), gleaned from their files, which included such gems as Philadelphia Bunnyface, Boadicia Basher and Ostrich Pockinghorn. Cobbledick, a surname from my wife's Cornish ancestry, was included. I myself come from a family where such first names as Claudius, Horace and Sarjeant were commonly inflicted on my ancestors. It made me wonder if, possibly, there might be a book to be compiled on unusual British names. I am pleased to say the answer proved to be a resounding 'yes'.

Fiction and fact

When I told my family and friends I was compiling a book of strange but true British names, almost all of them responded with, 'I was at school with someone called . . .' Some – though, sadly, not all – of the names they suggested turned out to be true, but I soon discovered that those that were represented only the tip of the onomastic* iceberg. Beneath the surface, hidden away in parish registers, birth, marriage and death records and official censuses, lie countless millions of undiscovered names spanning nine hundred years (the earliest here dates from 1109), from which I have excavated the few thousand that appear in this book.

And what names! Britain, the country that gave us toilets made by Thomas Crapper and a James Bond actor called Roger Moore, has a long tradition of odd and *double entendre* names that feature in our literature and comedy. The names invented, or adapted, by Charles Dickens represent just one stop on a

* *Relating to names*

comedic branch line that in the twentieth century gave us the Starkadders of *Cold Comfort Farm*; *The Goons* (Grytpype-Thynne and Willium Cobblers); the *Carry On* films (W. C. Boggs, Sidney Ruff-Diamond, *et al*); *Round the Horne* (J. Peasmold Gruntfuttock, Sid Rumpole, Dame Celia Molestrangler); *Monty Python* (Gervais Brookhamster, Raymond Luxury-Yacht – pronounced Throatwobbler Mangrove), Rowan Atkinson's school register sketch from *The Secret Policeman's Ball* (which includes several – Dint, Nibble, Mattock and Soda – that actually exist), and so on. However, even Dickens' most fanciful Sweedlepipes, Honeythunders and Fezziwigs do not come close to the reality of the aberrant but genuine first names, surnames and name combinations you are about to encounter.

Such factors as our tradition of eccentricity, linguistic changes, attempts by parents to come up with an original name and the blunders of illiterate scribes have combined to create the massive names catalogue of Britain, and *Potty, Fartwell & Knob* is the first ever attempt to present a selection of the strangest examples from this remarkable collection.

'There's one born every minute'

This has not been true in the UK for over a century: today, more than 1.2 babies are born every minute in England and Wales alone, and every one of them has to be named.

Some are born with strange surnames, some are blessed, or cursed, with unusual first or middle names. Occasionally we encounter such 'joke' names as Ben Dover (though there have been several real ones), or news reports of peculiar but inadvertent names, like the couple who as recently as 2004 innocently named their son 'Drew Peacock', before people started to say, 'You called him *what* . . . ?'

Aside from a few whimsical names – some bowing to the inevitable (if your surname is Christmas, you may as well call your kid 'Merry' – everyone else will) – ludicrously long examples and anagrams and related names, the majority were accidental, not deliberately designed to attract attention or raise a laugh. The ever-crazier names inflicted on the offspring of celebrities and the bizarre excesses of deed poll name changes have been avoided. I have also resisted delving into the realm of 'nominative determinism', the tendency for people to end up in professions appropriate to their names, as in the style of the famous I. Pullem, dentist, although I have included the occasional serendipitous discovery, such as Abraham Ball, castrator, such ironies as the birth of George Fatman in Broadbottom, Cheshire, and the weddings of Sherlock and Holmes, Slack and Bottom and Fucks and Allott and their ilk.

Where did these names come from?

Many surnames were originally descriptive – including those that refer to an individual's character or physical defects or are otherwise insulting – but the embarrassment associated with such names or those containing a *double entendre* depends on literacy and communications, which, before the modern era, were both undeveloped. Until recent times, most people were born, married and died within a few miles of their home. They probably could not read or write, so never sent or received letters, did not have any forms to fill out or phone calls to answer, did not travel abroad and hence did not need passports, so if someone happened to be called William Bollocks, it was perfectly possible for him to keep it quiet from the world beyond his family circle and so avoid being the subject of derision.

Some of the oddities result from the incongruity of the first and second names or the perhaps unwitting choice of a first name that when written as an initial teams aptly or inaptly with the surname – hence I. Pod and C. Rap (and I write as one whose name may be abbreviated to 'R. Ash').

Some bearers of strange names were perhaps immigrants whose names were unremarkable in their own countries, such as Low Fat, who married in Cardiff in 1905. However, other than such individuals, or a few immigrants who fetch up in British censuses, all the names are of British people.

Source material

After pornography, genealogy has become one of the most popular uses of the Internet, and it is only through access to online material that I have been able to research and compile this book – previously it would have been well-nigh impossible.

To unearth these names I have mined parish registers for records of baptisms, marriages and burials, wills and other legal documents, newspapers and phone books. The registration of births, marriages and deaths in England and Wales has been compulsory only since 1837. National censuses have been held every ten years since 1841 (though we currently have free access to those up to 1901 only).

These sources present information of variable detail: in the case of some baptisms, we may know the names of one or both parents; with marriages sometimes the name of the spouse; and with deaths and burials we often know the age. Census returns identify professions, but give ages rather than dates of birth, so birth years are *circa*, rather than precise.

Eureka!*

The frisson of discovering these names has been a constant pleasure. Surely no one can ever have been called Fanny Plenty – it's just too similar to *Goldfinger*'s Pussy Galore or *Austin Powers'* homage, Alotta Fagina – but, amazingly, there are several. Dick Head? Of course. Penis Hardon? Naturally. It is therefore almost disappointing to find that there is, for example, a Mary Dupp, but not a May Dupp, a John Time, but not a Justin Time, and not a single Helena Handcart. If only their parents had had more imagination.

Surely, some mistake?

Some peculiar names may have resulted from an error or mistranscription. In 1857 the Registrar-General reported that of 159,097 couples signing the marriage registers in England and

---

* *Eureka Jones, born Kingswinford, Staffordshire, c.1876*

Wales, 115,085 men wrote their names, but 44,013 (28 per cent of the total) made their marks. Among women, 97,332 signed and 61,765 (38 per cent) made their marks, the total rising to more than half in some counties. When so many of the adult population of the country could not even write their own names, it is no surprise that the registers contain some bizarre spellings, phonetic versions or inspired guesses. It is often impossible to discern whether an apparent dyslexic spelling of a name – some examples of which are included – was a clumsy error or a ploy to come up with a new name.

The census returns to which we have access are copies, not the originals, which were destroyed long ago, in handwriting that ranges from elegant copperplate to spidery scrawl, and contain many obvious errors. These have often been compounded when transcribed yet again into electronic databases. One of my own ancestors, whose not especially unusual first name was 'Drusilla', appears in the 1861 census as 'Priscilla' and in 1871 as 'Omsilla', while her daughter, also called Drusilla, appears as 'Prusella' in 1861 and 'Orusilla' in the 1871 census. Thus Pubica Prestridge (1841 census) turns out to be Isabella Partridge and Joseph Prickhead (1901 census) is disappointingly Joseph Pritchard. To avoid such traps, wherever possible original documents have been checked and, as a result, what might have been some splendidly dippy names, eliminated. A few may have slipped through the net, and I will be delighted to receive any corrections.

Census spoofs

There is evidence of occasional spoof entries in census returns. They were in all probability created by bored transcribers, such as the person who in the 1851 census of Islington, London, changed the name of a missionary called John Santo by the subtle addition of the word 'Clause'. The best-documented is perhaps the imaginative cast of characters inhabiting a Chelsea lodging house in 1881. It included Charles Bigtop – tiger slayer; Gustave Stinkpoor – turpentine boiler; Tanta Toppie – boy hairdresser; Henry Dandelion – horsehair plaiter; William Pitt –

clown; Cornelius Duskall – oat sorter, aged 91; Joseph Brown – urinal attendant; and 90-year-old Jimy [*sic*] Hillad – peacock carrier. Not far away, at the fictitious Paddington address of '16 Acacia Gardens', we find a 52-year-old 'international playboy', his 97-year-old wife and son (occupation – 'ponce') as well as a cosmopolitan army of servants, among them a Timbuktu-born butler, Persian governess, Russian gardener and a footman from Afghanistan.

Naming fashions

Naming fashions come and go over time. Though an unscientific sampling, certain years seem to have been especially strong for silly multiple names: 1842 and 1843, for example, produced Elizabeth Wrench Wrench, Mary Ann Morecock Morecock, Hairby Rook Rook, Harriot Whore Whore, Raper Raper and Edmund Crisp Crick Crick.

Certain locations are also notable for the oddity of their inhabitants' names: St George Hanover Square, London (the location of the baptisms and marriages of many members of my own family), registered such names as Charles Penis Horn and Emma Dyke Dyke. I can also corroborate the observations of researchers since the Victorian period who noted that Bury St Edmunds, Suffolk and Guildford, Surrey have a disproportionate abundance of strange names. I would also nominate Sculcoates, Yorkshire; Mitford, Norfolk; Portsea Island, Hampshire, and Blything, Suffolk.

Some names were not considered odd when they were created, but language marches on and linguistic changes mean that certain people find themselves lumbered with weird or *double entendre* names. As a result of such changes and increasing awareness, certain names have fallen out of favour or bizarre names altered and so filtered out of Britain's names corpus – which may explain, for example, why there is hardly anyone with the surname Titty after about 1830, and why the once hugely popular Fanny (as a given name, rather than a nickname for girls born 'Frances') all but vanished by the First World War. And you don't meet many people nowadays who have taken the bold decision to call their baby 'Gay'.

The uniqueness of some first names can be fairly simply explained as an aberration that never caught on. Only half a dozen people seem to have received 'Spearmint' as a first or middle name – all but one of them in 1906 – while only one person appears ever to have been baptized 'Bovril' (Bovril Simpson, who married in West Ham, 1911).

So good they named them twice

Some names are the human equivalents of the tautonyms encountered in the world of biology, where the genus and species names are identical, as with *Alces alces* (the moose), *Cygnus cygnus* (the whooper swan), *Ratus ratus* and *Gorilla gorilla* (you'll never guess). Can it just be down to pride in one's family name that leads so many parents to repeat it as their child's middle name – hence those noted above, along with Mabel Sexey Sexey, Henry Basher Basher, Bold Bold, James Brook Dust Dust, Lucinda Legassick Legassick and Albert Fluck Fluck?

Cruelty to children

It is impossible to fathom the psychology behind many naming decisions. Take, for example, those who have a weird name – Rhoda Boat, Henry Fuckalls, Henrietta Prick, Epaphreditus Eatty, Eva Brick, Prudentia Doolittle, Seraphim Hooker, Humiliation Hinde, Hercules Anthill, Golden Balls, Enoch Bottom Bray, Kitty Moose, Noble Wasp, Maude Ship, Finett Pissy, Lunabella C. Heagorty, Dansey Dansey, Large Bee and Grimwood Death, to name but a few – and promptly give their own offspring the same name. Are they proud of the names and desperate to see them carried on to the next generation, or is there perhaps a sense of, 'I had to put up with it – now you can too . . .'?

Names occasionally serve as a parental commentary on the latest and perhaps unwelcome addition to the family, hence Lewis Unexpected Smith, Not Wanted James Colvill, No More Durrant, One Too Many Gouldstone, Finale Eldridge, Franklin

Addenda Wilkins and (allegedly) That's It Who'd Have Thought It Restell.

The servant problem

Census returns in particular reveal that many of the bearers of 'embarrassing' names are servants. This is partly explained by their sheer numbers: at the time of the 1901 census there were 1,285,072 female servants out of a total female population of 16,804,347 in England and Wales – in other words, one woman in every thirteen was in service. There is also more than a hint of discrimination: masters and mistresses would often dub their staff with jokey or easily recalled variants of their real names, or nicknames that duly found their way into census returns.

Where have all the funny names gone?

Anyone undertaking genealogical research cannot fail to be moved by the constant reminders of high infant mortality before the twentieth century. All too often a birth or baptism is rapidly followed by a record of his or her death, so there was no chance of their passing their surname on by marriage, or, as noted above, by handing it on to their children as an often unwelcome gift.

Unusual surnames borne by women were lost when they were changed through marriage. In the 1841 census, there were fifteen people bearing the unfortunate surname 'Myass'. One of the last recorded, Ann Myass, married in 1886, thereby changing her name. By the time of the 1901 census, there were none. Or consider John Scum: we know he married in 1838, but there is no record of any Scum kids – did he and Mrs Scum not have any little Scums, or did they perhaps change their surname to something less pejorative?

Name changes are by no means a modern phenomenon: Joshua Bug's decision to change his name to Norfolk Howard was announced in *The Times* on 26 June 1862. Or John Robert Shittler, born in 1851 in Wimborne, Dorset, who married Martha Reeve in Kingston, Surrey, in 1877. Love conquers almost everything, but maybe not quite enough to spend the rest of your life as a

Shittler, and so, in 1884, Mr Shittler changed his family name to Rowden. Similarly, British people with the surname Hitler or Goering changed theirs during the Second World War, just as the Battenbergs had transmogrified into the Mountbattens in the First.

A sort of natural selection may have eliminated some surnames: most women would prefer not to marry if it meant thereby acquiring an embarrassing surname, so the name was not perpetuated, though some were not too lucky in their choices, often trading a ghastly surname for a worse one, as did Mary Madcap when in 1782 she married John Bastard. Then there was the girl with the curious name of Suck Stokes: at the time, perhaps no one gave a thought to the fact that, by her marriage to William Cocken (St Sepulchre, London, 1814), she would become Suck Cocken, and some forethought might have saved a girl who was allegedly but charmingly named Wild Rose from the unfortunate combination that resulted from her marriage to a Mr Bull. And pause for a moment to consider the devotion of Ann Smith, who loved William Fuck enough to marry him.

Past and present

Potty, Fartwell & Knob takes us on a tour of the major cities and tiny hamlets of a Britain peopled by so many oddly named characters that in some respects it appears another country or the setting of some surreal sitcom. Yet, while names of the past inevitably form the bulk of those that follow, the story has not ended: names such as Radar Oo, Princess Diana Frempong, Paris Harris, Phoenix Claw Unicorn, Jago Pirate Turner and Icicle Star Crumplin all date from the twenty-first century.

Finally, don't forget, I had only to disinter these names, and you have only to read – and, I hope – enjoy them. These people spent their lives with them!

Notes

- The humour derived from some names depends on the not unreasonable expectation that their owners' initials were used on occasion, Richard was commonly known as 'Dick', Philip as 'Phil', and so on.

- Some rely on their pronunciation – the seemingly innocuous 'Mike Hunt', for example, sounds like – well, you get the idea. If you don't get them, try saying them out loud (though perhaps not too loud, and not in a public place).

- Gender is noted where it is not obvious from the name or context, but the sex of some is impossible to interpolate from the available data.

- Apologies for the prevalence of Fannies but it was once one of the most common female names – and it is very funny.

- Especially when infant mortality was high, baptisms usually followed soon after births. Baptisms were entered in the parish register, so we know the date and location, and often the names of both parents; we generally don't know, but can reasonably assume that the place of birth was in the same locality.

- Place of birth is noted where known, but it is either omitted or given at county level only in some sources, such as early censuses; 'np' means no place and 'nd' no date is indicated in the source.

- The location of a registered birth is often the registration district – usually the nearest town with a register office – but not necessarily the exact place of birth, although these are recorded in census returns with either greater (down to parish level) or lesser ('London' or 'Dorset', for example) precision.

- 'Census' is for England unless otherwise stated.

- Locations and county names are as they were at the time of the record – in some instances, places may now be in different counties: for example, Barnet moved from Hertfordshire (1837–51) to Middlesex (1852–1946) and back to Hertfordshire (1946–65) before becoming part of Greater London (1965–present); Wokingham was in Wiltshire until 1845, but is now in Berkshire. Readers may be surprised to see occasional Irish entries, but from 1801 to 1922 Ireland was part of the United Kingdom.

Warning

The Author and Publishers can accept no responsibility if you use this book to choose your baby's name.

Russell Ash
Lewes, 2008
www.RussellAsh.com

Chapter One

Sue Age
Born Glasgow, Lanarkshire, c.1849 (Glasgow, 1851 Scotland census)

Zacharias Barf
Married Mary Cass, Lythe, Yorkshire, 15 October 1775

Anita Bath
Married Keith Clarke, Shrewsbury, Shropshire, 2001

Boadicea Belch
Baptized Rickmansworth, Hertfordshire, 2 May 1808

Alfred Ming Belcher
Born Henley-on-Thames, Oxfordshire, 1881

Burp Bendon
Born np, Somerset, c.1771 (Old Cleeve, Somerset, 1841 census)

Selina Bidet
Born Clerkenwell, London, 1839

James Craps Brown
Born Manchester, Lancashire, 1843

Urina Buckett
Born Isle of Wight, 1867

Ricard Burpy
Baptized Wesleyan Methodist, Frome,
Somerset, 26 October 1817

Shat Butler
(Male) Born np, Worcestershire, c.1834
(Oswaldslow, Worcestershire, 1841 census)

Farting Clack
Born London, c.1863 (Walthamstow, Essex, 1871 census)

Christopher Cockshit
Baptized Clayton with Frickley, Yorkshire, 14 October 1771

Turd Collar
Born np, Ireland, c.1821 (St George Hanover Square, London, 1841 census)

Iron Crapp
Born Idle, Yorkshire, c.1886 (Eccleshill, Yorkshire, 1901 census)

Arthur Brown Crapper
Born Sheffield, Yorkshire, 1867

Love Crapping
Married Edward Addicot, Brixham, Devon, 17 February 1712

Shitty Dikins
Born np, Buckinghamshire, c.1828 (Swanborne, Buckinghamshire, 1841 census)

Emete Douche
Married John Mantle, Crewkerne, Somerset, 11 January 1601

Fanny Dribble
Born Mile End, London, c.1836 (Bethnal Green, London, 1901 census)

Latrine Dubois
Born Lewisham, London, c.1890 (Lewisham, 1891 census)

Yelle Minnis Dump
Married Euphan Mitchell, Bo'Ness, West Lothian, 27 December 1660

John T. Dung
Born Coveney, Cambridge, c.1859 (Witcham, Cambridge, 1881 census)

Dick Fart
Married Susannah Blank, Chivelstone, Devon, 16 September 1788

Mary Fartarsley
Born Liverpool, Lancashire, c.1826 (Walton-on-the-Hill,
Lancashire, 1851 census)

John Fartas
Married Ales Hogg, St Nicholas, Newcastle upon Tyne,
Northumberland, 20 November 1651

Betsey Farting
Born Samford, Suffolk, 1843

Teresa Fartwangler
Born Usk, Monmouthshire, c.1828
(Cardiff, 1871 Wales census)

Mary Ann Fartwell
Born Wellington, Somerset, c.1829 (Thorne St Margaret, Somerset, 1851 census)

Fanny Farty
Born Rock, Worcestershire, c.1842 (Tenbury, Worcestershire, 1861 census)

Manure Ford
Born Rickmansworth, Hertfordshire, c.1831 (Harefield, Middlesex, 1851 census)

P. Freely
(Male) Born Liverpool, Lancashire, 1841

Farty Gladwish
Born Hastings, Sussex, c.1882 (Hastings, 1901 census)

Fanny Gush
Baptized Budleigh Salterton, Devon, 1 November 1871

Toilet Halkyard
(Female) Born Oldham, Lancashire, c.1839 (Northowram, Yorkshire, 1871 census)

Fartina Henwood
(Male) Born Rodbaston, Cheshire, c.1796 (Cheadle, Cheshire, 1851 census)

S. Hit
(Female) Born London, c.1862 (Kensington, London, 1871 census)

Emily Spew Hole
Born Barton Regis, Gloucestershire, 1885

Ellen Shitehead Holmes
Born Sheffield, Yorkshire, 1862

Urinal James
(Female) Born Llanllwni, Carmarthenshire, c.1889 (Llanllwni, 1891 Wales census)

Hannah Tinkle Jeffrey
Died Sunderland, Durham, 1838

Pissy Jordon
Born Manchester, Lancashire, c.1894 (Manchester, 1901 census)

Hew Lav
Baptized Wemyss, Fife, 30 October 1687

Fanny May Leak
Born Poplar, London, 1886

Willy Leak
Married Marjorie Homer, Rowley Regis, Staffordshire, 1 December 1576

Loo Loo
Born np, c.1877; died Greenwich, London, 1904

David Urine Looker
Born Swansea, Glamorgan, 1909

Sarah Pissey Loud
Married Bath, Somerset, 1874

Martha Bog McCall
Born np, Scotland, c.1872 (Hammersmith, London, 1891 census)

Patrick McFart
Born np, Ireland, c.1828 (New Monkland, Lanarkshire, 1851 Scotland census)

Willy McPee
Born Wigtown, Dumfries, c.1781 (Hackney, London, 1861 census)

William Widdle Moseley
Died Derby, 1854

Patience Muck
Baptized St Kew, Cornwall, 1 January 1779

Nathanael [*sic*] Odour
Married Sophia Chinick, St John the Evangelist, Whitwell-on-the-Hill,
Yorkshire, 18 October 1818

Poo Out
Died Stepney, London, 1888

Gleaner Grace Outhouse
Born Mutford, Suffolk, 1884

Lou Paper
(Female) Born Watford, Hertfordshire, c.1858
(Lambeth, London, 1891 census)

Piss Fisher Parkinson
Born np, Ireland, c.1781 (Holborn, London, 1841 census)

Caroline Eliza Passwater
Born Greenwich, Kent, 1861

Shit Paul
Born np, c.1811 (St Marylebone, London, 1841 census)

William Shit Payne
Born St Clement Danes, London, c.1799 (Shoreditch, London, 1861 census)
*'Shit' appears to have been added to the census return as an afterthought –
perhaps he did something to upset the enumerator.*

Ada Pee
Born Hereford, 1866

Pleasant Pee
(Female) Born Redgrave, Suffolk, c.1811 (Greenwich, Kent, 1871 census)

Thomas Peeless
Married Holborn, London, 1893

Bridget Phlegm
Married Dudley, Staffordshire, 1851

Adeliza Piddle
Baptized Holy Trinity, Gosport, Hampshire, 12 November 1803

Peter Piddle
Baptized Fowey, Cornwall, 2 April 1649

Elizabeth Piss
Married Robert Colt, Aldenham, Hertfordshire, c.1530

Emma Pisser
Married Robert Raven, St Anne, Soho, London, 31 December 1865

Dick Pissing
Baptized St Paul, Canterbury, Kent, 26 May 1705

Ellis Poo Poo
Born Leeds, Yorkshire, 1842

Penticost Pooe
Baptized Quethiock, Cornwall, 10 June 1576

Sarah Jane Soft Pooer
Born Byers Green, Durham, c.1893 (Byers Green, 1901 census)

Apostle Poop
Died Manchester, Lancashire, 1871

Florence Poopy
Born Yarmouth, Norfolk, c.1875 (Kingston upon Hull, Yorkshire, 1901 census)

John Chambers Potts
Born Tynemouth, Northumberland, 1854

Betty Potty
Died Clitheroe, Lancashire, 1870

Thomas Numbertwo Poulten
Born Holborn, London, 1892

Frank Privy
Born np, Devon, c.1854 (Horfield, Gloucestershire, 1881 census)

Percilla Puke
Married John Stawslee, Crediton, Devon, 2 February 1673

C. Rap
(Female) Born Bethnal Green, London, c.1831
(Bethnal Green, 1881 census)

Jimmy Riddle
Born Melrose, Midlothian, 19 March 1648

Shitwell Rogers
(Male) Born Cowick, Yorkshire, c.1827
(Ackworth, Yorkshire, 1881 census)

Lou Roll
Born Uxbridge, Middlesex, 1902

Enoch Shite
Born Pelsall, Staffordshire, c.1885
(Pelsall, 1901 census)

Thomas Shitt
Married Anne Eaton, Wellington, Shropshire,
16 October 1725

Cardilia Shitter
(Female) Born np, c.1833 (Fawley, Hampshire, 1841 census)

Gertrude Shitty
Born 'foreign parts', c.1829 (Somers Town, London, 1841 census)

Sarah Sick
Baptized Saxby, Leicestershire, 26 May 1811

Bogs Simons
Died Maidstone, Kent, 1853

Susan Slime
Born Dublin, Ireland, c.1820 (Islington, London, 1881 census)

Atty Sneeze
(Female) Born np, Ireland, c.1838 (Oldham, Lancashire, 1861 census)

Ann Sniff
Baptized St Nicholas, Liverpool, Lancashire, 4 March 1807

Betty Snot
Born np, Worcestershire, c.1796 (Worcester, 1841 census)

Rice Spew
Married Katherine Loughes, St Martin, Worcester,
Staffordshire, 1 May 1706

Crink Spittle
(Female) Born Stourbridge, Worcestershire, 1874

Richard Goodluck Spittle
Born Kingston, Surrey, 1903

Brown Spray
Born Thorne, Yorkshire, 1874

Dick Sprinkles
Born Castle Thorpe, Buckinghamshire, c.1804 (Castle Thorpe, 1871 census)

Ashford Squirts
(Male) Born Wellow, Nottinghamshire, c.1851
(Greasley, Nottinghamshire, 1871 census)

Sarah Squit
Married Thomas Wright, St Anne, Soho, London, 8 May 1717

Joshua Stink
Married Mary Bondock, St James, Duke's Place, London, 2 September 1686

Charles Stinker
Died Portsea Island, Hampshire, 1875

Shitty Strange
Born Haselbury, Dorset, c.1844 (Haselbury, 1851 census)

Betty Sweat
Married James Thompson, St Mary, Lancaster, Lancashire, 15 January 1776

Mary Sweaty
Baptized St Mary's, Aylesbury, Buckinghamshire, 27 April 1623

Susan Jane Puke Syms
Born Totnes, Devon, 1844

Sydney Shitehead Thompson
Born Leeds, Yorkshire, c.1900 (Leeds, 1901 census)

Ulalia Tinkle
Married Henry Stephens, Littleham by Bideford, Devon, 29 December 1699

Patrick Toilet
Born Blackburn, Lancashire, 1871 (Blackburn, 1871 census)

Latrine Topping
Born Warrington, Lancashire, c.1871 (Warrington, 1881 census)

Dick Trickle
Born np, Lancashire, c.1781 (Prescot, Lancashire, 1841 census)
His son was also called Dick Trickle.

Lancelot Shite B. Tristram
Born St George Hanover Square, London, 1898

Thomas Turd
Baptized St Matthew, Bethnal Green, London, 19 October 1788

Zenobia Urine
Baptized Wendron, Cornwall, 24 May 1799

Sally Vates
Born Billings, Lancashire, 12 August 1764

Thomas Dung Voce
Born Bourne, Lincolnshire, 1842

Sue Wage
Born Wensey, Wiltshire, c.1839 (Lewisham, London, 1891 census)

Ah Wee We
Born np, c.1869; died Hartlepool, Durham, 1909

Willy Weewell
Baptized Burslem, Staffordshire, 25 September 1785

Urinal Welburn
Born Garton, Yorkshire, c.1817 (Great Driffield, Yorkshire, 1881 census)

Fanny Wetter
Born St Austell, Cornwall, 1846

William Widdle
Baptized St Mary, Woodbridge, Suffolk, 31 March 1595

Marmaduke Windass
Born Hull, Yorkshire, 11 November 1817

James Windbottom
Born Salford, Lancashire, c.1853 (Salford, 1881 census)

Theophilus Windy
Born Weston, Lincolnshire, c.1830 (Weston, 1891 census)

Maria Wiper
Born Newcastle upon Tyne, Northumberland, 1901

Enema Bottomley Wood
Born np, c.1848; died Huddersfield, Yorkshire, 1904

Chapter Two

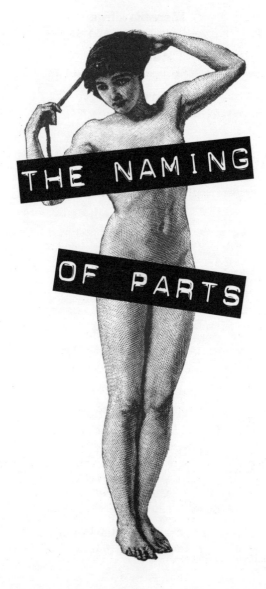

THE NAMING

OF PARTS

AN ANATOMY IN NAMES

Fanny Barelegs
Born Hitchin, Hertfordshire, 1869

Hugh Belly
Born np, Ireland, c.1801 (Liverpool, Lancashire, 1851 census)

Charles Bigfoot
Married Eleanor Cummin, Aycliffe, Durham, 15 November 1767

Annie Bodys
Born Neilston, Renfrewshire, c.1844 (Barrhead and Levern, 1901 Scotland census)
She had a daughter who was also Annie Bodys.

Septuagesima Bone Bone
Born Walsingham, Norfolk, 1875

Betty Bowel
Baptized Dalton, Dumfries, 16 February 1764

Harry Liver Brain
Born Wortley, Yorkshire, 1877

Semen Brain
(Male) Born East Dean, Gloucestershire, c.1865 (East Dean, 1901 census)

Belle Button
Born Salehurst, Sussex, c.1873 (Salehurst, 1891 census)

Rosie Cheek
Born Grays, Essex, c.1897 (Grays, 1901 census)

Thirza Chuff
Born Totnes, Devon, 1837
'Chuff' is one of those confusing slang words that, like 'Fanny',
can mean bottom or vagina.

John Thomas Colon
Born Bradford, Yorkshire, 1876

Pierce Deare
Married Elizabeth Portman, St Gregory by Paul's, London, 14 April 1635

Christopher Ears
Of Kenwyn, Cornwall (will, 1790)

Rochmar Elbow
Married John Lyon, St Martin-in-the-Fields, London, 29 May 1809

Hyman Finger
. Married Mile End, London, 1905

Rosina Knee Flower
Born Henley, Buckinghamshire, 1868

James Hoot Foot
Born Shaftesbury, Dorset, 1843

Phoebe Forehead
Baptized Shanklin, Isle of Wight, 6 April 1788

Tryphena Giblett
Born Easthampstead, Berkshire, 1859

Magdaline Gob
Married William Moncurr, Dundee, Angus, 22 June 1732

Bridget Groin
Died Bradford, Yorkshire, 1857

John Tummy Hague
Born Ecclesall Bierlow, Yorkshire, 1910

Orange Head
Born North Huish, Devon, c.1785 (Ugborough, Devon, 1861 census)

Dorothy Dimple H. Hermitage
Born Hastings, East Sussex, 1893

P. Hole
(Female) Married Wincanton, Somerset, 1842

Minnie Tongue Jags
Born Barton-upon-Irwell, Lancashire, 1886

Blanche Kidney
Born Brentford, Middlesex, 1898

I. Lash
(Male) Born Poplar, London, c.1890 (Wanstead, Essex, 1901 census)

Jemima Foot Legg
Born Dorchester, Dorset, 1841

Phelia Legg
Born np, Gloucestershire, c.1826 (Kempsford, Gloucestershire, 1841 census)

Soppy Leggs
(Female) Born Bethnal Green, London (Bethnal Green, 1901 census)

Oliver Livers
Born Birmingham, Warwickshire, c.1891 (Aston, Warwickshire, 1901 census)

Patrick Mandible
Born np, Ireland, c.1846 (Liverpool, 1881 census)

Amelia Mouth
Born Stepney, London, 1842

Naomi Nerve
Born Iden, Sussex, c.1824 (Playden, Kent, 1851 census)

Nellie Nose
Baptized St Mary Redcliffe, Bristol, Gloucestershire, 31 May 1877

Marie Ovary
Baptized Downton, Wiltshire, 4 April 1606

Lydia Pelvis
Baptized Bearstead, Kent, 24 January 1808

R. M. Pitt
(Female) Born Wolverhampton, Staffordshire, 1904

William Pulse
Died West Derby, Lancashire, 1880

Levina Sinus
Baptized Holy Trinity-Wesleyan Methodist, Shaftesbury,
Dorset, 12 September 1830

Hannah Skeleton
Born Great Boughton, Cheshire, 1867

Artery Smith
(Male) Born Bedstone, Shropshire, c.1899
(Bishops Castle, Shropshire, 1901 census)

Esther Cowley Sperm
Born np, c.1836; died Tynemouth, Northumberland, 1891

Joannes Mauritius Spleen
Baptized Gosport, Hampshire, 24 June 1789

Lymph Stanley
Born Croydon, Surrey, c.1881 (Ealing, Middlesex, 1901 census)

Caroline Stomach
Born Rotherham, Yorkshire, 1878

Lung Tack
Died West Derby, Lancashire, 1907

Jeani Talia
Born np, France, c.1864 (St Andrew, Devon, 1891 census)

Tobias Thumb
Baptized Greystoke, Cumberland, 16 August 1690

Truelove Toe
Born Barrow upon Soar, Leicestershire, 1848

Bold Tongue
Married Bury, Lancashire, 1846

Sarah Tonin
Married Thomas Clark, St Dunstan, Stepney, London, 1813

Pearl Tooth
Born Steeples, Derbyshire, 1930

Mary Jaws Turner
Born Berwick, Northumberland, 1849

Betsey Wrinkle
Married Bolton, Lancashire, 1837

PLEASANT TITTY AND HER BOSOM CHUMS

◆

Sarah Baps
Married James Linsall, Debden, Essex, 16 October 1688

Rebecca Baretitt
Born np, Lincolnshire, c.1826 (Billingborough, Lincolnshire, 1841 census)

Eliza Boobies
Married Tiverton, Devon, 1861
*Boobies is mainly a Devon name – a whole family of Boobies was
recorded in Poltimore at the time of the 1841 census.*

Edith D. Boobs
Born Wharfedale, Yorkshire, 1917

Triphena Bosom
Baptized St Mary the Virgin, Dover, Kent, nd July 1592

Jane Breast
Baptized St Matthew's, Douglas, Isle of Man, 4 February 1787

Seymour Bust
Born Halstead, Essex, 1841

Jemima Busty
Married Denis Boston, Hampton-in-Arden, Warwickshire,
25 November 1819

Myboob Bux
Born Kensington, London, 1859

Mary Buxom
Born Snitter, Northumberland, c.1840
(Bothal Demesne, Northumberland, 1861 census)

Chesty Carroll
(Male) Born Dublin, Ireland, c.1847 (Rotherham, Yorkshire, 1861 census)

Ellen Bristol Dancer
Born Stoke-on-Trent, Staffordshire, 1860

Jugs Ferner
Born np, Scotland, c.1896 (East Ham, Essex, 1901 census)

Hannah Globes
Born 26 January 1791; baptized Wentworth, Yorkshire, 6 March 1791

Emma Hooters
Born London, c.1839 (St Marylebone, London, 1851 census)

Miss Hooters was recorded in the 1851 census as a twelve-year-old nurse in the Baker Street home of bookseller and printer John G. Griffin.

Fanny Knocker
Born np, c.1829; died Dover, Kent, 1899

Lucy Mammary
Born np, Norfolk, c.1844 (Southwark, London, 1891 census)

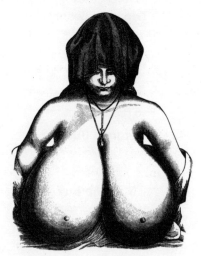

Melons Meakin
Married Basford, Nottinghamshire, 1897

Mary Melons
Married Thomas Jones, Talgarth, Breconshire, 19 February 1798

Elizabeth Nipple
Baptized St Mary Major, Exeter, Devon, 8 December 1772

Elizabeth Norks
Married Edward Nock, Aston, Warwickshire, 28 June 1758

Elsie Stitz
Born Chorlton, Lancashire, 1892

George Bunney Teat
Died Melton Mowbray, Leicestershire, 1839

Bosom Thaxter
(Male) Born Barningham, Norfolk, c.1811 (Gresham, Norfolk, 1851 census)

Tits Tillies
(Male) Born Rockingbourne, Hampshire, c.1878
(Fordingbridge, Hampshire, 1891 census)

Phebe Tit
Baptized Thundridge, Hertfordshire, 8 March 1790

Fanny Titball
Born Tetcott, Devon, c.1857 (Tetcott, 1871 census)

Willy Titcock
Born np, Bedfordshire, c.1807 (Toddington, Bedfordshire, 1851 census)

Funny Titman
Born Rowell, Northamptonshire, c.1833
(Rowell, 1851 census)

Fanny Titsworth
Born Messingham, Lincolnshire, c.1856
(Gainsborough, Lincolnshire, 1891 census)

Charles Dud Titt
Born Wandsworth, London, 1909

Sarah Tittie
Baptized Sturry, Kent, 27 December 1667

Pleasant Titty
Baptized St John, Margate, Kent, 3 April 1768
She was named after her mother, so there was a
pair of Pleasant Tittys in the family.

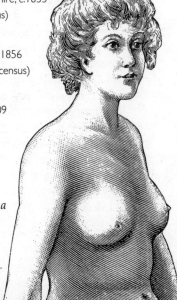

Doris Topless
Born Sculcoates, Yorkshire, 1902

Ann Udder
Married Robert Andrew, Buckland Monachorum, Devon, 5 September 1720

Allice [*sic*] Whoppers
Baptized St Nicholas, Gloucester, 22 December 1578

Juggy Williams
(Female) Married John Price, Almeley, Herefordshire, 24 May 1792

and

Juggy Williams
(Male) Baptized Llywel, Breconshire, 25 July 1819

ANUS HORRIBILIS: THE BOTTOM LINE

In his book The Compleat Practical Joker *(1953), American humorist
H. Allen Smith relates:*

*'In London, some years ago, a man named Pierce Bottom, weary of
jokes about his name, spent several days combing through the telephone
directories, seeking people who had "bottom" in their names. He found
dozens – Bottom, Bottomley, Winterbottom, Throttlebottom, Greenbottom, Sidebottom, Higginbottom, and so on. He arranged for a dinner
to be served in a sub-basement of a London building, and sent engraved
invitations to all the "bottoms". Most of them showed up, but Pierce
Bottom did not, and the guests found that each of them had to pay his
own check. The entrée was rump roast.'*

*The story's authority is somewhat undermined by the fact that there
is no evidence that anyone called 'Pierce Bottom' ever existed (not to
mention 'Throttlebottom' and 'Greenbottom'), and in all probability it
should be filed in the category of 'urban folktale'. The* Oxford
Dictionary of National Biography *credits the same tale to practical
joker Horace De Vere Cole (1881–1936), as does the biography of his
wife, Mavis. True or apocryphal? We leave you, the reader, to decide –
but there's no denying 'bottom' names are pretty funny.*

Maria S. Aas
Born London, c.1821 (Penge, Surrey, 1871 census)

Jemima Allass
Born np, c.1861; died Barnsley, Yorkshire, 1893

Fanny Allbutt
Born Lincoln, 1852

Hephzibah Ann Anus
Born City of London, 1850

Ursula Anus
Baptized Ponteland, Northumberland, 6 May 1610

Hugh Arse
Born Saint Mary Steps, Exeter, Devon, 1701

Arse was uncommon but not unknown as a surname in the sixteenth century: a John Arse (born c.1543) was recorded marrying a Marie Day in Rothley, Leicestershire, on 6 July 1568 – and how thrilled she must have been to find herself thenceforth known as 'Marie Arse'. From the seventeenth century we have a Dorothy Arse from Barnstaple, Devon, while in the eighteenth a whole family of Arses, probably of Spanish origin, resided in Milton Bryan, Bedfordshire, where Exequiel, son of Manuel Arse and Carmen Sagaseta, was baptized on 21 March 1877. His was the last Arse birth to be recorded, however, and by the time of the 1881 census, we find only an 'M. D. Arse', born in Germany in about 1855, a baker living in Holborn, London. The last of the British Arses had apparently all died of shame, changed their names, or perhaps emigrated to Bolivia, Mexico or Costa Rica where – numerically, at least – the Arses are much bigger.

Anus Arslanyan
Born np, 1917; died Bexley, Kent, 2004

Hannah Arsol
Baptized Glasbury, Brecon, 9 June 1733

Caroline Ass
Born Kensington, London, 1849

Dick Assman
Born Birmingham, Warwickshire, c.1797 (Lambeth, London, 1851 census)

Hannah Aynus
Born North Walsham, Norfolk, c.1847
(Barnham Broom, Norfolk, 1861 census)

Arsabella Bending
Born Payhembury, Devon, c.1818
(Feniton, Devon, 1851 census)

Harquless George Bootyman
Died Hull, Yorkshire, 1899

Amelia Brown Bottom
Born Islington, London, 1876

Anice Bottom
Baptized Thornhill by Dewsbury, Yorkshire, 14 May 1837

Arthur Henry Anulus Bottom
Baptized Sheffield, Yorkshire, 25 December 1859

Elizabeth Wildgoose Bottom
Baptized Bakewell, Derbyshire, 22 January 1826

Etta Bottom
Born Huddersfield, Yorkshire, c.1871
(Almondbury, Yorkshire, 1901 census)

Henry Goozee Bottom
Born Holborn, London, 1869

Huga Bottom
Born Nystad, Finland, c.1871
(Chief Mate of ship *Pallas*, Wallsend,
Northumberland, 1901 census)

James Bottom Bottom Bottom*
Born Wakefield, Yorkshire, 1852

Joseph Liverpool Bottom
Born Great Boughton, Cheshire, 1842

* That's three Bottoms

Nora Bottom
Born Ecclesall Bierlow, Yorkshire, 1905

Original Bottom
Born Lockwood, Yorkshire, 1846

Popsie Bottom
(Female) Born np, Kent, c.1891 (Kensington, London, 1891 census)

Silence Bottom
Married Thomas Mason, Chesterfield, Derbyshire, 26 October 1735

Sugden Green Bottom
Died Bradford, Yorkshire, 1855

Zippah Bottom
(Female) Born Whitley, Yorkshire, c.1832 (Thornhill, Yorkshire, 1901 census)

Huga Bottome
Baptized St Margaret's, Leicester, 10 March 1615

Favouretta Bottomley
Born Halifax, Yorkshire, 1891

Total Bottomley
(Male) Born Manningham, Yorkshire, c.1858
(North Bierley, Yorkshire, 1861 census)

Truly Constant Bottomley
Born np, c.1842; died Halifax, Yorkshire, 1907

James Seymour Bottoms
Born Ampthill, Bedfordshire, 1898

A. Harry Botty
Born Bethnal Green, London, 1884

Enoch Bottom Bray
Born Golcar, Yorkshire, c.1813 (Lindley cum Quarmby, Yorkshire, 1861 census)
At the time of the 1861 census, cartwright Enoch Bottom Bray was the head of a household that comprised his son, also called Enoch Bottom Bray, as well as Ann, Fred, George, John and Nancy – all of whom had 'Bottom' as their middle name.

Botty Brown

(Female) Born Bolton, Lancashire, c.1790 (Bolton, 1851 census)

Fanny Bum

Born np, Oxfordshire, c.1839 (Binfield, Oxfordshire, 1841 census)

Rose Bum

Born Shoreditch, London, c.1891 (St Mary Stratford, Bow, London, 1901 census)

Violet Bum

Born Birmingham, Warwickshire, c.1897 (Aston, Warwickshire, 1901 census)

Willy Bum

Born np, Derbyshire, c.1836 (Glossop, Derbyshire, 1861 census)

Will Bumass

Born Birmingham, Warwickshire, c.1892 (Birmingham 1901 census)

Fanny Bumbot

Born St Pancras, London, c.1848 (Lambeth, London, 1871 census)

Letitia Bumfastland

Born Holborn, London, c.1855 (Holborn, 1901 census)

Dick Bumfitt

Born Chorlton, Lancashire, 1898

Willy Bumgardner

Born Whicham, Cumberland, 18 October 1881

Willy Bumkum

Born Callington, Cornwall, c.1888 (Callington, 1891 census)

Engelbert J. Bummer

Born Hull, Yorkshire, c.1847 (Holy Trinity, Yorkshire, 1871 census)

Bertha Bumming

Born Kingsclere, Hampshire, c.1878 (Kingsclere, 1901 census)

Harry Bummy

Born Liverpool, Lancashire, c.1873 (West Derby, Lancashire, 1901 census)

Fanny Bumpass

Born Brackley, Buckinghamshire, 1842

Annus Bumphrey
(Female) Born Broomhill, Northumberland, c.1860
(Ashington, Northumberland, 1891 census)

Hugh Bums
Born Glasgow, Lanarkshire, c.1897 (Glasgow, 1901 Scotland census)

Dick Bumshead
Born Lambeth, London, c.1828 (Westminster, London, 1891 census)

Mary Bumsick
Born Glasgow, Lanarkshire, c.1841 (Barrhead, Renfrewshire, 1901 Scotland census)

Isabella Bumup
Born Newcastle upon Tyne, Northumberland, c.1824
(Westgate, Northumberland, 1851 census)

Little Bunns
(Female) Born Spalding, Lincolnshire, c.1815
(Whittlesey, Cambridgeshire, 1871 census)

Annie Trollope Butt
Married Wandsworth, London, 1892

Bijou Butt
Born Okehampton, Devon, c.1860 (Gloucester, 1891 census)

Harry Butt
Married Martha Maidment, Mere, Wiltshire, 26 April 1752

Matilda Payne Butt
Married Warminster, Wiltshire, 1839

Sexey Butt
Born Dundry, Somerset, c.1803 (Hanham, Gloucestershire, 1851 census)

Seymour Butt
Born Bath, Somerset, 1875

Sarah Buttholes
Born Finchley, London, c.1876 (Willesden, London, 1891 census)

Anthony Buttocks
Married Dorothy Thompson, Marske-by-the-Sea, Yorkshire, 24 January 1662

Susanah Ashworth Anus de Boothfould
Buried Newchurch in Rossendale, Lancashire, 11 April 1723

Maria Entry
Born Publow, Somerset, c.1813 (Bedminster, Somerset, 1861 census)

Fanny Fairbottom
Born Bridlington Quay, Yorkshire, c.1858 (Bridlington, 1861 census)

Bumming Frederick
Born Great Hanningfield, Suffolk, c.1830 (Colchester, Essex, 1901 census)

Sahara Arse Hayward
Born Bottseford, Wiltshire, c.1851
(St George Hanover Square, London, 1891 census)

William A. S. Hole
Born Burton upon Trent, Staffordshire, c.1887
(Buckhurst Hill, Essex, 1901 census)

Ambrose Hughbottom
Born np, England, c.1830 (Edinburgh, 1861 Scotland census)

Anus Hughes
Died St Asaph, Denbighshire, 1847

Annie Tush King
Born Shoreditch, London, c.1834 (Shoreditch, 1861 census)

Arundel Anus King
Born np, c.1847; died Wellington, Somerset, 1904

Anus Lane
Born Marylebone, London, 1879

Iva Longbottom
Born Balby, Yorkshire, c.1899 (Selby, Yorkshire, 1901 census)

Lightfoot Longbottom
(Male) Born North Bierley, Yorkshire, 1900

James Loveass
Married Elizabeth Seward, St George, Exeter, Devon 24 February 1833

Cato McAnus
(Female) Born Leeds, Yorkshire, c.1889 (Leeds, 1891 census)

Joseph McArse
Born South Shields, Durham, 1917

Willy McBum
Born Glasgow, Lanarkshire, c.1870 (Litherland, Lancashire, 1891 census)

Isabella Mybum
Born Guernsey, Channel Islands, c.1834 (Ilminster, Somerset, 1851 census)

Ann Nus
Married John Dixon, St Peter-at-Leeds, Leeds, Yorkshire,
4 February 1671

Maria Orefice
Born Holborn, London, 1895

Alice Pinckass
Married Perranarworthal, Cornwall, 29 September 1711

Wonderful Ramsbottom
Born Dewsbury, Yorkshire, 1855

Nanny Rawbottom
Baptized Aston, Yorkshire, 5 April 1795

Joseph Man Rear
Baptized Heckington, Lincolnshire, 27 May 1820

Jane Rockbottom
Born Birmingham, Warwickshire, c.1811 (Birmingham, 1841 census)

Minnie Rosebottom
Born Ashton-under-Lyne, Lancashire, c.1888
(Ashton-under-Lyne, 1901 census)

Mary Roughbottom
Baptized St Mary, Oldham, Lancashire, 17 January 1731

Benjamin Rump Rump
Born Aylsham, Norfolk, 1884

Lotta Rump
Born Flegg, Norfolk, 1902

Mary Sanus
Married Samuel Wilkinson, Birstall, Yorkshire, 29 July 1824

Mary Sarse
Born Holt, Worcestershire, c.1851 (Kempsey, Worcestershire, 1871 census)

Anal Saw
Born Lewisham, London, 1913

Lincoln Entwistle Shipperbottom
Born Bolton, Lancashire, 1894
Almost all Shipperbottoms come from Bolton.

Obadiah Shoebottom
Baptized Rushton Spencer, Staffordshire, 26 March 1769

Eliza Shovebottom
Married Richard Allport, St Phillips, Birmingham, Warwickshire,
3 October 1842

Benigna Shufflebottom
Died Haslingden, Lancashire, 1867

Asseley Sidebottom
Married William Shaw, Mottram-in-Longdendale, Cheshire, 3 September 1774

Arson Skidmore
Married Gloucester, 1849

Sarah Smallass
Married John Watson, Tivetshall St Mary, Norfolk, 21 May 1751

Mary A. Stripperbottom
Born Bolton, Lancashire, c.1834 (Tonge with Haulge, Lancashire, 1891 census)

Arsley Swell
Baptized St Martin-in-the-Fields, London, 7 July 1745

Sarah Thickbottom
Died Wakefield, Yorkshire, 1879

Fanny Tush

Born Hull, Yorkshire, c.1849 (Sculcoates, Yorkshire, 1871 census)

Ann Whiteass

Baptized St Bridget, Chester, Cheshire, 21 March 1685

Arseman Whitteron

Born Plumpton, Yorkshire, c.1881 (Spofforth, Yorkshire, 1891 census)

Mary Windbottom

Born Salford, Lancashire, c.1855 (Salford, 1881 census)

Alice Winkbottom

Born Clifton, Lancashire, c.1871 (Clifton, 1891 census)

Enema Bottomley Wood

Died Huddersfield, Yorkshire, 1904

Mary Zarse

Born np, Cornwall, c.1811 (Mevagissey, Cornwall, 1841 census)

◆

HAIR-RAISING NAMES

Rosalind Silver Beard

Born Edmonton, Middlesex, 1883

Sexa Beard

Born Axbridge, Somerset, 1855

Storm Beard

Married Bath, Somerset, 1839

Wealthy Beard

Married Gloucester, 1867

Fanny Beardshear

Born np, Nottinghamshire, c.1806 (Blyth, Nottinghamshire, 1841 census)

Betty Butterworth Beaver

Baptized St Michael, Ashton-under-Lyne, Lancashire, 8 January 1843

Harry Beaver
Baptized St Mary Portsea, Hampshire, 21 November 1812

Fanny Bevercomb
Born Wareham, Dorset, 1843

Brown Bush
Married Susan Turner, Bunwell, Norfolk, 23 October 1759

Curley Bush
(Male) Born Aldeburgh, Suffolk, c.1841 (Aldeburgh, 1851 census)

Fanny Bush
Married Francis Cox, Ringwood, Hampshire, 7 February 1824

Frances Rude Bush
Born West Ham, Essex, 1882

John Pecker Bush
Born Leeds, Yorkshire, 1883

Shave Copsey
Died Sudbury, Suffolk, 1852

Fanny Cutbush
Born Lewisham, London, 1839

Semen Fur
Born np, 1913; died Bradford, Yorkshire, 2004

Rhoda Furbelow
Born Chippenham, Wiltshire, 1864

Annie Goatee
Married Droxford, Hampshire, 1880

Fanny Hair
Born Walsall, Staffordshire, 1868

Alice Haircut
Married Moses Cowcill, Deane, Lancashire, 27 February 1856

Pubecca Hare
Born np, Kent, c.1831 (Minster, Kent, 1841 census)

Hairy Head
Born Dover, Kent, c.1878 (Dover 1891 census)

Merkin King
Born Nassington, Northamptonshire, c.1837 (Nassington, 1871 census)
A merkin is a pubic wig worn by prostitutes. The word first appeared in print in English in 1617.

Hairy Mann
Married Dover, Kent, 1894

Fanny Merkin
Born Thingoe, Suffolk, 1845

Hairy Percy Muckley
Born Kings Norton, Staffordshire, 1891

Archimedes Muff
Married Dewsbury, Yorkshire, 1848

Harry Muff
Born Bradford, Yorkshire, 1857

Catherine Pube
Married Thomas Jenkyn, Redruth, Cornwall, 1540

Susan J. Pubeblank
Born Bigbury, Devon, c.1862 (Bigbury, 1871 census)

Harry Pussey
Born Croydon, Surrey, c.1863 (Croydon, 1901 census)

Bald Scutt
Born np, Lancashire, c.1840 (Middleton, Lancashire, 1841 census)

Jane Shaven Self
Born Clifton, Gloucestershire, 1841

Fanny Shaver
Married Stockton-on-Tees, Durham, 1842

Peter Twatt Shearer
Married Hampstead, London, 1900

William Dundreary Stevens
Born St George Hanover Square, London, 1862
Lord Dundreary is the bewhiskered character in Our American Cousin, *the play Abraham Lincoln was watching when he was assassinated in 1865; bushy sideburns became known as 'Dundrearys'.*

Mary Trimbush
Married Benjamin Ireland, St Mary, Portsea, Hampshire,
17 February 1806

Wiggy Watkin
Born np, Breconshire, c.1786
(Aberystwyth, Monmouthshire, 1851 Wales census)

Ada Whisker Whisker
Born Walsingham, Norfolk, 1876

Fanny Wig
Born Hartley Wintney, Hampshire, 1838

Wilbart Charlesworth Wigfull Wigfull
Born Wortley, Yorkshire, 1846

THE C-WORD

◆

Perhaps surprisingly, despite its super-taboo status, 'cunt' and its variants crop up as both a first name and surname in Britain. It appeared within a number of British names in the medieval period: a Simon Sitbithecunte was recorded in Norfolk in 1167 in a Pipe Roll (a financial record), the boastfully named John Fillecunt was noted in a Lancashire Assize Roll of 1246, Robert Clevecunt in a Yorkshire Subsidy Roll of 1302 and Bele Wydecunthe in a Norfolk Subsidy Roll of 1328. Here are some more recent examples:

Mary Allcunt

Born Demerara, British Guiana, c.1815 (Chelsea, London, 1881 census)

Cunt Berger

Born np, Germany, c.1878 (Sunderland, Durham, 1901 census)

Cuntin Churles

Born np, Yorkshire, c.1861
(Chorlton-on-Medlock, Lancashire, 1891 census)

Cuntha Cronch

(Female) Born np, Middlesex, c.1834
(St Marylebone, London, 1841 census)

A. Cunt

(Female) Baptized St James', Colchester, Essex, 1 March 1684

Fanny Cunt

Born Colchester, Essex, c.1839 (Hastings, East Sussex, 1891 census)
Fanny Cunt lived in the seaside resort of Hastings with a bunch of Cunts: her son Richard (one hopes otherwise, but must assume he was known as 'Dick Cunt') and her daughters Ella and Violet Cunt, all of whom were born in Cape Colony (South Africa), and their brother Alfred Cunt, born in New Zealand. Fanny is described as 'living on her own means' – presumably she had acquired her unfortunate surname through marriage and returned from the colonies with her four children, but apparently minus Mr Cunt.

Harry Cunt
Born Runcorn, Cheshire, c.1874

(mate of ship *Thistle*, Mersey, Lancashire, 1901 census)

As the captain claimed his name was Robert Ball, Harry (Hairy?) Cunt may possibly have been a joke played on a naïve census enumerator.

Richard Harry Cunter
Born Romford, Essex, 1880

Worthy Cuntilla
Born Broughton, Wiltshire, c.1825 (Walcot, Somerset, 1861 census)

Lancelot S. Cuntin
Born Ely, Cambridgeshire, c.1899 (Ely, 1901 census)

Mary Cunting
Born Alverstoke, Hampshire, c.1837 (Portsea, Hampshire, 1861 census)

Joseph Cuntingdon
Born Portsea, Hampshire, c.1823 (Portsea, 1851 census)

Christian Cuntlay
(Female) Born Ellon, Aberdeenshire, c.1835

(Cruden, Aberdeenshire, 1871 Scotland census)

Ellen Cuntly
Born np, Ireland, c.1877 (Kensington, London, 1901 census)

James Cunts
Baptized Bank Street Unitarian Church, Bolton-le-Moors,
Lancashire, 28 May 1757

Sarah Cuntsman
Born Hull, Yorkshire, c.1859 (Hull, 1871 census)

Mary Cuntwall
Born Westminster, London, c.1834 (St Martin-in-the-Fields, London, 1851 census)

Margaret Cunty
Married John Hurley, St Anne, Soho, London, 26 March 1798

Cunty Hoel
Born Warnham, Cheshire, c.1849 (Walton-on-the-Hill, Lancashire, 1871 census)

Cunty Hoel was the wife of Dick Hoel.

Mary Ann Cunt Hunt

Born Cheriton Fitzpaine, Devon, c.1829 (Thorverton, Devon, 1851 census)

Mary Ann and George F. Cunt Hunt were the parents of a girl baptized three months earlier with the same rhyming name as her mother.

Mike Hunt

Born Chippenham, Wiltshire, 1842

Fannie Kunt

Born Clipston, Nottinghamshire, c.1873 (Kirkby, Nottinghamshire, 1891 census)

Temperance Kunt

(Female) Born Banwell, Somerset, c.1824 (Banwell, 1851 census)

Adolph Kunty

Born np, Germany, c.1864 (Derby, 1891 census)

Hervey le Cunte

Of Norwich, Norfolk (will, 1320–21)

Christina Cuntisharks Meikle

Born Lesmahgow, Lanarkshire, c.1861 (Lesmahgow, 1901 Scotland census)

Cunny Overend

(Female) Born Birkenhead, Cheshire, c.1870 (Birkenhead, 1871 census)

Cunny is a diminutive of cunt; it exists to this day as a rare surname, principally in the Manchester area.

Cunt Pepper

(Male) Born Smallthorne, Staffordshire, c.1828 (Burlsem, Staffordshire, 1851 census)

Emma Scunt

Born Harrow, Middlesex, c.1845 (Stepney, London, 1861 census)

Cuntliffe Fanny Vidal

Born Creeting St Mary, Suffolk, c.1887 (Creeting St Mary, 1891 census)

Cunton Wass

(Male) Born Barton, Lincolnshire, c.1868 (Barton, 1871 census)

Kunt Zonar

Born np, Scotland, c.1828 (Gorbals, Lanarkshire, 1841 Scotland census)

THE UPS AND DOWNS OF 'FANNY'

Eagle-eyed readers will note the prevalence of 'Fanny' names throughout. This is as much a reflection of its popularity as of its double entendre *potential. 'Fanny' gradually replaced Frances as a baptismal name, rather than a nickname, from the second half of the eighteenth century, John Cleland's popular novel,* Fanny Hill: Memoirs of a Woman of Pleasure, *dating from 1748, perhaps contributing to its success. It peaked in the 1870s, when more than 5,000 girls were given the name every year, but then began a steady decline which perhaps reflected the rise in the use of 'fanny' as a slang word for the female genitals (its earliest recorded such use in print appeared in the September 1879 issue of the salacious magazine* The Pearl, *with the phrase, 'You shan't look at my fanny for nothing' – quite so). Thereafter, it became progressively less common, so that by the time it featured in songs and ribald jokes in the trenches of the First World War, it had all but fallen out of use. By the Second World War, scarcely anyone was given the name 'Fanny'. The 1944 British film* Fanny by Gaslight, *based on the novel of that name by Michael Sadleir, received such an outraged reaction*

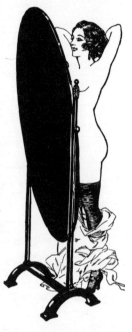

that in the US it was retitled Man of Evil *– even though it did not mean quite the same thing. The American use of 'fanny' for the bottom dates from the 1920s, the differing meaning resulting in occasional confusion. (On the author's first visit to the USA in the early 1970s, he was astonished when a woman told him that she preferred not to wear jeans because, she claimed, she had 'an enormous fanny'.) Here is just a sampling of the Fannies of yesteryear:*

Fanny Action
Baptized Claverley, Shropshire, 22 April 1747

Fanny Affection
Born np, c.1815 (Watford, Hertfordshire, 1871 census)

Fanny Beaver
Born Bourne, Lincolnshire, 1839

Fanny Box
Born Chippenham, Wiltshire, 1839

Fanny B. Bythesea
Born np, India, c.1847 (Bath, Somerset, 1881 census)

Loveday Fanny Cocks
Born Liskeard, Cornwall, 1849

Fanny Coil
Born Chester, Cheshire, 1898

Fanny Crease
Born Reading, Berkshire, c.1878 (Reading, 1901 census)

Fanny Crevice
Baptized Old Swinford, Worcestershire, 16 September 1838

Fanny Crotch
Baptized St Martin at Palace, Norwich, Norfolk, 13 July 1624

Fanny Crumpler
Born Poole, Dorset, 1856

Fanny Bollock Cullis
Married Islington, London, 1856

Fanny Dogger
Born Norton, Hertfordshire, c.1859 (Norton, 1871 census)

Fanny Eighteen
Born Great Glemham, Suffolk, c.1863 (Reading, Berkshire, 1901 census)

Fanny Fanny
Baptized St Pancras, London, 1837

Quadruna Fanny Fewster
Born Stockton-on-Tees, Durham, 1893

Fanny Fidget
Died Portsea, Hampshire, 1868

Fanny Filler
Born St Olave, Southwark, London, 1892

Fanny Flasher
Married Victor Grenbaum, Humberside, Lincolnshire, 1920

Fanny Flick
Born Clerkenwell, London, 1842

Fanny Flow
Born Newport, Isle of Wight, c.1844 (Chelsea, London, 1901 census)

Fanny Fridge
Born Kensington, London, c.1851
(Wandsworth, London, 1901 census)

Fanny Funk
Born Whitechapel, London, 1859

Fanny Funt
Born St Leonard, Shoreditch, London, c.1853 (St Leonard, 1881 census)
*As was said of the surname of Allen Funt (1914–1999),
the creator of the TV show* Candid Camera*, 'Funt' is neither
one thing nor another.*

Fanny Gash
Baptized Syston, Lincolnshire, 29 July 1838

Fanny Growcock
Born Bourne, Lincolnshire, 1852

Fanny Gussett
Born Kenilworth, Warwickshire, c.1859
(Duddeston cum Nechells, Warwickshire, 1871 census)

Fortunate Fanny Hinder
Born Cirencester, Gloucestershire, 1884

Fannys [*sic*] Hole
Born Farnham, Surrey, c.1867 (Westminster, London, 1891 census)

Fanny Honey
Buried Padstow, Cornwall, 12 November 1891

Fanny Humpage
Born Dudley, Staffordshire, 1876

Fanny Ing
Born Thame, Oxfordshire, 1854

Fanny Lather
Married Tonbridge, Kent, 1873

Fanny Lingo
Born Bedford, 1852

Fanny Lips
Married John Christophers, Falmouth, Cornwall, 13 April 1823

Fanny Lover
Married Marylebone, London, 1850

Fanny Lust
Born Lewes, Sussex, 1844

Fanny Alotta Mould
Born np, c.1858; died Newmarket, Suffolk, 1868

Fanny Organ
Born Frome, Somerset, 1838

Fanny Party
Born np, Cumberland, c.1813 (Wimbledon, Surrey, 1871 census)

Fanny Passage
Born Sheerness, Kent, c.1865 (Gillingham, Kent, 1891 census)

Fanny Jane Penis
Born Gloucester, 1842

Fanny Pie
Married Robert Marsh, Wigan, Lancashire, 1923

Fanny Pimp
Born Sleaford, Lincolnshire, 1876

Fanny Plenty
Born Shoreditch, London, 1867

Fanny Pounder
Born Manchester, Lancashire, 1879

Fanny Pussephette
Born np, Hertfordshire, c.1833 (Flamstead, Hertfordshire, 1841 census)

Fanny Pussey
Born np, Yorkshire, c.1817 (Holderness, Yorkshire, 1841 census)

Nine Fanny Rogers
Married Whitchurch, Shropshire, 1905

Many Fanny Salisbury
Born Wrexham, Denbighshire, 1898

Fanny Pink Simons
Married Spilsby, Lincolnshire, 1859

Fanny Softness
Married Samuel Cohen, Mile End, London, 1925

Fanny Spong
Born Woking, Surrey, 13 March 1858

Pubete Fanny Steel
Born Morley, Yorkshire, c.1887 (Morley, 1901 census)

Fanny Strain
Born Dudley, Staffordshire, 1867

Fanny Tingle
Born Worsley, Lancashire, 1848

Fanny Warmer
Married Newent, Gloucestershire, 1875

Fanny Warning
Born np, Northamptonshire, c.1862 (Kensington, London, 1881 census)

Fanny Washer
Married Axbridge, Somerset, 1846

Fanny Wonder
Married Whitechapel, London, 1907

Fanny Worker
Baptized Ridgmont, Bedfordshire, 6 June 1824

*See also: The Names of the Game, Reverse
Names and throughout for yet more Fannies.*

MORE LADIES' PARTS

Clit Beatley
Born Carlton, Lincolnshire, c.1797
(Grainthorpe, Lincolnshire, 1871 census)

Yoni Boland
Born Epping, Essex, 1911
*'Yoni' is Sanskrit for 'divine passage', but is often
misinterpreted as meaning 'vagina'.*

Vegina Mode Bradley
Born Bishop Auckland, Durham, 1876

Charlotte Crotch
Born Norwich, Norfolk, 1846

Elizabeth Flaps
Baptized St Andrew Holborn, London, 31 March 1695

Pinkus Gash
(Male) Born np, Russia, c.1888 (Spitalfields, London, 1891 census)
Pinkus was the son of Fanny and Isaac Gash.

Labia Hood
Born Nottingham, c.1843
(Snelland, Nottinghamshire, 1861 census)

M. Inge
(Female) Born Eastry, Kent, 1840

Hyacinthe Labia
Born np, France, c.1865 (St Peter Port, Guernsey, 1891 Channel Islands census)

Minkie Miles
Born Hammersmith, London, c.1895 (Fulham, London, 1901 census)

Harry Minge
Born West Derby, Lancashire, 1911

Caroline Minky
Baptized St Dunstan, Stepney, London, 14 November 1860

Vagina Prior
Born Chelsea, London, nd (Chelsea, 1881 census)

Seymour Pussy
Baptized St Laurence, Catsfield, Sussex, 18 June 1836

John Thomas Quim
Born Bolton, Lancashire, 1875

Pudendiana Ryan
(Female) Born np, India, nd (Bury, Lancashire, 1891 census)

Eliza Scrack
Born Cuckfield, Sussex, 1873

Lucy Snatch
Married Robert Colley, St Dunstan, Stepney, London, 11 June 1644

Euphemia Twat
Baptized Walls, Shetland, 1800

There were forty-eight Twats in Orkney and Shetland at the time of the 1841 census. In this same year, in his poem Pippa Passes, *Robert Browning included the line 'Cowls and twats', later explaining to the editor of the* Oxford English Dictionary *that he thought a 'twat' was a kind of hood worn by nuns. He was wrong.*

Jamima Twat
Born Tingwall, Shetland, 12 November 1833

Philadelphia Twat
Baptized Walls, Shetland, 1793

Emelie Vegina
Born Longeuil, Canada, c.1848 (Golcar, Yorkshire, 1881 census)

◆

COCK-EYED NAMES: CLEVER DICKS, PRICKS AND WILLIES

John Thomas Badcock
Baptized Great Bowden, Leicestershire, 18 June 1868

Mildred Rose Baldcock
Born Holborn, London, c.1862 ('prostitute', Paddington, London, 1881 census)

There was little euphemism or political correctness in Victorian census returns: individuals were routinely described as 'prostitute', 'brothel keeper' or 'criminal', or even 'idiot', 'imbecile' or 'lunatic'.

Dick Barecock
Baptized Stagsden, Bedfordshire, 29 August 1790

Betsy Cockin Beevers
Died Huddersfield, Yorkshire, 1852

Dick Bellend
Baptized St Mary Magdalene, Bermondsey, London, 6 February 1848

Willy Bicardick
Baptized Franham, Yorkshire, 10 July 1576

Dick Bigrigg
Born Gateshead, Durham, 1893

Jane Cock Burgers
Born Camborne, Cornwall, c.1817 (Camborne, 1861 census)

Fanny Cleaver
Baptized St Michael, Coventry, 8 June 1755

A 'fanny cleaver' is a slang term for a large penis.

Alice Ada Cock
Born Wapping, London, c.1846 (Covent Garden, London, 1871 census)

Dick Willy Cock
Born Plymouth, Devon, 1853
His name is a rare example of a penile triple.

Epiphany Bullock Cock
Born St Austell, Cornwall, 1844

Everard Cock
Born Wells, Somerset, 1890

Faithful Cock
Married St Columb Major, Cornwall, 1 January 1708

George Alfred Pink Cock
Born Shoreditch, London, 1852

Hugh Cock
Married Charlotte Over, Mevagissey, Cornwall, 19 June 1825

John Thomas Cock
Born np, c.1859; died Penzance, Cornwall, 1894
One of at least twenty-three John Thomas Cocks born in the period 1837–1902.

Lovely Cock
(Female) Born np, Cornwall, c.1781 (Mylor, Cornwall, 1841 census)

Tinie Cock
Born Pembroke, 1861

William Curling Cock
Born Dover, Kent, 1861

Rose Cockhead
Born Bladon, Oxfordshire, c.1874 (Begbroke, Oxfordshire, 1901 census)

Champagne Cocks
Born Medhurst, Kent, April 1906

Frederick Seymour Cocks
Born Darlington, Durham, 1882
Labour MP for Broxtowe, Nottinghamshire, 1924–54, known as Seymour Cocks.

Henry Lovedy Cox Cocks

Born np, Gloucestershire, c.1821 (Hackney, London, 1871 census)

Ophelia Cocks

Born np, Oxfordshire, c.1800 (St Marylebone, London, 1871 census)

Bellend Cokella

(Female) Born np, Ireland, c.1840 (Ramsbottom, Lancashire, 1871 census)

Adora Dick

Married Simon J. Pomphrey, Bath, Somerset, 1989

Dick Dick

Born Coylton, Ayr, 19 February 1856

Effing Dick

(Male) Born Glasgow, Lanarkshire, c.1848 (Glasgow, 1861 Scotland census)

Hugh Dick

Born Sheffield, Yorkshire, 1904

Little Dick

Born Northroad, Cheshire, c.1851 (Wolstanton, Staffordshire, 1881 census)

Thomas Hardy Dick

Born Sculcoates, Yorkshire, 1883

William Hardy Dick

Born Sculcoates, Yorkshire, 1883

With Thomas Hardy Dick above, there were two Hardy Dicks born in the same town in the same year.

Ann Dickcock

Married Roger Willis, St James', Southbroom, Devizes, Wiltshire, 1 October 1738

Willie Manhood Dickerson

Born King's Lynn, Norfolk, 1864

Odd Dicks

Died Thrapston, Northamptonshire, 1886

Benjamin Dickus

Married Daventry, Northamptonshire, 1838

Fans of Monty Python's Life of Brian *may wish to know that his is the closest recorded name to that of the celebrated Biggus Dickus.*

Harry Dong
Born Birmingham, Warwickshire, c.1847
(Edgbaston, Warwickshire, 1861 census)

John Thomas Dong
Born Bradford, Yorkshire, c.1868 (Bradford, 1901 census)

Darling Donger
Born Muston, Leicestershire, c.1899 (Muston, 1901 census)

Willy Donger
Born Barnstaple, Devon, 1855

Dick End
Married Sarah Hunt, Lacock, Wiltshire, 21 July 1755

Isabel Ender
Born np, Perthshire, c.1796 (Alyth, Perthshire, 1841 Scotland census)

P. Enis
(Male) Born np, Lancashire, c.1806 (Manchester, Lancashire, 1841 census)

Dick Everhard
Married Frances Lee, Billesley, Warwickshire, 11 September 1653

Harry Goldcock
Born Hackington, Kent, c.1891 (Canterbury, Kent, 1891 census)

Prick Green
(Male) Born Preston, Lancashire, c.1863
(Clitheroe, Lancashire, 1881 census)

John Thomas Grewcock
Born Ashby-de-la-Zouch, Leicestershire, 1879

Helmet North Guest
Born Hull, Yorkshire, 1889

Mealota Hardcock
Born np, Norfolk c.1832 (Spotland, Lancashire, 1861 census)

Catharine Harddick
Baptized Ollerton, Nottinghamshire, 7 June 1725

John Knobs Henry
Born Cookstown, Ireland, c.1837 (Greenwich, Kent, 1881 census)

Love Hiscock
Baptized Mere, Wiltshire, 18 April 1825

Mike Hock
Born Wigan, Lancashire, 1892

Charles Penis Horn
Married St George Hanover Square, London, 1845

Ivor Horn
Born Cardiff, Glamorgan, 1907

Prick Hucklesbury
Born Framlingham, Suffolk, c.1811 (Woodbridge, Suffolk, 1871 census)

William Dick Inches
Born Alyth, Perth, 25 August 1830

Dick Knob
Married Elizabeth Flower, Beeston, Nottinghamshire, 14 November 1682

Nathaniel Knob
Born Bristol, Somerset, c.1868 (Battersea, London, 1891 census)

Henri Le Dong
Married Amy L. Williams, Swansea, Glamorgan, 1915

Dick Less
Born Stepney, London, c.1861 (Limehouse, 1891 census)

Letitia P. Lingam
Born Cosgrove, Northamptonshire, c.1858 (Birkenhead, Cheshire, 1901 census)
The lingam is the male counterpart of the yoni – see Yoni Boland, above.

Willy Long
(Female) Born Luton, Bedfordshire, c.1896 (Luton, 1901 census)

Willy Longcock
Born np, 1833 (Lambeth, London, 1861 census)

George Longdong
Born Frodingham, Yorkshire, c.1858 (Frodingham, 1861 census)

Elizabeth Lovescock
Baptized St Giles without Cripplegate, London, 21 February 1727

Fred Knoblock Lowcock
Married Keighley, Yorkshire, 1890

Dick Manhood
Baptized Glemsford, Suffolk, 17 May 1657

Wanger Rhoda Mantropp
(Female) Born Lowestoft, Suffolk, c.1874 (Swaffham, Norfolk, 1901 census)

Willy McCock
Married Jean Harper, St Cuthbert's, Edinburgh, Midlothian,
21 December 1760

Jemima Merrycock
Married Joseph Scott, St Margaret's, King's Lynn, Norfolk, 6 September 1829

Mary Ann Morecock Morecock
Born Wokingham, Berkshire, 1842

Willy Muscle
Baptized Holme, Huntingdonshire, 31 May 1685

Pat Mycock
Born Burton upon Trent, Staffordshire, 1927

Harriet Nicewonger
Born Ilkeston, Derbyshire, c.1876 (Ilkeston, 1891 census)

P. Nile
(Male) Born St Austell, Cornwall, 1897

Juan P. Nis
Baptized Blanchland, Northumberland, 30 April 1837

William Nocock
Born np, Surrey, c.1837 (Oxted, Surrey, 1841 census)

Hugh Organ
Born Port Glasgow, Renfrewshire, 18 June 1769

John Thomas Organ
Born Newport, Monmouthshire, 1856

Chris Peacock
Born Askrigg, Yorkshire, 1837

Claude Pecker
Born Atcham, Shropshire, 1897

Zilpah Penis
(Female) Born Witton, Wiltshire, c.1791 (South Newton, Wiltshire, 1851 census)

Fanny Penix
Born Elsecar, Yorkshire, c.1889 (Elsecar, 1901 census)

Marianne Penus
Married John Claudius Bitton, St Botolph, London, 29 February 1736

John Penusardon
Born Pancrasweek, Devon, c.1814 (Pancrasweek, 1851 census)

Harry Chopper J. Percy
Born Gravesend, Kent, 1879

Cyril Twocock Peters
Born Gravesend, Kent, 1906

Dick Prick
Born np, c.1790; died Machynlleth, Powys, 1870

Hugh Prick
Born np, Shropshire c.1801 (Oswestry, Shropshire, 1851 census)

Misericordia Prick
Married Susanna Land, Stansfield, Suffolk, 4 July 1731

Willy Prickhard
Born Bootle, Lancashire, c.1878 (Hythe, Kent, 1901 census)

Dick Prickwell
Baptized St Botolph without Aldgate, London, 16 December 1669

Hugh Penis Pritchard
Born np, 1915; died Caernarfon, Gwynedd, 1990

Curly Dick Radcliffe
Born Swansea, Glamorgan, 1904

Dick Rampant
Father of Mary Rampant, baptized Dorking, Surrey,
21 February 1713

Dick Ramrod
Born Swansea, Glamorgan, c.1847
(Merthyr Tydfil, Glamorgan, 1861 Wales census)

P. Rick
(Male) Married Ann Gouding, St Dunstan, Stepney, London,
29 March 1835

Mike Rotch
Born np, Ireland, c.1817 (Stockport, Cheshire, 1861 census)

Penis Rough
Born np, Ireland, c.1831 (Liverpool, Lancashire, 1871 census)

Elizabeth Scock
Married Phillip Postle, Great Yarmouth, Norfolk, 29 September 1745

George Silvercock
Born Bethnal Green, London, c.1857 (Bethnal Green, 1881 census)

Willie Skin
Married Spilsby, Lincolnshire, 1907

Oliver Slowcock
Baptized St Mary Whitechapel, Stepney, London, nd May 1778

Dick Smallpiece
Baptized Cranley, Surrey, 6 October 1793

John Willie Soft
Born Macclesfield, Cheshire, 1893

Gladys Treblecock Stanton
Died Neath, Glamorgan, 1908

Dick Surprise
Born np, Cheshire, c.1822 (Chester, Cheshire, 1851 census)

John Todger
Born Gringham, Dorset, c.1825 (Weston-super-Mare, Somerset, 1891 census)

Hugh Tool
Born np, Cumberland, c.1850 (Wolsingham, Durham, 1881 census)

John Thomas Tool
Born Weardale, Durham, 1873

John Long Toole
Born Stonehouse, Devon, c.1842 (Devonport, Devon, 1871 census)

Willy Treblecock
Born St Marylebone, London, 1850

John Shaw Twilley
Born Helmsley, Yorkshire, 1873

James Twococks
Born Bermondsey, London, 1861

Hugh Wang
Baptized St Oswald, Durham, 14 February 1568

Minnie Wanger
Born Stepney, London, 1872

Willie Warmer
Born Mitford, Norfolk, 1883

Dick Whatcock
Married Sarah Fletcher, Edgbaston, Warwickshire, 27 February 1731

Any Willie
Born Pembroke, 1862

Hugh Willy
Baptized Old Kilpatrick, Dunbarton, 3 November 1743

John Thomas Willy
Baptized St George the Martyr, Southwark, London, 25 December 1812

Willy Willy
Born np, Ireland, c.1844 (Kensington, London, 1851 census)

Zippora Willy
Baptized Warmington, Warwickshire, 23 December 1785

Dick Willyman
Married Jennet Smythe, Snaith, Yorkshire, 12 February 1597

Dick Wiper
Born np, 1913; died Dewsbury, Yorkshire, 1998

A Load of Balls

Abraham Ball
Born Greasley, Nottinghamshire, c.1811 ('castrator', Greasley, 1881 census)

Ball Ball
Born Tisbury, Wiltshire, 1890

Ellis Poo Ball
Born Leeds, Yorkshire, 1842

George Slack Ball
Born Nottingham, 1847

Lackary Ball
Born Coleshill, Hertfordshire, c.1808 (Amersham, Buckinghamshire, 1871 census)

Ophelia Ball
Born Ashby-de-la-Zouch, Leicestershire, 1874

Titty Ball
Born Cobridge, Staffordshire, c.1884 (Hanley, Staffordshire, 1901 census)

William Loose Ball
Married Holsworthy, Cornwall, 1888

Benjamin Balls Balls
Born Newmarket, Cambridgeshire, 1875

Christmas Balls
Born Docking, Norfolk, 1886

Comfort Balls
Married Mitford, Norfolk, 1879

Ellen Merry Balls
Born Lexden, Essex, 1879

Golden Balls
Baptized Aylsham, Norfolk, 26 September 1813
His son was also called Golden Balls.

Happy Balls
Born Blything, Suffolk, 1878

Harry Balls
Married Thingoe, Suffolk, 1869

Horatio Finer Balls Balls
Born St Luke, London, 1842

John Mean Balls
Died Blything, Suffolk, 1869

Minnie Balls
Born West Ham, Essex, 1870

Norah Balls
Born North Shields, Northumberland, c.1887
(Tynemouth, Northumberland, 1901 census)

Violet Minnie Balls
Born St Pancras, London, 1896

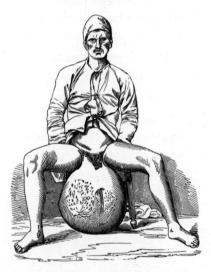

Willy Hugh Balls
Born Kensington, London, 1874

Myball Barton
Born np, Lancashire, c.1816 (Preston, Lancashire, 1841 census)

Dick Bollock
Married Dorathy [sic] Marten, St Mabyn, Cornwall, 16 June 1659

Fanny Bollock
Born Battersea, London, c.1850 (Battersea, 1851 census)

William Bollocks
Married Anne Hodges, Withington, Herefordshire, 13 November 1574

Arnold Eunuch
Married Ann Mabie, Sherburn-in-Elmet, Yorkshire, 25 January 1701

Balls Garrett
Born Leiston, Suffolk, 11 May 1810

William Gonad
Baptized Fyfield, Wiltshire, 7 August 1774

Selina Goolie
Born Bromfield, Shropshire, c.1863
(Malvern, Worcestershire, 1901 census)

Harry Balls Gouldstone
Born West Ham, Essex, 1865

Mahala Honeyballs
Baptized Fordham, Essex, 10 March 1811

Sidney Herbert Knacker
Baptized St Mary the Virgin, Dover, Kent, 13 January 1803

Ann Bollock Lovelace
Married Dorchester, Dorset, 1861

Ada McBollock
Born Birmingham, Warwickshire, c.1881
(Birmingham, 1881 census)

John Nadger
Married Elizabeth Lund, Plumpton, Lancashire, 31 January 1704

Amelia Testes
Born np, Kent, c.1857 (Kensington, London, 1881 census)

Chapter Three

THE NAMES OF THE GAME

On the Job

Sarah Amorous
Married Jonathan Everit, Wheathampstead, Hertfordshire,
1 August 1780

Isabella Anal
Married David Moneypenny, St Andrews and St Leonards, Fife,
4 December 1835

Charlotte Anally
Baptized St John Portsea, Hampshire, 24 January 1813

Alice Banger Banger
Born Bridport, Dorset, 1888

Fanny Dicks Beebe
Born Thrapston, Huntingdonshire, 1860

Eliza Bondage
Baptized St George the Martyr, Southwark, London,
1 March 1812

Daily Boner
(Female) Born Hernhill, Kent, c.1898 (Hernhill, 1901 census)

Emma Hedwig M. Bonk
Married Westminster, London, 1888

Anne Pretty Johns Bonker
Married Kingsbridge, Devon, 1842

Lizzie Bonking
Born Hannington, Surrey, c.1878 (Clerkenwell, London, 1891 census)

Rebecca Bonks
Baptized St Pancras, London, 17 November 1839

Rogers Boys
Born Newport, Monmouthshire, c.1848 (Newton Abbot, Devon, 1901 census)

Dorothy Brothel
Married Henry Shipp, Wigtoft, Lincolnshire, 21 March 1705

Erasmus Bugger
Born North Shields, Northumberland, c.1876 (Hackney, London, 1901 census)

Mary Buggery
Born Stourbridge, Worcestershire, 1852

Fanny Buster
Born St Albans, Hertfordshire, c.1866 (St Albans, 1891 census)

Fanny Carnal
Baptized Feniton, Devon, 24 June 1733

Fanny Cathouse
Born Darnham, Wiltshire, c.1868 (Alfreton, Derbyshire, 1881 census)

Fanny Chaffer
Born Westhampnett, Sussex, 1864

John Benjamin Fister Christian
Born Eastry, Kent, 1859

William Deviant Christie
Born Hackney, London, 1845

Dick Clutcher
Baptized St James Westminster, London, 23 October 1575

Rhoda Cock
Married Thomas Lovack, South Lopham, Norfolk, 9 February 1815

Ellen Fanny Cockaday
Born Norwich, Norfolk, 23 June 1880

Percy Cockfit
Born Chelmsford, Essex, 1867

Mary Cockfull
Died Huddersfield, Yorkshire, 1852

Ulaya Cockin
Baptized St Agnes, Cornwall, 9 December 1673

Anne Cocklove
Married Richard Taylor, St Gregory by Paul's, London, 23 February 1608

Dick Cockout
Baptized Manchester Cathedral, Manchester, Lancashire,
17 May 1796

Fanny Cockup
Born Dartford, Kent, 1840

Jane Coldtart
Married West Derby, Lancashire, 1857

Dick Comes
Born Thorpe, Surrey, c.1798 (Thorpe, 1851 census)
Dick Comes was the father of Willy Comes.

Fanny Comes
Baptized Witton-cum-Twambrooks, Cheshire, 25 October 1857

Fanny Coming
Born Crewe, Cheshire, c.1847
(Brackley St Peter, Northamptonshire, 1881 census)

Dick Condom
Born St Marylebone, Middlesex, c.1845 (St Marylebone, 1851 census)

Fanny Congress
Born Spalding, Lincolnshire, c.1819 (Spalding, 1891 census)

Fanny Creamer
Born Pocklington, Yorkshire, 1872

Susanna Cum
Married Thomas Louch, Ottery St Mary, Devon, 11 June 1806

Isabella Deviant
Born np, c.1806 (Portsea, Hampshire, 1841 census)

Henry Cock Dicker
Born np, c.1822; died Plymouth, Devon, 1880

Susan Harde Dicker
Born Brixton, Devon, c.1855 (Totnes, Devon, 1871 census)

John Large Dickin
Married Wem, Shropshire, 1870

Fanny Dicking
Baptized Helion Bumpstead, Essex, 17 February 1721

Fanny Dickwell
Born Butterwick, Lincolnshire, c.1859 (Leake, Lincolnshire, 1861 census)
Fanny was the daughter of Willy Dickwell Snr and sister of Willy Dickwell Jnr.

Jenet Dildo
Married William Withington, Eccles, Lancashire, 1614

Bridget Dogging
Born np, Ireland, c.1869 (Barony, Lanarkshire, 1891 census)
The etymology of the British slang term 'dogging' – engaging in sex in public places – has not yet been definitively established, but one school of thought claims it derives from the common response of men caught in search of such activities, as participant or voyeur, 'I was just walking the dog…'

Willy Droop
Born Steinhagen, Germany, c.1866 (Camberwell, London, 1891 census)

Harlot Duncan
Married Glanford Brigg, np, Lincolnshire, 1867

S. Emen
(Female) Born Brill, Buckinghamshire, c.1790
(Tring, Hertfordshire, 1851 census)

Horny Ende
Born np, Warwickshire, c.1830
(Birmingham, Warwickshire, 1841 census)

Emma Erecter
Born np, c.1863 (Sheffield, Yorkshire, 1901 census)

Phil Fanny
Born Gorton, Lancashire, c.1800 (Gorton, 1851 census)

Rhoda Fanny
Born Widnes, Lancashire, c.1876 (Eccleston, Lancashire, 1891 census)

Fanny Feeling
Born np, Hampshire, c.1801 (Northwood, Hampshire, 1841 census)

Frank Felch
Died Bedford, 1869
*Felching is a sexual practice too rude to explain in a
family book such as this.*

Fanny Felcher
Born Pattinghager, Staffordshire, c.1874
(Worfield, Shropshire, 1851 census)

Charlotte Fillass
Born Shoreditch, London, 1860

Fanny Filling
Born Horsham, Sussex, c.1832 (Lingfield, Surrey, 1901 census)

Fanny Finger
Born Ide Hill, Kent, c.1859 (Blacklands, Sussex, 1891 census)

Fanny Fister
Born Weymouth, Dorset, c.1859 (Parkstone, Dorset, 1891 census)

Mary Y. Fisting
Born np, Essex, c.1839 (Radipole, Dorset, 1871 census)

Thomas Flasher
Married Mary Barrett, Nethley, Yorkshire, 15 April 1786

Ebenezer Flirt
Born np, Middlesex, c.1865 (St Pancras, London, 1881 census)

Freelove Flower
Born Bath, Somerset, 1849

John Carnal Fox
Married Stoke-on-Trent, Staffordshire, 1851

Lucy Ada Frig
Baptized Stowe Nine Churches, Northamptonshire,
10 September 1874

Fanny Frigger
Died Beckley, Northiam, Sussex, 17 March 1849

Martha Margaret Getiton
Married Plymouth, Devon, 1885

Robert Goldspunk
Born np, Middlesex, c.1837 (Bethnal Green, London, 1841 census)

Christiana Gush Good
Born Stoke Damerel, Devon, 1865

Mary Goodlay
Married George Brown, Rougham, Suffolk, 19 November 1741

Cum E. Gook
(Female) Born London, c.1833
(St George Hanover Square, London, 1851 census)

N. Gorge
(Female) Born np, Norfolk, c.1840 (Larling, Norfolk, 1841 census)

Dick Gothard
Born Ely, Cambridgeshire, 1838

L. E. Gover
(Female) Born South Stoneham, Hampshire, 1894

Sibella Grope
Baptized Manaccan, Cornwall,
28 December 1829

Harris Groper
Born St George in the East, London, 1902

Fanny Growcock
Born Bourne, Lincolnshire, 1852

Randy Guest
Born np, Sussex, c.1795
(Wadhurst, Sussex, 1841 census)

Martha Gusher
Born Pershore, Worcestershire, c.1858
(Pershore, 1871 census)

Dorothy Needs Guy
Born Penzance, Cornwall, 1899

S. Hag
Married Henry Beerlin, St Mary the Virgin,
Dover, Kent, 2 January 1800

S. Hagger
(Female) Baptized Great Chishall, Essex, 7 May 1646

Dick Hardon
Buried Auckland, Durham, 25 April 1571

Ivor Hardon
Born Llansamlet, Glamorgan, c.1878
(Swansea, Glamorgan, 1891 Wales census)

Penis Hardon
(Male) Born np, Ireland, c.1811 (Fulham, London, 1851 census)

Dorcas Harlot
Died Northampton, 1879

Kissy Hoare
Born London, c.1879 (Shanklin, Isle of Wight, 1901 census)

Ophelia Fanny Hole
Born Bristol, Gloucestershire, 1859

Phyllis Hole
Born Greenwich, London, 1906

Phyllis Private Holes
Born Eastbourne, East Sussex, 1893

Seraphim Hooker
(Male) Born Exeter, Devon, c.1796 (Exeter, 1851 census)

Love Hoore
(Female) Baptized Holsworthy, Devon, nd January 1583

Roger Horny
Baptized Lindridge, Worcestershire, 1628

Fanny Humper
Born Clerkenwell, London, c.1842
(St Luke, Old Street, London, 1851 census)

Hannah Humping
Born np, Shropshire, c.1800 (Sedgley, Shropshire, 1881 census)

Willy Inass
Born Inverness, c.1835 (Inverness, 1861 Scotland census)

Martha Incest
Born Whitechapel, London, c.1899 (West Ham, Essex, 1901 census)

Dick Ing
Baptized Long Crendon, Buckinghamshire,
1 February 1858

Lothario Othello Ingham
Born Sculcoates, Yorkshire, 1880

Raper Jagger
Born Leeds, Yorkshire, 1842

Carnal Jarvis
Born Wisbech, Cambridgeshire, 1852

Mary Jezebel
Baptized Loversall, Yorkshire, 6 June 1756

Fanny Jiggles
Born Ampthill, Bedfordshire, 1859

Fanny Juice
Baptized St Margaret, Westminster, London, 12 March 1650

Dick Justin
Baptized St Andrew, Holborn, London, 4 October 1685

Hardon King
Born np, c.1828 (St James, Clerkenwell Green, London, 1841 census)

Harlot Kingdon
Born Plymouth, Devon, 1839

Fanny Kiss
Died Epping, Essex, 1874

Merrie Tart Knox
(Female) Born np, Fifeshire, c.1770
(St Ninians, Stirlingshire, 1851 Scotland census)

Phil Lander
Born Stoke Damerel, Devon, 1846

Analey Larking
Died Sevenoaks, Kent, 1843

E. C. Lay
(Female) Born Lizard, Cornwall, c.1862
(Pendeen, Cornwall, 1871 census)

Francis Pervert Leconte
Born Holborn, London, 1887

Mo Lester
(Male) Born Wigan, Lancashire, 1875

Kerenhappuch Letch
Married Elijah Davey, Great Yarmouth, Norfolk, 30 July 1827

Clementina Labia Lever
Born Nottingham, 1897

Priscilla Lewd
Born np, Lincolnshire, c.1806 (Boston, Lincolnshire, 1841 census)

Ogshort Boner Lewis
(Male) Born Holyhead, Anglesey, c.1865 (Holyhead, 1881 census)

James Higginson Lovebody
Baptized St Peter's, Liverpool, 1 September 1830

Dick Lover
Baptized Thakeham, Suffolk, 22 April 1591

Alberta Lovetoy
Born Windsor, Berkshire, c.1879 (Plumstead, London, 1891 census)

I. Lovit
Married Mary Mothersell, Harlington, Bedfordshire, 13 June 1710

Lucy Lube
Born Preston, Lancashire, c.1830 (Formby, Lancashire, 1881 census)

John Bonker Luscombe
Born np, c.1816; died Plympton St Mary, Cornwall, 1897

Jet Lust
Born np, Oxfordshire, c.1840 (Drayton, Oxfordshire, 1841 census)

Herbert Lusty Lusty
Born Stroud, Gloucestershire, 1902

Thomas Fondle Manning
Married Yarmouth, Norfolk, 1848

James McAnal
Born np, Ireland, c.1801 (Liverpool, Lancashire, 1841 census)

Phil McCracken
Born Lewisham, Kent, 1876

Willy McCum
Born Bolton, Lancashire, 1840

Archibald McRim
Born Chorley, Lancashire, 1865

Kenneth McShager
Born np, Scotland, c.1811
(Glasgow, Lanarkshire, 1841 Scotland census)

Roger Mee
Died Bolton, Lancashire, 1856

Annie Milf
Born Birmingham, Warwickshire, c.1864 (Edgbaston, Warwickshire, 1881 census)
'Milf' is a recently-coined acronym for 'Mother I'd Like to Fuck'.

Thomas Molester
Born np, Middlesex, c.1834 (Hackney, London, 1841 census)

Mary Jane Loves Moore
Born Whitehaven, Cumbria, 1860

Roger Dicks Moore
Married East London, 1852

Comes More
Born np, Middlesex, c.1821
(Covent Garden, London, 1841 census)

Dick Myass
Baptized Hornsea, Yorkshire, 26 January 1804

Roger Mycock
Born np, 1913; died King's Lynn, Norfolk, 1997

Fanny Nookey
Baptized Ashcott, Somerset, 28 July 1872

Nicholas Orgy
Baptized St Martin-in-the-Fields, London, 26 December 1626

Elizabeth Spunk Oxley
Born Dewsbury, Yorkshire, 1871

Humping M. C. Palmer
(Male) Born Newbury, Berkshire, c.1872 (Newbury, 1881 census)

Nancy Passion
Born St George in the East, London, 1904

Elizabeth Sex Pechey
Born Docking, Norfolk, 1846

Vincent Pedo
Married Sophia Weatherwise, St Leonard, Shoreditch,
London, 5 February 1827

George Spurt Percival
Born Camberwell, London, 1852

Trannie Pickup
(Female) Born Portsmouth, Hampshire, c.1853
(Grays, Essex, 1901 census)

George Pimp
Born Sleaford, Lincolnshire, 1860

Alice May Poke
Born Sheffield, Yorkshire, 1896

Fanny Poker
Born Henley-on-Thames, Oxfordshire, c.1877
(Remenham, Berkshire, 1901 census)

Fanny Porn
Born Nutley, Hampshire, c.1849 (Nutley, 1861 census)

Dick Pounder
Born Sculcoates, Yorkshire, 1903

Porndance Powell
(Female) Born Blackwell, Worcestershire, c.1841
(Sedgley, Staffordshire, 1871 census)

Harlot Price
(Male) Born np, Shropshire, c.1832 (Clun, Shropshire, 1841 census)

Ada Prick
Born np, c.1878; died Sheffield, 1907

Simon Prickadvance
Married Mary Lullham, Peasmarsh, Sussex, 8 May 1682

Fanny Pricklove
Born Waltham Abbey, Essex (Sewardstone, Essex, 1851 census)

Mary Anne Prickup
Born Newton Moor, Cheshire, c.1827 (Dukinfield, Lancashire, 1861 census)

Ray Pugh
Born Ashton-under-Lyne, Lancashire, 1898

Dick Pumper
Born Clee Hills, Shropshire, c.1826
(Kingswinford, Staffordshire, 1851 census)

Fanny Pumper
Born Mile End, London, c.1879
(St George in the East, London, 1881 census)

Amoral Bessie Purchase
Born Langport, Somerset, 1891

Roger Quicklove
Baptized St Mary, Whittlesey, Cambridgeshire, 11 June 1629

Mary Rampant
Baptized Dorking, Surrey, 21 February 1713

Raper Raper
Born Bridlington, Yorkshire, 1843

Large Mounting Ratcliffe
Born Haslingden, Lancashire, c.1885 (Haslingden, 1901 census)

Richard Ravish
Baptized St Mildred Poultry without St Mary Colechurch,
London, 6 September 1685

Dick Rider
Born Hungerford, Berkshire, 1839

William Horny Robinson
Born Hull, Yorkshire, c.1847 (Hull, 1901 census)

G. Roper
(Male) Baptized St Margaret, Westminster, London, 22 May 1552

Loveday Rutter
Buried Wendron, Cornwall, 16 February 1783

Willie Rutting
Born London, c.1882 (Chertsey, Surrey, 1891 census)

Come Saladin
Died Southampton, Hampshire, 1888

Annie Scandal
Born Leeds, Yorkshire, c.1883 (Hunslet, Yorkshire, 1891 census)

Shafter Scorer
(Male) Born Hetton-le-Hole, Durham, c.1866
(Broom, Durham, 1901 census)

Mary Screws
Married Edward Taylor, Canterbury, Kent, 2 January 1710

Sod Self
(Male) Born Bromley, Kent, c.1899 (Bromley, 1901 census)

Willy Semen
Born Stirling, c.1854 (Stirling, 1871 Scotland census)

Lucy Sex
Born Dorking, Surrey, 1844

William Sexace
Born Brighton, Sussex, c.1825
(South Malling, Sussex, 1851 census)

Mabel Sexey Sexey
Born Stockport, Cheshire, 1893

George Sexy
Born Bakewell, Derbyshire, 1843

Fanny Shafter
Born Durham, c.1811 (Durham, 1841 census)

Petronella Shafter

Married Edward Ellett, Ashburton, Devon, 19 September 1637

Thirza Shagg

Born np, Gloucestershire, c.1821 (Old Sodbury, Gloucestershire, 1841 census)

Mary A. Shagger

Born Poplar, London, c.1876 (Bromley, London, 1891 census)

Fanny Shaggs

Born Datchworth, Hertfordshire, c.1832 (Hertford, 1851 census)

Titus Shagin

Born np, Russia, c.1875 (Shoreditch, London, 1901 census)

Dick Shagshaft

Born Islington, London, c.1861 (Shoreditch, London, 1881 census)

John Shagshutt

Married Betty Bate, St Peter's Collegiate,
Wolverhampton, Staffordshire, 25 July 1813

Emma Shagwell

Born Brixton Hill, Surrey, c.1828 (Kentish Town, London, 1891 census)

Dick Shaker

Baptized Fenny Compton, Warwickshire, 5 November 1772

Cuthbert Cumson Simpson

Born Tynemouth, Northumberland, 1880

Hugh Sin

Married Jane Entwistle, St Laurence, Chorley, Lancashire,
27 February 1738

Jane Sinful

Born St Albans, Hertfordshire, 1843

Ethel S. X. Sinner

Born London, c.1876 (St George in the East, London, 1891 census)

Anne Slag

Baptized Hope, Derbyshire, 25 October 1693

Salome Slapper
Born Chipping Sodbury, Gloucestershire, 1891

Virtue Slip
Born Bath, Somerset, 1846

Jane Slut
Baptized Roos, Yorkshire, 28 March 1643

Mary Slutty
Born Birmingham, Warwickshire, 1832

Fanny Smut
Baptized Coldwaltham, Sussex, 4 August 1872

Hester Snogs
Baptized West Hanney, Berkshire,
19 February 1797

Dick Sodom
Baptized Coseley in Sedgley,
Staffordshire, 4 July 1836

G. Spot
(Male) Baptized Edinburgh,
Midlothian, 1 July 1621

Willy Spunk
Born Buxhall, Suffolk, c.1810
(Combs, Suffolk, 1881 census)

Amelia Ann Spurting
Baptized St Paul, Deptford, Kent, 5 March 1845

Ada Maud Squirtes
Married Medway, Kent, 1890

Semion Staines
(Male) Born Maldon, Essex, c.1863
(Maldon, 1871 census)

Benjamin Stiff Stiff
Born Samford, Suffolk, 1893

Henry Stiffens
Born 4 March 1805; baptized St Botolph without Aldgate,
London, 31 March 1805

Enoch Porn Stoner
Born np, c.1851 (Bilston, Staffordshire, 1851 census)

Willie Stretch
Born Winsford, Cheshire, c.1894
(Chadderton, Lancashire, 1901 census)

Fanny Stretcher
Born Gloucester, 1877

Constable J. Stripper
Born Burnley, Lancashire, c.1872
(Habergham Eaves, Lancashire, 1881 census)

Jane Strips
Born Portsea Island, Hampshire, 1845

Charlotte May Stuff
Born Greenwich, London, 1894

Amorous Swain
Died Halifax, Yorkshire, 1843

Fanny Sweetlove
Born Eastry, Kent, 1837

Angelina Swinger
Born Downham, Norfolk, 1879

Dick Swinger
Born np, Norfolk, c.1821
(King's Lynn, Norfolk, 1841 census)

Hannah Swive
Born Stockport, Cheshire, 1843

'Swiving' is an Old English term for sexual intercourse. Germaine Greer once attempted to resurrect its use as a gender-neutral expression, in the sense that it was a mutual act – people swive together, rather than a man doing something to a woman – but it failed to catch on.

Jane Tarty
Born Biggleswade, Bedfordshire, c.1861
(St George, London, 1881 census)

Wanton Thurston
Married Poplar, London, 1867

Fanny Tickler
Born Withern, Lincolnshire, c.1859 (Grimsby, 1881 census)

Fanny Trollope Tilley
Died Kensington, London, 1851

Kinky Tily
Born Cupar, Fifeshire, c.1815
(Dundee, Angus, 1851 Scotland census)

Melony Tramp
Married Nicholas Williams, Honiton, Devon, 19 April 1742

Fanny Trembling
Born Calne, Wiltshire, 1893

Silly Trollope
Born Doncaster, Yorkshire, c.1894 (Doncaster, 1901 census)

S. Trumpet
(Female) Born Tynemouth, Northumberland, 1862

Semen Tugwell
Born Westonbirt, Gloucestershire, c.1794
(Frampton Cotterell, Gloucestershire, 1861 census)

Henry Twiceaday
Married Allice [sic] Crosfield, Aldingham, Lancashire,
17 September 1723

Willie Twitcher
Born Wandsworth, London, 1890

Jane F. Ucker
Born Dunstable, Bedfordshire, c.1801
(Sandy, Bedfordshire, 1871 census)

Jack Ulate
Born Dudley, Worcestershire, c.1835
(Burntwood, Staffordshire, 1861 census)

Samuel Uphard
Born Elton, Lancashire, 1861 (Elton, 1861 census)

Alexander Climax Whitehouse
Born Ashton, Warwickshire, 1904

Alice Whore
Married Francis Smyth, Brinklow, Warwickshire, 17 January 1604

Harriot Whore Whore
Born Ross, Herefordshire, 1843

Christiana Whores
Married Johes [sic] Touse, St George, Wilton, Somerset,
25 April 1585

Charles Hardd [sic] Willy
Born Middleton, Yorkshire, c.1880 (Middleton, 1891 census)

Elizabeth Experience Withall
Born Hackney, London, 1856

BRIGHTON GAY, NANCY BOYS
AND BIGGERDYKES

◆

George F. Aggot
Born Liverpool, Lancashire, c.1897 (Toxteth, Lancashire, 1901 census)

Bent Beaumont
Born Ashton-under-Lyne, Lancashire, 1845

Gay Beaver
Born St Pancras, London, c.1897
(St Marylebone, London, 1901 census)

Nancy Bender
Born Lambeth, London, 1902

Barbara Lezza Berrington
Born np, 1903; died Windsor, Berkshire, 1984

Liz Bian
Born np, Hertfordshire, c.1786 (Hitchin, Hertfordshire, 1841 census)

Fanny Biggadyke
Baptized Whaplode, Lincolnshire, 24 May 1744

A. Biggerdyke
(Female) Born Moulton, Lincolnshire, c.1809
(Spalding, Lincolnshire, 1861 census)

Henry L. J. Bisex
Born np, Gloucestershire, c.1845 (Clerkenwell, London, 1901 census)

John T. Bothways
Born Stapleford, Nottinghamshire, c.1856 (Willington, Derbyshire, 1881 census)

Lezzie Box
Born St Luke, Finsbury, London, c.1874 (St Luke, 1891 census)

Nancy Boys
Born Brighton, Sussex, c.1842 (Brighton, 1871 census)

Charles Bumboy
Born Lexden, Essex, 1844

Delita Dyke
Married Matthew Fisher, Alverstoke, Hampshire, 24 November 1844

Dorcas Wanklin Dyke
Born Gloucester, 1843

Emma Dyke Dyke
Born St George Hanover Square, London, 1896

Jane Gay Dyke
Born Pilton, Somerset, c.1848 (Keynsham, Somerset, 1881 census)

Rhoda Dyke
Born Pewsey, Wiltshire, 1869

Thomas Loveless Dyke
Born Poole, Dorset, 1882

Wilfred Titanic Dyke
Born np, 1912; died Chorley, Lancashire, 1985

Alfred Want Dykes
Born Hackney, London, 1865

George Tabernacle Fagg
Born Chelsea, London, 1859

Marmaduke Faggott
Baptized Selby, Yorkshire, 12 November 1797

Lesby Fannawell
Born Shirebrook, Derbyshire (Warsop, Nottinghamshire, 1851 census)

Brighton Gay
Married Helston, Cornwall, 1881

Henry Gay Gay
Born Bedwelty, Monmouthshire, 1884

Sarah Gaybeard
Married Robert Briggs, Westbury on Trym, Gloucestershire, 9 July 1807

Thomas Gaycock
Baptized St Bride's Fleet Street, London, 29 March 1723

Oscar Gaylard
Born Plymouth, Devon, 1884

Mary Anne Gaylove
Baptized Sandy, Bedfordshire, 21 May 1820

Emma G. Gay Guy
Born Lichfield, Staffordshire, c.1831 (Lichfield, 1851 census)

Camp Henry
Born Islington, London, c.1840 (Islington, 1901 census)

Queer Selina Victoria Hert
Born Hamworthy, Dorset, c.1879 (Branksome, Dorset, 1901 census)

Adam Homo
Married Christian Somerval, Dalziel, Lanarkshire,
27 January 1705

Faggy Jennings
(Female) Born np, Buckinghamshire, c.1781
(Chesham, Buckinghamshire, 1841 census)

Homo Jones
Born Cardigan, 1877

Fanny Sappho Pogson
Born Christchurch, Hampshire, 1886

Roger Poof
Married Elizabeth Brown, Salisbury,
Wiltshire, 4 October 1604

Henry Queer
Born Kirkintilloch, Dunbarton,
7 May 1809

Gayman Rackstraw
Married Wandsworth, London, 1899

Lezza Scragg
Born Burslem, Staffordshire, c.1860
(Burslem, 1861 census)

Albert Gay Sexton
Born Thurning, Norfolk, *c.*1866
(Thurning, 1871 census)

William Shirtlift
Born Rotherham, Yorkshire, 1859

Joseph Faggot Tempest
Born Houghton-le-Spring, Durham, 1888

M. Vaseline
(Male) Born Le Havre, France, *c.*1864
(Southampton, Hampshire, 1881 census)

Lesbiana Wharton
Born Ross, Herefordshire, *c.*1803
(Chelsea, London, 1881 census)

ONE OF THE BUCKINGHAM FUCKINGHAMS?*

Since 'fuck' has been permitted in print only since the Lady Chatterley
*trial of 1960, and remains taboo, it is surprising to discover its
long-standing use as a personal name.*

Samuel Fucker Chivers
Born Bath, Somerset, c.1809 (Bath, 1861 census)

Emma Fuck Fisk
Died Stepney, London, 1834

Amelia Fuck
Born Leeds, Yorkshire, 1905

Charlotte Fuck
Born np, c.1799; died Kingsclere, Hampshire, 1870

Rob Fuck
Born Isle of Man, c.1841 (Isle of Man, 1871 census)

Henry Fuckalls
Born Colchester, Essex, c.1815 (Lambeth, London, 1851 census)
His son was also called Henry Fuckalls.

Violet Fuckard
Born Battersea, London, 1900 (Enfield, Middlesex, 1901 census)

Fanny Fucker
Born np, Wiltshire, c.1825 (Salisbury 1851 census)

Mercy Fucker
Born np, Kent, c.1835 (Mayland, Essex, 1861 census)

Willie Fucker
Born Langtree, Devon, c.1859
(Moretonhampstead, Devon, 1871 census)

There are no Buckingham Fuckinghams – made you look, though

Dick Fuckett
Married Marie Dore, Shalfleet, Wellow, Isle of Wight,
17 November 1581

Archibald Fucking
Born np, England, c.1904; passenger on *Albania*,
arrived New York, 13 November 1924

Henry Fuckingham
Born Ab Kettleby, Leicestershire, c.1797 (Matlock, Derbyshire, 1851 census)

Harold P. Fuckly
Born np, Northamptonshire, c.1895 (Kettering, Northamptonshire, 1901 census)

Sarah Fuckman
Born Westbere, Essex, c.1815 (Shoreditch, London, 1851 census)

Charlotte Fucknote
Born Henfield, Sussex, c.1826 (Henfield, 1891 census)

Crolet N. Fuckott
(Female) Born Paddington, London, c.1898 (Paddington, 1901 census)

Lucy Fucks
Married Thomas Ward, Sileby, Leicestershire, 24 July 1757

Sarah Fuckwell
Born Retford, Nottinghamshire, c.1855 (Sheffield, Yorkshire, 1871 census)

Elizabeth Fuk
Born St Olave, Southwark, London, 1877

Minnie Fukins
Born London, c.1847 (Aldington, Kent, 1861 census)

Millisant [*sic*] Fukk
Married Nicholas Symons, West Clandon, Surrey,
2 November 1579

Sarah Fukker
Baptized Hartley Wespall, Hampshire, 12 March 1754

William Fukmadge
Married Joan Crann, Netherbury, Dorset, 22 September 1818

Golde Fuks
Married Mile End, London, 1905

Thomas Fukup
Born Blackburn, Lancashire, c.1874 (Hyde, Cheshire, 1901 census)

Hugh Fuqua
Born np, Ireland, c.1821 (Liverpool, Lancashire, 1851 census)

Bessie Fux
Married Bristol, Gloucestershire, 1896

Sarah Fuxcock
Born London, c.1807 (Edgbaston, Warwickshire, 1861 census)

Jane Fuxlonger
Born London, c.1803 (Lambeth, London, 1871 census)

Fuck Hunt
(Male) Born np, c.1834 (St Mary Newington, Surrey, 1841 census)

Fuk Yu Lee
Born np, 1940; died Leeds, Yorkshire, 1991

Andrew Le Fuckinjon de Cadet
Married Elizabeth Blackmore, Chapel of the Holy Trinity, Middlesex, 12 June 1678

Yau Fuk Man
Born np, 1953; died Banbury, Oxfordshire, 1992

Alice Phuck
Baptized Salwarpe, Worcestershire, 5 March 1863

F. Uckwell
Born Barton, Oxfordshire, c.1859 (Steeple Barton, Oxfordshire, 1861 census)

Fuckley John Wilkinson
(Female) Born Ferrybridge, Yorkshire, c.1801 (Selby, Yorkshire, 1871 census)

Phuker William
Born np, Staffordshire, c.1791 (Betley, Staffordshire, 1841 census)

SO LONG, SUCKERS: AN ORAL SURVEY

Etta Beaver
Born Bradford, Yorkshire, 1895

Dick Chew Bishop
Born Burnley, Lancashire, 1868

Dick Blower
Baptized Roxwell, Essex, 19 September 1559

Job Blower
Born Stockton, Shropshire, 27 August 1727

Fanny Blows
Baptized Bassingbourn, Cambridge, 5 August 1860

Vincent Suck Chamberlain
Born Forehoe, Norfolk, 1845

Isuck Chandler
Born np, Surrey, c.1840 (Carshalton, Surrey, 1841 census)

Emily Etta Cock
Born Sleaford, Lincolnshire, 1884

Nora Cock
Born Greenwich, London, 1900

Rosetta Cock
Married Stoke Damerel, Devon, 1888

Sukey Cock
Married Samuel Brown, St Mary, Truro, Cornwall, 27 March 1826

Munch Cox
(Female) Born np, Devon, c.1791 (Ottery St Mary, Devon, 1841 census)

Bethiah Cunlick
Born Beaminster, Somerset, 1844

Henrietta Dick
Born Birkenhead, Cheshire, 1900

Nora Dick
Born Strickland Roger, Westmorland, c.1898
(Strickland Roger, 1901 census)

Fanny Diver
Born Blything, Suffolk, 1838

Rosetta Donger
Baptized St John the Evangelist, Bury St Edmunds,
Suffolk, 5 October 1873

Dick Eater
Born Ruislip, Middlesex, c.1829
(Ruislip, 1851 census)

Fanny Eater
Born np, c.1816
(Hampstead, London, 1841 census)

Eatme Edwards
(Female) Born np, c.1827
(Amlwch, Anglesey, 1841 census)

Henrietta Fanny
Born np, Cheshire, c.1860
(St Martin, Cheshire, 1871 census)

Nora Fanny
Born Grantham, Lincolnshire, c.1873
(Leyton, Essex, 1901 census)

Margaret Fellather
Born Acton Dene, Northumberland, c.1875
(Ingleton, Durham, 1891 census)

Isabel G. Gobbledick
Married Keir Hardy, Exeter, Devon, 1986

Henry Gobbler
Baptized St Martin, Birmingham, Warwickshire, 31 May 1787

Mary Gobbles
Born Croydon, Surrey, c.1859 (Hastings, Sussex, 1881 census)

Dick Gobling
Born Croydon, Surrey, c.1810 (Lewisham, London, 1881 census)

Sarah Godown
Baptized St Dunstan, Stepney, London, 1 April 1710

Fanny Goodhead
Born Burton upon Trent, Staffordshire, 1848

Samuel Sucking Gordon
Born Romford, Essex, 1881

Fanny Greathead
Born Birmingham, Warwickshire, 1873

Ellen Good Head
Married Stoke-on-Trent, Staffordshire, 1862

Isaac Hunt
Baptized Bethersden, Kent, 29 June 1634
He was the son of Isaac Hunt.

Blo Job
Born Llanelly, Carmarthenshire, 1892

Fanny Lapper
Born Shoreditch, London, 1841

Harriot Orala Laywell
Born Stepney, London, 1840

William Lickass
Baptized Chatteris, Cambridge, 13 May 1694

Dick Licker
Born Oldham, Lancashire, c.1845
(Oldham, 1861 census)

Messy Licker
(Female) Born Chorley, Lancashire, c.1803
(Manchester, 1861 census)

Fanny Licking
Born Leeds, Yorkshire, 1848

Eliza Lickwell
Born np, Somerset, c.1821 (Walcot, Bath, 1841 census)

Connie Linger
Born Wolverhampton, Staffordshire, c.1889
(Birmingham, Warwickshire, 1891 census)

Ronnie Lingus
Born Burntwood, Lancashire, 1957

Dick Muncher
Born Welshampton, Shropshire, c.1838
(Horseman's Green, Flintshire, 1891 Wales census)

Sally Orally
Born np, Ireland, c.1831 (Wolverhampton, Staffordshire, 1861 census)

Rosetta Peniss
Born Kensington, London, 1867

Henrietta Prick
Born Liverpool, Lancashire, c.1845 (St Luke, London, 1871 census)

Suca Prick
Born Reed, Suffolk, c.1753

Roger Rimmer
Baptized St Botolph, Aldgate, London, 30 May 1658

Jean Slurper
Born np, Banffshire, c.1821 (Gamrie, Banffshire, 1841 Scotland census)

Hyman Suck
Born Leeds, Yorkshire, 1899

Deborah Suckall
Born Leeds, Yorkshire, 1879

Matilda Suckcock
Born np, Warwickshire, c.1840 (Aston, Warwickshire, 1841 census)

Dick Sucker
Baptized Weobley, Herefordshire, 21 January 1719

Ann Suckerman
Married Thomas Cocksedge, Ingham, Suffolk, 16 October 1740

Sully Suckhole
(Male) Born St Petersburg, Russia, c.1868 (Whitechapel, London, 1891 census)

Willie Sucking
Born Elham, Kent, 1882

Rebecca Suckit
Married William Webbe, Burmarsh, Kent, 24 November 1614

Charles William Suckoff
Married Elizabeth Stevens, St Dunstan, Stepney, London,
14 September 1856

Dick Suckwell
Born np, c.1785 (Potterspury, Northamptonshire, 1841 census)

Sara Sux
Baptized Knapton, Norfolk, 31 October 1705

Sarah Swallows
Married John Wass, Fishlake, Yorkshire, 1733

Fellat Tidser
Born np, Essex, c.1835 (Chelsea, London, 1851 census)

Fanny Tongue
Born West Bromwich, Staffordshire, 31 July 1881

Sucky Trevithick
Born np, Cornwall, c.1903 (St Ives, Cornwall, 1841 census)

Thomas Blows Valentine
Born Aston, Warwickshire, 1861

Eta Willey
Born Upottery, Devon, c.1888 (Upottery, 1891 census)

Suck Worthy
Married Joseph Carter, St Mary, Rotherhithe, London, 1799

HOPELESS W. ANKERS

W. Anker
(Male) Baptized Wonersh, Surrey, 28 July 1877

James Masters Bates
Born Daventry, Northamptonshire, 1868

Mastin Bates
(Male) Born London, c.1866 (Scredington, Lincolnshire, 1881 census)

Dick Beater
Born Norwich, Norfolk, c.1835 (Wisbech, Norfolk, 1851 census)
At the time of the census, young Dick Beater was a sixteen-year-old prisoner in Wisbech jail.

Willy Beatoff
Born np, Somerset, c.1821 (Yeovil, Somerset, 1841 census)

Fanny Frigger
Baptized Hawkhurst, Kent, 29 November 1776

Dick Handler
Baptized Earls Colne, Essex, 29 December 1585

Wank Hardy
Born Idle, Yorkshire, c.1892 (Idle, 1901 census)

Jack Hoff
Born Thetford, Norfolk, 1910

Grace Tosser Makins
Married Grimsby, Lincolnshire, 1905

Fanny Cock Manuel
Born Feock, Cornwall, c.1828 (Feock, 1861 census)

John Thomas Massage
Married Maria Catharine Bond, Old Church, St Pancras, London, 17 June 1780

Jack Off
Married Sarah Clarke, St Peters, Thetford, Norfolk, 28 December 1773

Jane Panter Onan

Born Potterspury, Northamptonshire, 1890
*Pedants claim that what the Biblical Onan did was not masturbation – but
the* Oxford English Dictionary *defines onanism as 'masturbation'.*

Alfred Henry Pullcock

Born np, Surrey, c.1811 (Brighton, Sussex, 1851 census)

Wanker Sayer

(Female) Born Northallerton, Yorkshire, c.1855 (Northallerton, 1861 census)

Fiddle Sehmens

Born np, Buckinghamshire, c.1821 (Aylesbury, Buckinghamshire, 1841 census)

Willy Stroker

Died Salford, Lancashire, 1872

Dick Tosser

Married Rebaka [sic] Tothill, Ideford, Devon, 13 April 1685

Dick Wacker

Born np, Essex, c.1781 (Dagenham, Essex, 1841 census)

Thomas Wank

Born np, c.1838; died Chorley, Lancashire, 1886

Willie Harriet Wank

Born Leytonstone, Essex, c.1868 (Wanstead, Essex, 1871 census)
*His surname is bad enough, but he was also given his mother's
first name as his middle name.*

Willy Wanker

Born Angus, Scotland (Dundee, 1841 Scotland census)

Easter Wanking

Baptized Wigmore, Herefordshire, 7 February 1822

Fanny Wankman

Born Colchester, Essex, c.1789 (Stepney, London, 1851 census)

Bertram H. Wankwell

Born Bournemouth, Hampshire, c.1900 (Bournemouth, 1901 census)

Chapter Four

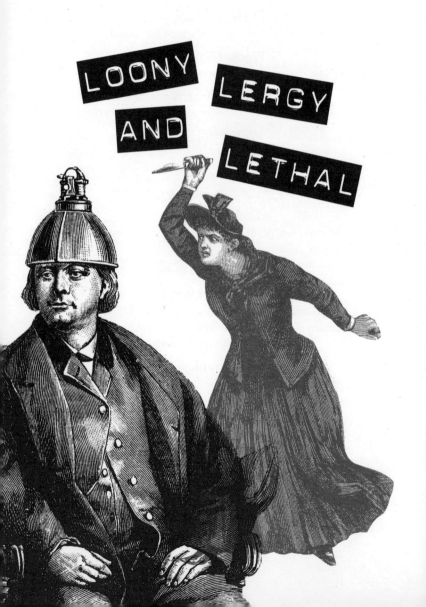

CRAZY NAME, CRAZY GUY

Elizabeth Barmy
Married William King, Letheringsett, Norfolk, 1702

John Moron Battey
Born np, Derbyshire, c.1879 (Cudworth, Yorkshire, 1901 census)

Lettuce Bedlam
Married James Hill, Nottingham, 10 November 1596

Bernard Daft Butler
Born Prescot, Lancashire, 1907

Daft Coggins
Born Nottingham, 1859

Freak E. Cox
(Male) Born Carshalton, Surrey, c.1877 (Carshalton, 1891 census)

Alice Crackers
Born Hull, Yorkshire, c.1871 (St Margaret, Leicestershire, 1891 census)

Ada Crazy
Baptized Thorpe Acre and Dishley, Leicestershire, 4 April 1869

Dick Daft
Baptized St Thomas, Ardwick, Manchester, Lancashire,
2 February 1873

Mary Dope
Baptized Rathkeale, Limerick, Ireland, 17 August 1746

Isaac Dopey
Married Hannah Shaw, Bonsall, Derbyshire, 24 February 1803

Loon Alexander Edgar
Born Eastry, Kent, 1893

Loonie Fattelay
Married Lewisham, London, 1908

Mad Fontheim
Married Hampstead, London, 1903

George Freaky
Baptized Worplesdon, Surrey, 25 December 1814

Nutty Haddock
Died Plomesgate, Suffolk, 1859

Jane Hairbrain
Married George Lilburn, Eglingham, Northumberland, 1801

Mad Hatter
Born Wigginton, Oxfordshire, c.1879 (Northfield, Worcestershire, 1901 census)
Coincidentally, Oxfordshire was the location of Lewis Carroll's
Alice in Wonderland.

Edwin M. Headcase
Born Grasmere, Westmorland, c.1867 (Toxteth Park, Lancashire, 1891 census)

Kathleen Psycho Houghton
Born Oxford, 1878

Mania Hyman
Born Bethnal Green, London, 1903

John Idiot
Married Hailsham, Sussex, 1848

Maniac Keene
Born Chertsey, Surrey, c.1860 (Chertsey, 1861 census)

Mad Looney
Born np, 7 March 1910; died np, Warwickshire, 1894

Easter Loony
Baptized Maughold, Isle of Man, 11 November 1744

John Loopy
Born np, Ireland, c.1816 (Tadcaster, Yorkshire, 1841 census)

George Mad
Married Jane Cole, Cucklington, Somerset, 1 February 1699

Mary Madcap
Married John Bastard, Wells-next-the-Sea, Norfolk, 9 July 1782

Elijah Madhouse
Born Lye, Worcestershire, c.1816 (Lye, 1881 census)

Temperance Madly
Died Monmouth, 1881

Isaac Madman
Married Elizabeth Sewell, St Andrew, Rugby, Warwickshire, 16 November 1811

John Mental
Married Elizabeth Martin, Seaborough, Somerset, 16 January 1609

Lozies Moron
Born Bromsgrove, Worcestershire, 1878

Barm E. Neale
(Male) Born Holloway, London, c.1835 (Hove, Sussex, 1861 census)

Tommy Nuts
Born np, c.1833; died Burnley, Lancashire, 1896

Edith Hard Nutter
Died Hackney, London, 1864

Handle Nutter
Born Burnley, Lancashire, 1871

Joyce Moody Nutter
Born np, 1925; died Braintree, Essex, 2001

Sugar Nutter
Born Burnley, Lancashire, 1853

Mad Parrott
(Female) Born Piedmont, Italy, c.1821
(St George Hanover Square, London, 1861 census)

Beatrice Retard
Born St Pancras, London, c.1877 (St Pancras, 1881 census)

William Joseph Lunatick Rogers
Married Stepney, London, 1856

Mary Ann Stupid
Born np, Middlesex, c.1821 (St Dunstan in the West,
London, 1841 census)

Batty Treasure
(Female) Born Midsomer Norton, Somerset, c.1795
(Midsomer Norton, 1861 census)

MEDICAL MONIKERS

Elizabeth Agony
Married Wrexham, Denbighshire, 1849

Rehab Allwright
(Female) Born Cholsey, Oxfordshire, c.1843 (Cholsey, 1851 census)
Rehab's siblings include Parfet and Quiet.

Margaret Aspirin
Married Noah Wareham, Bowdon, Cheshire, 1 May 1831

Sarah Bandage
Married John Chase, St Martin-in-the-Fields, London, 20 May 1823

Bridget Blackeye
Married Richard Jones, London, 1 May 1617

Benjamin Blister
Married Wantage, Berkshire, 1847

Jack Acne Blunsden
Born np, 1926; died Merton, Surrey, 1988

Clara Spotty Broughton
Born Ongar, Essex, 1843

Charity Clap
Baptized Branscombe, Devon, 11 June 1643

Piles Edycle Cradock
Born np, Somerset, c.1840
(West Derby, Lancashire, 1861 census)

George Typhus Elliott
Married Toxteth Park, Lancashire, 1896

Frances Flu
Married Anne Richardson, Westminster, London, 18 March 1724

William Gangreen [sic]
Born St Pancras, London, c.1824
(St Marylebone, London, 1851 census)

Margaret Coma Garland
Born West Bromwich, Staffordshire, 1904

Betsy Getsick
Born Prestwich, Lancashire, 1894

Elizabeth Prettijohn Gleet
Baptized Combe Street Independent, Lyme Regis, Dorset, 24 July 1819
*It is hard to imagine how a word that refers to a discharge
associated with a sexually transmitted disease might also
be a surname.*

Hernia Harker
Born Bolton, Lancashire, 1887

Dicky Hart
Born Mile End, London, c.1888 (Bethnal Green, London, 1891 census)

Barbaray [*sic*] Headache
Baptized Wonston, Hampshire, 16 August 1576

Comfort Health
(Male) Born Buckhurst Hill, Essex, c.1828
(Bethnal Green, London, 1871 census)

Henry Hiccups
Born Westbury-on-Severn, Gloucestershire, 1852

Isabella Itch
Married John Heyworth, Newchurch-in-Rossendale, Lancashire, 8 June 1875

Dick Itchcock
Born np, Huntingdonshire, c.1856
(Basford, Nottinghamshire, 1881 census)

Viral Beatrice James
Born Wells, Somerset, 1907

James Boil Johns
Born Sherborne, Dorset, 1907

Merrie Leper
Born 'foreign parts', c.1801 (Glasgow Bridegate, 1841 Scotland census)

Martha Lergy
Married Ormskirk, Lancashire, 1865

Syphilla Mears
(Female) Born Exeter, Devon, c.1848 (Exeter, 1881 census)

Samuel Measles
Baptized Welford-on-Avon, Gloucestershire, 8 April 1747

Agony Minchin
Born Bradfield, Berkshire, 1860

Richard Mumps
Born Salford, Lancashire, 1864

John Pox Oliver
Born Yaxley, Huntingdonshire, c.1866 (Yaxley, 1891 census)

Constant Pain
(Female) Born Hackney, London, 1901 (Hackney, 1901 census)

Edward Steady Pain
Born Dover, Kent, 1891

Benjamin Sharpe Paine
Born np, c.1845; died Brentford, Middlesex, 1875

Priscilla Piles
Baptized St Andrew by the Wardrobe, London, 11 February 1736

Instance Ann Pill
Born Cardiff, Glamorgan, 1871
and another:
Instance Ann Pill
Born St Austell, Cornwall, 1878

Mary Pimple
Born Bridport, Dorset, 1852

Emily Frances Plague
Married Stroud, Gloucestershire, 1865

Bessie Pox
Married George Falconer, Gifford, East Lothian, 13 December 1670

Phoebe Puss
Married Joseph Bramble, Boldre by Lymington, Hampshire, 13 January 1786

Cupid Rash
Born Linton, Cambridgeshire, 1852

Dick Rash
Born Chesterton, Cambridgeshire, 1872

Emma Royds
Born Bury, Lancashire, 1854

Leper Scarlett
(Male) Born Tuddenham, Suffolk, c.1845 (Tuddenham, 1901 census)

Frank Senilitee [*sic*]

Born Bury, Suffolk, c.1879 (Great Yarmouth, Norfolk, 1901 census)

Mary Sexwart

Born Marylebone, London, c.1828 (Swaffham, Norfolk, 1851 census)

R. Sitch

(Female) Born Lambeth, London, 1883

Ann Sneezy

Married Robert Clark Tetford, St Giles without Cripplegate, London,
15 December 1794

Frederick Henry Spasm

Married Prescot, Lancashire, 1894

Mary Ann Squints

Married Shoreditch, London, 1852

Hugh Swelling

Born np, Ireland, c.1811 (Kilbirnie, Ayrshire, 1851 Scotland census)

Hoarse J. Titshall

(Male) Born Letheringham, Suffolk, c.1872
(Dennington, Suffolk, 1881 census)

Prudence Toothaker

Married William Avery, St Olave, Southwark, London, 26 January 1789

Daniel Twinge

Born St George Hanover Square, London, 1886

Dick Wart

Born np, Northamptonshire, c.1811
(Silverstone, Northamptonshire, 1841 census)

Nerve Wart

(Male) Born Holborn, London, c.1822 (Holborn, 1851 census)

Virus Wheelhouse

(Female) Born Hebden Bridge, Yorkshire, c.1839 (Hebden Bridge, 1901 census)

FROM GRIMWOOD DEATH TO PHIL GRAVES

John Hell Bell
Died West Derby, Lancashire, 1854

Jet Morticia Black
Born np, 1961; died Birmingham, 1998

John Bury Bury
Born Chorlton, Lancashire, 1846

Mary Carcass
Born Reading, Berkshire, c.1863
('Punch and Judy performer', Horsham, Sussex, 1881 census)

James Cemetery
Died Liverpool, Lancashire, 1844

Samuel Lowery Coffin Coffin
Born Hoo, Kent, 1843

Violet Corpse
Born Whitby, Yorkshire, 1891

Helen A. Deadbody
Born np, Northamptonshire, c.1875 (St John, Cheshire, 1881 census)

Archibald Deadly
Born Paddington, London, c.1875
(St Gregory by Paul's, London, 1891 census)

Grimwood Death
Born np, c.1810; died Hartismere, Suffolk, 1884
Several generations of Grimwood Deaths are recorded, the most recent
(spelling his surname 'De'Ath') dying in 2002.

Lazarus Death
Born Cambridge, 1844

Macro Death
Born Bury St Edmunds, Suffolk, 15 August 1827

Ritzpah Death
(Female) Born London, c.1879 (Diss, Norfolk, 1891 census)

Thomas Jolly Death
Died Epsom, Surrey, 1908

Jacob Decay
Married City of London, 1861

Daniel Demon
Married Louize Beniel, St James, Duke's Place, London, 10 August 1692

Dominick Doom
Born np, Somerset, c.1845 (Whitchurch, Herefordshire, 1861 census)

Ann Ghostly
Died Gloucester, 1870

Hyatt Ghoul
Born np, 1932; died Westminster, London, 2004

Phil Graves
Died Rotherham, Yorkshire, 1879

Fatal Frederick Grucutt
Born Walsall, Staffordshire, 1858

Minnie Hangman
Born Chatham, Kent, c.1882 (Chatham, 1891 census)

Isaac Hearse
Born Axbridge, Somerset, 1852

Christian Killer
Baptized Kinnoul, Perth, 28 September 1784

John Lightning Morgue
Born np, c.1809; died St Saviour, Southwark, London, 1884

Mary Murder
Married John Gurrutt, Thurlaston, Leicestershire, 31 December 1881

David Tomb Robb
Born Liverpool, Lancashire, 1845

Sarah Satan
Baptized Layham, Suffolk, 13 September 1778

Stanley Slaughter Slaughter
Born Aylsham, Norfolk, 1893

Lethal Margaret Stothert
Born Castle Ward, Northumberland, 1875

Chapter Five

A GALLIMAUFRY* OF NAMES

A dish made by hashing up odds and ends of food; a hodge-podge, a ragout; a heterogeneous mixture, a confused jumble, a ridiculous medley; a promiscuous assemblage (of persons)
OXFORD ENGLISH DICTIONARY

Catherine Pizza Alexander
Married Plomesgate, Suffolk, 1847

Marmalaid [*sic*] Frederick Allen
Born South Shields, Durham, 1885

Ann Apple
Married William Parrott, St Alfege, London Wall, London, 5 May 1792

You say . . .
Tom Ato
Born Sleaford, Lincolnshire, 1867

I say . . .
Tom Ayto
Baptized Grantham, Lincolnshire, 28 November 1808

Herodias Pert Bacon
Born Blofield, Norfolk, 1884

Jane Fat Bacon
Born Rippingale, Lincolnshire, c.1811
(Rippingale, 1851 census)

Roy Baguette
Born np, 1945; died Cheshire, 2004

Bagel Baker
Born np, Middlesex, c.1816 (Shoreditch, London, 1841 census)

Catherine Banana
Born Barnsley, Yorkshire, 1876

Minnie Bar
Baptized Galston, Ayr, 25 June 1761

Mince Bates
Born np, Cambridgeshire, c.1863 (Bloomsbury, London, 1881 census)

Caroline Isabel Bathbun
Baptized St Mary the Virgin, Reading, Berkshire, 3 May 1846

Caleb Bean Bean
Born West Ashford, Kent, 1837

Rhubarb Bean
Born np, 1916; died Bury St Edmunds, Suffolk, 2002

Christopher Strong Beer
Baptized Stoke Damerel, Devon, 17 April 1768

Oliver Beer
Born Salisbury, Wiltshire, 1853

Bertha Bread Binns
Born Wakefield, Yorkshire, 1886

John William Biscuit
Born Oldham, Lancashire, 1870

Jane Bisto
Married Thame, Oxford, 1842
An A. Bisto is also recorded, but not an A. H. Bisto.

Mary Caramel Boot
Born Manchester, Lancashire, 1891

Barbary Booze
Baptized St Mary, Carlisle, Cumberland, 6 June 1686

Maud Stale Bun
Born Sunderland, Durham c.1851
(Sunderland, 1871 census)

Lettuce Burger
Died Bristol, Gloucestershire, 1839

Pleasure Butter
(Female) Born London, c.1834 (Holborn, London, 1871)

Christopher Buttermilk
Married Eleanor Walker, Morland, Westmorland, 7 June 1796

Peculiar Buttery
Married Wolverhampton, Staffordshire, 1871

Herbert Cabbage
Born Leyburn, Yorkshire, 1873

Bertha Bacon Cafe
Baptized Stoke-next-Guildford, Surrey, 1 April 1811

Deliverance Smith Cafe
Married Anna Nichols, South Leith, Midlothian, 9 August 1830

Mango Cairns
Died Lambeth, London, 1840

Ambroseus Cake
Baptized Belstone, Devon, 17 October 1613

Fanny Cake
Born Wareham, Dorset, 1848

Harry Eiffel Cakebread
Born St Pancras, London, 1889

Mary Louisa Canape
Born Holborn, London, 1841

Flossie Candy
Born Shepton Mallet, Somerset, c.1858 (Wincanton, Somerset, 1871 census)

James Booze Cave
Died Hull, Yorkshire, 1882

Almodad Cheese
Baptized Rochford, Worcestershire, 25 October 1741

Princess May Cheese
Born West Bromwich, Staffordshire, 1896

Eel Cherry
Married Aston, Warwickshire, 1875

Charles Chips
Baptized St Dunstan, Stepney, London, 9 October 1808

Sarah Chocolate
Baptized Cranley, Surrey, 14 October 1693

Agnes Chutney
Born np, Angus, c.1827 (Dundee, Angus, 1841 Scotland census)

Mary Suet Cobley
Born Hastings, Sussex, c.1850 (Hastings, 1851 census)

Cornelius Coffee
Baptized Phillack, Cornwall, 16 November 1868

Pestrop Cola
(Male) Born Barton-upon-Irwell, Lancashire, c.1831
(Barton-upon-Irwell, 1881 census)

Alma Dumpling Collins
Born Ticehurst, Kent, 1855

Prune Cossey
(Male) Born Mile End, London, c.1874 (West Ham, Essex, 1881 census)

Faithful Christian Cream
Born Chesterton, Cambridgeshire, 1851

Susannah Butter Crease
Born Taunton, Somerset, 1849

Ernest Milk Cremer
Born Norwich, Norfolk, 1876

Walter Cress
Born Cricklade, Wiltshire, c.1858 (Cricklade, 1871 census)

Fortunatus Crisp
Married Lewes, Sussex, 1859

Pleasance Crisp
Baptized Clenchwarton, Norfolk, 22 March 1814

Frances Crumpet
Married Thomas Walters, Tipton, Staffordshire, 5 February 1804

Millie Cucumber
Born Whitechapel, London, 1885

Demosthenes Cuppa
Married City of London, 1886

Jam Curry
Married Tiverton, Devon, 1854

Virtue Bible Curry
Born np, *c.*1790; died Thanet, Kent, 1875

Alexander Custard
Baptized Plympton St Mary, Devon, 6 December 1621

William Spam Dadd
Born Skelton, Yorkshire, *c.*1881 (Skelton, 1901 census)

Happy Wine Dainty
(Female) Born Rugby, Staffordshire, *c.*1821
(Willenhall, Staffordshire, 1861 census)

Theophilis Tripe Damphey
Born Chard, Somerset, 1862

Louisa F. De la Sausage
Born Kentish Town, London, *c.*1844 (Enfield, Middlesex, 1871 census)

Al Dente
Born Whitechapel, London, *c.*1900
(St Botolph, Aldersgate, London, 1901 census)

Lilly Diet
Born Kilwinning, Ayrshire, 2 September 1772

Emily Dinner D. Dinner
Born Launceston, Cornwall, 1906

Ann Drybread
Married Thomas Harberd, St Simon and St Jude,
Norwich, Norfolk, 15 July 1615

Emma Jenefer [*sic*] Egg Egg
Born East Stonehouse, Devon, 1849

Fred Egg
Born Lymington, Hampshire, 1858

Mercy Egg
Married Dartford, Kent, 1849

Richard Bacon Eggar
Born Alton, Hampshire, 1861

Henry Mussel Farm
Born np, Lincolnshire, c.1873
(Chesterfield, Derbyshire, 1891 census)

Low Fat
Married Cardiff, Glamorgan, 1905

Damson Fish
(Male) Born Darwen, Lancashire, c.1850 (Darwen, 1871 census)

Philetus Fish
(Male) Born Uxbridge, Middlesex, 1844

Sue Flay
Born Wellington, Somerset, 1871

Colly Flower
Father of Rebecca Flower, married St Anne, Soho, London, 1797

Molasses Frill
Born Londonderry, Ireland, c.1811 (Liverpool, Lancashire, 1861 census)

Melchisedeck Fritter
Married Jone [sic] Deane, St James, Clerkenwell Green, London,
26 December 1630

Margarine Fryer
(Female) Born Durham, c.1831 (Darlington, Durham, 1841 census)

Gentle Fudge
Stoke Climsland, Cornwall (will, 1662)

Normal [sic] Cecil Fudge
Born Gloucester, 1891

Spencer Puff Gammon
Born Uckfield, Sussex, 1848

Prudence Pineapple Goodall
Born Stoke-on-Trent, Staffordshire, 1989
She is believed to be a unique British-born Pineapple.

Bernard Haggis
Born Barnet, Hertfordshire, 1894

Chocolatte [*sic*] Hales
Born Kingston upon Thames, Surrey, *c.*1851
(Bromley, London, 1901 census)

Henry Stunner Ham
Born St Thomas, Devon, 1860

Petronella Hamburger
Born Islington, London, 1876

Spearmint Hardy
Born Blandford, Dorset, 1906

Joseph Aero Hart
Born Rochford, Essex, 1907

Sarah Omelet Henley
Born Westminster, London, 1863

George Luncheon Hewitt
Born Greenwich, Kent, 1846

William Soup High
Died Sunderland, Durham, 1840

Catherine Highball
Married Francis Southall, Ribbesford, Worcestershire,
1 October 1818

George Raspberry Hogarth
Born Tynemouth, Northumberland, 1898

Lawrence Mash Instance
Born Tendring, Essex, 1871

James Jam
Buried Camborne, Cornwall, 9 August 1772

Eliza Fruit Jarritt
Born Kensington, London, 1868

Kind Jelly
Married Sarah Philips, St Mary, Alverstoke, Hampshire,
17 September 1754

Watercress Joe
(Male) Born np, c.1829 (Burslem, Staffordshire, 1881 census)

Apple Jordan
Born Milton, Kent, 1853

Jane Juice
Married Samuel Dawson, Faversham, Kent, 25 February 1676

George Ketchup
Baptized All Saints, Sudbury, Suffolk, 24 January 1803

Edith Mary Hudson Whis Key
Born Lofthouse, Yorkshire, c.1877 (Lofthouse, 1891 census)

Raspberry King
Born Freebridge Lynn, Norfolk, 1853

Cecil De Winton Kitcat
Born Portsea, Hampshire, 1900

Moses Lard
Born Preston, Lancashire, c.1837 (Preston, 1851 census)

Daisy Lasagna
Born np, 1907; died Wandsworth, London, 1988

Basil Leaf
Born York, 1895

Nunquam Leek
Born Leominster, Herefordshire, 1919

Emmeline Hole Lemon
Born Barnstaple, Devon, 1889

Lemon Lemon
Married City of London, 1885

Orange Lemon
Born Kingston, Surrey, 1871

Lucy Licquorice
Born np, 1905; died King's Lynn, Norfolk, 1997

Piggy Liver
Born np, Lancashire, c.1827 (Radcliffe, Lancashire, 1841 census)

Louisa Loaf
Born Middlesbrough, Yorkshire, 1897

Elizabeth Macaroni
Born London, c.1810 (Weybridge, Surrey, 1881 census)

Sarah Jane Pant Marrows
Born Caistor, Lincolnshire, 1865

Pretty Mash
(Female) Born np, Lancashire, c.1826 (Preston, Lancashire, 1841 census)

Margaret Coffee Maxwell
Born West Derby, Lancashire, 1893

Tomato May
Born Lambeth, London, 1889 (Lambeth, 1891 census)

Walter Mellon
Born Salford, Lancashire, 1839

Mary Magdalene Milk
Married William Hopkins, St John, Hackney, London, 27 April 1751

Posthumous Mince
Died Greenwich, Kent, 1839

Andrew Cheesy Molt
Born St Albans, Hertfordshire, 1871

Trifle Muddock
Married Hartismere, Suffolk, 1853

Sop Muffin
Born Bedford, 1846

Joseph Twaddle Mustard
Born Tynemouth, Northumberland, 1897

Alfred Kipper Negus
Born Redruth, Cornwall, 1887

Carry Apricot Nicholls
Born Kingsbridge, Devon, 1885

Nacky Noodle
(Male) Born South Shields, Durham (Leeds, Yorkshire, 1901 census)

Hazel Nutt
Born Holborn, London, 1894

P. Nutt
Born Macclesfield, Cheshire, 1859

A more recent Peter Nutt, a Scunthorpe schoolteacher, tired of being known to his pupils as P. Nutt, changed his surname to Knuddsen.

Flossie Gross Oats
Born Penzance, Cornwall, 1890

Comfort Offal
(Female) Baptized Welland, Worcestershire, 8 April 1756

Mary Potage Oliver
Born Laceby, Lincolnshire, c.1849
(St James, Lincoln, 1871 census)

Edward Singular Onion
Born Shepton Mallet, Somerset, 1871

George Onion Onions
Born Aberystwyth, Cardiganshire, 1879

Mary Picken Onions
Born Wellington, Shropshire, 1844

Ann Orange
Married William Royston, St Dunstan,
Stepney, London, 30 June 1755

Cinderella Orange
Born Wakefield, Yorkshire, 1843

Lemon Orange
Baptized Newcastle-under-Lyme, Staffordshire, 28 July 1723

P. Orridge
(Female) Born Chesterfield, Derbyshire, 1894

Mary Spangle Osborn
Born Eastbourne, Sussex, c.1886 (Eastbourne, 1891 census)

Frederick Cheese Painter
Born Lambeth, London, 1859

Lucy Pancake
Married Thomas Drew, Deene, Northamptonshire,
30 December 1733

Asher Pasta
Born Twickenham, Middlesex, c.1724

Henrietta Peach
Born Burton upon Trent, Staffordshire, 1875

Matilda Peach Peach
Born Yeovil, Somerset, 1882

Agnes Etta Pepper
Born Ipswich, Suffolk, 1881

Gordon Salter Pepper
Born Blything, Suffolk, 1876

Truth Peppercorn
Born Edmonton, Middlesex, 1860

Genius Pickles
Born Bradford, Yorkshire, 1855

Your Pickles
(Male) Born Todmorden, Lancashire, c.1846
(Todmorden, 1871 census)

Agneta Pie
Baptized Belton, near Epworth, Lincolnshire, 4 July 1562

Raisin Plumb
(Male) Born Cambridgeshire, c.1839
(West Wratting, Cambridgeshire, 1841 census)

Cashew Poole
Born Birmingham, Warwickshire, 1877

George Pork
Married Jane Wetlock, Cathedral Church of St Thomas of Canterbury,
Portsmouth, Hampshire, 30 July 1827

Theophilus Porridge
Baptized Gravesend, Kent, 22 September 1752

Florence Gooseberry Pratt
Born Whitechapel, London, 1868

Strawberry E. Presnell
Married St Olave, Southwark, London, 1888

Ralph Prune
Baptized Christ Church, Greyfriars, Newgate, London, 22 August 1549

Fanny Pudding
Born Preston, Somerset, c.1847 (Yeovil, Somerset, 1861 census)

Hephzibah Pudding
Married Newington, London, 1845

Butter Reynolds
Married Mile End, London, 1876

Joseph Rhubarb
Married Elisabeth Steward, St Mary in the Marsh,
Norwich, Norfolk, 10 January 1736

Mary Sandwich Rice
Born Cockermouth, Cumberland, 1874

Charlotte Russe
Born Liverpool, Lancashire, c.1842 (Woodhey, Cheshire, 1901 census)

Hans Sandwich
Born np, Germany, c.1858 (Birkenhead, Cheshire, 1881 census)

Elizabeth Sausage
Married John Magennis, Chatham, Kent, 24 June 1812

Annie Seed
Baptized St John Preston, Lancashire, 17 August 1862

Patti Serrie
(Male) Born np, Ireland, c.1816
(Cadder, Lanarkshire, 1841 Scotland census)

Banana Bill Shaw
Born np, 1919; died np, Lincolnshire, 2003

Blu Sherry
(Male) Born Liverpool, Lancashire, c.1873 (Liverpool, 1901 census)

Bovril Simpson
Married West Ham, Essex, 1911

William Souffle
Died Newcastle upon Tyne, Northumberland, 1871

Abraham Soup
Married Agnesse Messenger, Burbage, Leicestershire,
23 January 1606

William Radish Southgate
Born Fincham, Norfolk, c.1833 (Bethnal Green, London, 1861 census)

Sarah Spam
Born Durham, c.1760 (Bishop Wearmouth, 1841 census)

Min Spiess
Born Laverton, Gloucestershire, c.1876
(Snowshill, Gloucestershire, 1891 census)

Abraham Spinach
Born Bethnal Green, London, 1889

Martha Stew
Baptized Nantwich, Cheshire, 22 April 1827

Getta Supper
Born St Giles, London, 1905

Jam [*sic*] Organ Sweet
Born Gravesend, Kent, 1892

Catherine Beetroot Tapper
Born Newton Abbot, Devon, 1891

Eunice Tart
Baptized Brierley Hill, Staffordshire, 6 August 1820

Ambrose Tea
Baptized St Botolph, Aldersgate, London, 16 August 1727

Benjamin Teapot
Born Neath, Glamorgan, 1858

This Benjamin Teapot started a short-lived local trend – two others born in Neath in 1867 and 1878 received the same name.

Agnes Semolina Thrower
Born Newcastle upon Tyne, Northumberland, 1889

Len Tills
Born Stockton-on-Tees, Durham, 1905

T. Time
(Male) Baptized Crowle, Lincolnshire, 4 August 1855

Sarah Toffee
Born Gravesend, Kent, c.1862 (Clerkenwell, London, 1881 census)

Thomas Treacle
Born Abergavenny, c.1874 (Abergavenny, 1881 Wales census)

John Gustavus Trifle
Married St George in the East, London, 1858

Jane Loosemore Tripe
Married City of London, 1884

Tripe Trips
Born Exeter, Devon, 1872

Violet Trout
Born Devonport, Devon, 1900

Elizabeth Truffle
Baptized Bradfield St Clare, Suffolk, 8 April 1731

Whitehead Turnip
Baptized Bolsover, Derbyshire, 31 December 1825

James Coke Twist
Born Prescot, Lancashire, 1852

Delicia Veal
Born Bideford, Devon, 1839

Valkyrien Odour Veal
(Male) Born South Stoneham, Hampshire, 1871

Thomas Vegetable
Born Tettenhall, Staffordshire, c.1825
(Birmingham, Warwickshire, 1851 census)

Alborac Vinegar
(Male) Born np, Wiltshire (Downton, Wiltshire, 1841 census)

Mary Vodka
Baptized St Saviour, York, 21 March 1639

Joseph Waffle
Born Withingham, Lancashire, c.1784
(Walton-le-Dale, Lancashire, 1851 census)

Mineral Waters
Born Shoeburyness, Essex, c.1893 (Shoeburyness, 1901 census)

Charles Cranberry Winfield
Married Gloucester, 1850

Salami Wingate
(Female) Born Alford, Lincolnshire, c.1842 (Alford, 1851 census)

Chapter Six

BEASTLY NAMES

Lewis Lobster Abbs
Born Erpingham, Norfolk, 1884

William Rat Adah
Born Liverpool, Lancashire, 1862

Baboon Dalbert Anson
(Female) Born np, Scotland, c.1844 (Clewer, Berkshire, 1871 census)

Annie Ant
Born Whitechapel, London, 1879

Hercules Anthill
Baptized St Peter Southgate, Norwich, Norfolk, 7 June 1711

Abraham Ape
Baptized Staindrop, Durham, 4 January 1669

Liz Ard
Born np, Ireland, c.1824 (Waltham Abbey, Essex, 1871 census)

Hamster C. Armatys
(Male) Born Clerkenwell, London, c.1853 (Headingley, Yorkshire, 1901 census)

Anne Asp
Married John Tarling, Epping, Essex, 4 September 1655

Adder Attack
Born Hull, Yorkshire, c.1866
(Sculcoates, Yorkshire, 1881 census)

Cockle Ayton
Born Depwade, Norfolk, 1842

Benjamin Baboon
Married Mile End, London, 1897

Diehappy Badger
(Female) Born West Bromwich, Staffordshire, c.1860
(West Bromwich, 1861 census)

Minty Badger
Married Southam, Warwickshire, 1866

Smiley Badger
(Female) Born Napton, Warwickshire
(Southam, Warwickshire, 1901 census)

Mary Balamb
Born np, c.1811 (St Giles-in-the-Fields, London, 1841 census)

Cat Basket
Married Robert Girling, St Matthew, Ipswich, Suffolk, 19 November 1764

Rupert Bear
Born Stratford, Essex, c.1878 (Harrow, Middlesex, 1881 census)

Teddy Bear
Born np, 1912; died Maidstone, Kent, 1998

Savage Beare
Baptized St John, Portsea, Hampshire, 3 September 1795

Gary M. (The Most Honourable) Beaver
Married Nargis S. Caan, West Surrey, 2001

Bea Bee
Born Windsor, Berkshire, 1866

Large Bee
(Male) Born np, Nottinghamshire, c.1829 (Nottingham, 1891 census)
His son was also called Large Bee.

Ladybird Bingley
Born Kensington, London, 1871

Baby Bird
(Male) Born Shotlow, Norfolk, c.1829 (St Marylebone, London, 1871 census)
An unusual name for a 42-year-old farrier and father of eight children.

Charles Game Bird
Born Holborn, London, 1881

Crapper Bird
Born Bury, Lancashire, 1870

Dicky Bird
Born Edmonton, Middlesex, 1894

Earle Bird
Born Wandsworth, London, 1894

Moggy Birdwistle
Born np, Middlesex, c.1832 (Finsbury, London, 1841 census)

Otter Bloodworth
Died Peterborough, Northamptonshire, 1842

Cod Bohling
Died Whitechapel, London, 1880

Lizard Booth
Born Sheffield, Yorkshire, 1838

John Snail Borrell
Born Chorlton, Lancashire, 1882

Margerie Budgie
Married William Coles, Solihull, Warwickshire, 9 February 1571

Anger Bull
Buried St Dionis Backchurch, London, 22 December 1680

Bastard Bull
Died Plomesgate, Suffolk, 1839

Thomas Bulldog
Born np, Yorkshire, c.1851
(Priest Hutton, Lancashire, 1901 census)

Easter Bunny
(Female) Born np, Yorkshire, c.1826
(Bradford, Yorkshire, 1841 census)

Steadfast Bunny
(Female) Born Bristol, Gloucestershire, c.1808
(Hubberston, Pembrokeshire, 1861 Wales census)

William Mole Burrow
Born Wellingborough, Northamptonshire, 1853

Moose Burrows
(Female) Born Bolton, Lancashire, c.1862
(Bolton, 1871 census)

Fly Burt
Born Plymouth, Devon, 1897

Isaac Worm Butcher
Born Blything, Suffolk, 1843

Violet Mice Butcher
Born Wandsworth, London, 1908

Betty Butterfly
Born Spursholt, Hampshire, 1751

Sir Anthony Wass Buzzard
Born St George Hanover Square, London, 1902

Harris Vole Candle
Born Jersey, Channel Islands, c.1820
(Westbury on Trym, Gloucestershire, 1871 census)

Tom Cat
Baptized St Michael's, Withyham, Sussex, 16 October 1624

Wolf Bear Chalvony
Born St George in the East, London, 1910

Ann Chevye
Baptized Sedbergh, Yorkshire, 1 January 1615

Kerrenhappuch Chick
(Female) Baptized Thornecombe, Dorset, 17 March 1756

Quintus Chicken
Married Eliza Gillon, Colchester, Essex, 1878

Richard Chimp
Married Anne Wells, St Albans Abbey, Hertfordshire,
22 April 1679

Ethel Chinchilla
Born Aston, Warwickshire, 1900 (Aston, 1901 census)

Sloth Cleaver
(Male) Born Dunstable, Bedfordshire, 1861 (Dunstable, 1861 census)

Pubens Cockle
(Male) Born Northampton, c.1869 (Northampton, 1891 census)

Anna Conder
Born Mile End, London, c.1794 (West Ham, Essex, 1851 census)

Claude Crabb
Born London, c.1875 (Stratford, London, 1901 census)

Mungo Creature
Baptized Holm and Paplay, Orkney, 2 April 1769

Jane Crocodile
Born np, c.1822 (Blandford, Dorset, 1841 census)

Job Pickering Crow Crow
Born Ecclesfield, Yorkshire, 1840

Nightingale Cuckoo
Died Westminster, London, 1838

Jack Daw
Born Bermondsey, London, c.1872 (Bermondsey, 1901 census)

Shark Dawson
Died Bradford, Yorkshire, 1852

Thomas Fox Decent
Born Dover, Kent, 1837

Dorothy Spider De La H. Maddocks
Born Ross-on-Wye, Herefordshire, 1890

Emily Wevil Dennett
Born Nantwich, Cheshire, 1882

Mammallia Dobson
Born Yeadon, Yorkshire, c.1861 (Yeadon, 1881 census)

Elizabeth Dodo
Baptized Bristol, Gloucestershire, 12 July 1738

Cat Dog
Baptized Dundee, Angus, 13 November 1679

Zephaniah Donkey
Baptized St Peter's, Liverpool, Lancashire, 2 April 1827

Jane Ding Dove
Born np, c.1827; died Spalding, Lincolnshire, 1898

Ginsel Dragon
Married James Alexander, Erskine, Renfrewshire,
12 June 1759

Donald Duck
Born Edmonton, Middlesex, 1899
Donald Duck was the brother of Rhoda Duck.

Love A. Duck
Born Helmsley, Yorkshire, 1820

Snowdrop Eagle
Born St Olave, Southwark, London, 1894

Charlotte Earwig
Baptized St Mary, Marylebone Road, London, 29 May 1772

Vermin Eastwood
(Female) Born Burnley, Lancashire, c.1841 (Blackpool, Lancashire, 1861 census)

Mammal Edwards
Died Pontypool, Monmouthshire, 1846

Ann Eel
Baptized Watlington, Oxfordshire, 16 February 1812

Fanny Elephant
Born Liverpool, Lancashire, 1908

Elle Fant
Born Durham, 1861

Vixen Faulkner
(Female) Born Edmonton, Middlesex, 1889

Fanny Ferret
Born Bideford, Devon, 1877

Mary Ann Fieldmouse
Married Wolverhampton, Staffordshire, 1877

Fish Fish
Born Salford, Lancashire, 1840

Happy Fish
Died Wangford, Suffolk, 1837

John Pilot Fish
Born Loddon, Norfolk, 1839

Milliner Flea
Married Samuel Jewell, St Mary Magdalene, Taunton,
Somerset, 5 September 1695

Mary Stoat O. Float
Born Plymouth, Devon, c.1828 (Plymouth, 1851 census)

Locust Fosburg
(Female) Born Leatherhead, Surrey, c.1887
(Camberwell, London, 1891 census)

Foxy Fox
(Male) Born np, 1947; died Bangor,
Caernarvonshire, 1999

Wolf Fox
Born Whitechapel, London, c.1876
(Whitechapel, 1881 census)

Zany Fox
Born St Pancras, London, 1908

William Frog
Born Holborn, London, 1849

Newt Gawthrop
Married North Bierley, Yorkshire, 1901

Gazelle George
Married Flegg, Norfolk, 1873

Merry Gibbons
Died Stepney, London, 1846

Magpie Ginger
Born np, c.1849; died Sedbergh, Yorkshire, 1902

George Gnat
Born np, Norfolk, c.1796 (Castle Acre, Norfolk, 1841 census)

Edward James Goat Goat
Born Norwich, Norfolk, 1843

Gertrude Obedience Goose
Born Yarmouth, Norfolk, 1898

Mary Grasshopper
Baptized St Giles without Cripplegate, London, 7 February 1762

Adolfine Grebe
Born St Marylebone, London, 1888

Edwin Bullock Guzzle
Baptized Blakeney, Gloucestershire, 11 March 1826

Thomas Chicken Hair
Born Tynemouth, Northumberland, 1838

John Hamster
Married Elizabeth Pearson, Sheffield Cathedral,
Sheffield, Yorkshire, 2 February 1784

Piggy Hart
Born Chorley, Lancashire, 1852

Joseph Hedgehog
Baptized Bromyard, Herefordshire, 15 January 1745

Bland Herring
Born Caistor, Lincolnshire, 1851

Cycle Herring
Born Madeley, Shropshire, c.1897 (Shifnal, Shropshire, 1901 census)

Rembrandt Herring
Born Downham Market, Norfolk, c.1841
(Battersea, London, 1881 census)

Priscilla Hippo
Baptized St Matthew, Bethnal Green, London, 13 October 1782

Sun Fat Fish Ho
Rochdale, Lancashire (phone book, 1977)

Stormy Petrel Hodgson
Born Stepney, London, 1892

Trout Holdsworth
Born Skipton, Yorkshire, 1885

Ass Holmes
Born Skipton, Yorkshire, 1866

Hornet Hunk
(Female) Born West Cowes, Isle of Wight, c.1812
(Northwood, Hampshire, 1881 census)

Moth Hunt
(Male) Born np, Middlesex c.1821 (Hillingdon, Middlesex, 1841 census)

John Jaguar
Married Wigan, Lancashire, 1878

Larva Beatrice Jeffries
Born Hereford, 1892

Lamprey Karney
Born Eastry, Kent, 1838

Ali Katt
(Female) Born Axminster, Devon, c.1819
(Lyme, Dorset, 1871 census)

Don Key
Born Norwich, Norfolk, 1885

Turtle King
Married Sheffield, Yorkshire, 1887

Albatross Louisa Kingston
Born Cookham, Berkshire, 1891

Benjamin Pig Kirkham
Born Boston, Lincolnshire, c.1860 (Boston, 1881 census)

Cat Kitten
Born Lawhitton, Cornwall, c.1820
(Launceston, Cornwall, 1851 census)

Adder Knaggs
Born Stockton-on-Tees, Durham, 1855

Martian Lamb
Born London, c.1860 (Woolverstone, Suffolk, 1861 census)

Snake H. Lawless
Married Tequilla-Jack Daniel, Southampton, Hampshire, 2001

Dolphin Leach
Died Camberwell, London, 1911

Zebra Leek
Died Birmingham, Warwickshire, 1865

John James Leveret White Leveret
Born Leicester, 1860

Kitty Litter
Born Martson, Cheshire, c.1839
(Wincham, Cheshire, 1851 census)

Lucina Lizard
Baptized St Dunstan, Stepney, London, 22 April 1717

Mary Lobster
Born Ilkeston, Derbyshire, c.1817 (Ilkeston, 1881 census)

Mole Lory
Born Chertsey, Surrey, 1882

Grizall Louse
Baptized Loudon, Ayr, 4 February 1781

Emu Luckwill
Born Williton, Somerset, 1864

Creature Lugger
Buried Sheviock, Cornwall, 23 May 1613

Pilchard Macksey
(Male) Born Liverpool, Lancashire, c.1871
(Litherland, Lancashire, 1891 census)

Ginger Magpie
Born np, c.1849; died Sedbergh, Yorkshire, 1902

Emma Mammal
Born Eldingdon, Warwickshire, c.1834
(Birmingham, Warwickshire, 1851 census)

Rabbit Martin
(Male) Born np, Hampshire, c.1835 (Otterbourne, Hampshire, 1841 census)

Cat Mews
Born np, c.1839; died Hexham, Northumberland, 1911

Ming Mole
Born np, Buckinghamshire, c.1781 (Ashendon, Buckinghamshire, 1841 census)

William Scrambler Moles
Born np, c.1885; died Kings Norton, Worcestershire, 1909

Winnie Weasel Mollinson
Born Chelsea, London, 1859

Grace Monkey
Baptized Sithney, Cornwall, 3 March 1839

Kitty Moose
Baptized Stourton, Wiltshire, 17 April 1825

Henrietta Mosquito
Born np, c.1884; died Toxteth Park, Lancashire, 1914

Dotty Moth
(Female) Born Warwickshire, c.1889 (Kenilworth, Warwickshire, 1901 census)

Moth John K. Moth
Born Bagworth, Leicestershire, 1845

Micky Mouse
Married Dorothy Collett, Totternhoe, Bedfordshire, 13 May 1641

Elk Mutter
Born Pitminster, Somerset, c.1856 (Corfe, Somerset, 1901 census)

Pascow Newt
Baptized St Dominick, Cornwall, 17 May 1619

Chimp Norman
Born np, 1909; died Dacorum, Hertfordshire, 1999

Blanche Zoo Nules
Born Great Bentley, Essex, c.1862 (Colchester, Essex, 1871 census)

Joseph Bug Nunn
Born Stow, Suffolk, 1841

Puffin Annabelinda O'Hanlon
Born Oxford, March 1985

Maudlin Orang
Married Isaac Lepley, St Dunstan, Stepney, London, 28 February 1700

Otter Otters
Died Mile End, London, 1868

Ann Owl
Baptized Wellington, Shropshire, 13 August 1797

Reufrozina Oyster
Born St Cuthbert's, North Shields, Northumberland, 5 February 1897

Beaver Panter
Died Kettering, Northamptonshire, 1849

Fine Orick Parrot
Born Stanbridge, Bedfordshire, c.1851
(Leighton Buzzard, Bedfordshire, 1871 census)

Polly Parrot
Baptized Luddington, Lincolnshire, 21 June 1778

Philomena Mary Pelican
Born 7 April 1920; died Hounslow, London, 1988

Matilda Pigeon Pigeon
Born St Giles, London, 1874

Ernest Piggy
Born Woolwich, Kent, c.1859 (Minster-in-Sheppey, Kent, 1881 census)

Reuben Toad Pinkney
Born Whitby, Yorkshire, 1847

Sara Pismire
Married St Cuthbert, Bedford, 10 April 1666
A pismire is another word for the common ant.

Benjamin Squirrel Pitt
Born Stockport, Cheshire, 1892

Ostrich Pockinghorn
Married St Stephens by Saltash, Cornwall, 1792

Rich Poodle
Married Lydia Carpenter, Shipton-under-Wychwood, Oxfordshire, 1836

John Possum
Married Elizabeth Roy, Holy Trinity, Gosport, Hampshire, 23 May 1717

John Prawn
Baptized Kilspindie, Perth, 13 March 1737

Peacock Prettyman
(Male) Baptized St Botolph, Aldgate, London, 18 August 1727

Mary Python
Married George Sephton, Aughton by Ormskirk, Lancashire,
14 September 1818

Esther Rabbit
Born Gouldstone, Kent, c.1836 (Orpington, Kent, 1861 census)

Henery [sic] Racoon
Born Stanford-le-Hope, Essex, c.1831 (Dagenham, Essex, 1881 census)

Fanny Mary Cuckoo Rawbone
Died Lambeth, London, 1837

Annie Rhino
Married Merthyr Tydfil, Glamorgan, 1881

Wandering Robin
Born c.1858; died Hartlepool, Durham, 1898

Charles Pelican Roebeuck
Married East Stonehouse, Devon, 1856

Hairby Rook Rook
Born Spilsby, Lincolnshire, 1843

Chris Sallis
Baptized Littleport, Cambridgeshire, 17 November 1804

Porridge Salmon
Born Brackley, Northamptonshire, 1840

Sofa Salmon
Born Dunmow, Essex, 1859

Dinah Saw
Baptized St Lawrence, Chobham, Surrey, 18 October 1818

Thomas Sheep Shanks
Born np, c.1796 (Holy Trinity, Coventry, 1841 census)

Charles E. Crunk Shark
Born np, Scotland, c.1874 (Stoke Charity, Hampshire, 1891 census)

John Shelfish
Baptized St Katharine by the Tower, London, 19 January 1691

Cuckoo Hope Shipperson
Born Barnet, Middlesex, 1891

Sarah Jane Shrew
Baptized St Mark, Dukinfield, Cheshire, 5 December 1847

Isabella Shrimp
Baptized St Stephen Coleman, London, 23 November 1718

Mary Winkle Shufflebotham
Born Macclesfield, Cheshire, 1843

Goat Skippen
Died Wangford, Suffolk, 1858

Jane Skunk
Baptized Ottringham, Yorkshire, 13 August 1570

Sarah Slug
Married Roger Hill, Westbury, Wiltshire, 10 April 1757

Alice Snake
Married Joseph Millard, Thornford, Dorset, 3 June 1621

Jane Perfect Sparrow
Born Mere, Wiltshire, 1859

Mary Spider
Married Mathew Tompson, Grantham, Lincolnshire, 3 July 1732

Joseph Squid
Born St George in the East, London, c.1864
(Bethnal Green, London, 1881 census)

Charity Squirrel
Baptized Swimbridge, Devon, 5 February 1565

Bat Stack
Born Merthyr Tydfil, Glamorgan, 1858

Robert Shuffle Starling
Born Plympton St Mary, Devon, 1845

Sophia Stoat
Born Islington, London, 1879

Symen Swine
Married Katherine Tegue, St Thomas the Apostle,
Exeter, Devon, 2 August 1698

Faithfull Tadpole
Baptized St John the Evangelist, Dublin, 11 November 1665

Ann Teater
Born Lamberhurst, Sussex, c.1854 (Tonbridge, Kent, 1881 census)

Thomas Tiger
Married Elizabeth Stout, St Mary, Beverley, Yorkshire, 23 December 1694

Jemima Tortoise
Baptized Swafield, Norfolk, 6 April 1794

Horse Browe Trist
Born np, c.1800; died Godstone, Surrey, 1877

Fanny Pony G. Trubody
Born Bedwelty, Monmouthshire, 1881

Debby Turkey
Married Thomas Jackson, Holy Trinity, Gosport, Hampshire, 14 October 1805

Shady Turtle
(Female) Born Southwell, Nottinghamshire, 1892

Jane Dingo Voisey
Died Pembroke, c.1806

Darrel Vole
Baptized St Botolph, Colchester, Essex, 6 July 1705

Mary Ann Vulture
Married Caistor, Lincolnshire, 1863

Henry Beast Waddingham
Born Howden, Yorkshire, 1842

Jonah Wales
Born Walsall, Staffordshire, 1858

Elizabeth Wallaby
Baptized Spennithorne, Yorkshire, 7 March 1780

Noble Wasp
Baptized St Mary at Coslany, Norwich, Norfolk, 27 February 1773

Alice Weasel
Born Poplar, London, 1880

Brightweed Whale
Baptized Lezant, Cornwall, 28 January 1585

Clement Sparrow Wham
Baptized Nardwell, Suffolk, 7 November 1839

Mary Ape Wild
Born Wolverhampton Staffordshire, c.1834
(Wolverhampton, 1871 census)

Wildgoose Wildgoose
(Male) Born Bakewell, Derbyshire, c.1846 (Bakewell, 1851 census)

Eliza Auroch Willet
Born Dulwich, London, c.1829 (Lambeth, London, 1901 census)
*The auroch was a cow-like animal that once roamed
across Europe, but became extinct in 1627.*

Whale Windsor
Died Coventry, Warwickshire, 1864

Hamlet Winkle
Baptized Burslem, Staffordshire, 1 May 1808

Wolf Wolf
Born St George in the East, London, 1886

Dodo Woodcock
Married Atcham, Shropshire, 1903

Unity Worm
Married John Speller, Salcombe Regis, Devon, 4 November 1805

Mao Worms
Married West Derby, Lancashire, 1908

Margaret McOstrich Yeoman
Born Camberwell, Surrey, 1886

Alice Zebra
Married Westminster, London, 1864

FLORA BRITANNICA

Leafy Babb
Died Bideford, Devon, 1904

Blossom Bassam
Born Maidstone, Kent, 1892

Margarett [*sic*] Beanblossom
Born Finsbury, London, 1826; died 1903

Holly Berry
Born Barnsley, Yorkshire, 1880

Pete Bog
Married Eliza Young, St Pancras, London, 1812

Flowery Bolliski
Died Leeds, Yorkshire, 1875

Olive Branch
Born West Ham, Essex, 1880

Rose Bush
Born Shoreditch, London, 1864

Elegant Verbena Edwards
Born Thetford, Norfolk, 1902

Jeannie Machine Flower
Born np, Scotland, *c.*1859 (Surbiton, Surrey, 1901 census)

Oleander George Freestone
(Male) Born np, Cambridgeshire, *c.*1849
(Cambridge, 1861 census)

Field Flowers Goe
Born Coningsby, Lincolnshire, *c.*1798
(Louth, Lincolnshire, 1861 census)

Gladiolus Gooch
Born Smallburgh, Norfolk, 1896

Sophia Grass Grass
Born Thetford, Norfolk, 1862

Ever Green
Born Lexden, Essex, 1847

Theresa Green
Baptized Motcombe, Dorset, 23 September 1804

Sycamore Hyam
Married City of London, 1878

Arminel Lavender
Offerton, Cheshire (will, 1812)

Vine Leaf
Born York, 1896

Dan D. Lyons
Born Cardiff, Glamorgan, 1891 (Cardiff, 1891 Wales census)

Innocent Mandrake
Married Magdalene Young, St George, Mayfair, London, 17 March 1753

Lavender Marjoram
Born Mitford, Norfolk, 1848

Pete Moss
Baptized Acton by Nantwich, Cheshire, 22 June 1679

Matilda Mushroom
Married John Shanks, Skirlaugh, Yorkshire, 1848

Dahlia Zsta [*sic*] Norris
Born West Ham, Essex, 1890

Sunny Orchard
Died Poole, Dorset, 1837

Pansy Daffodil Parcell
Born South Stoneham, Hampshire, 1902

Flora Plant
Born Walsall, Staffordshire, 1870

Poppy Primrose Purple
Born Mitford, Norfolk, 1907

Lawn Ridding
Born Keighley, Yorkshire, 1880

Seaflower Rolls
Born Cookham, Berkshire, 1875

Seaflower was the sister of Benbow, Bluebell, Daisy, May,
Ocean and Snowdrop Rolls.

Calculus Sage
Born Foleshill, Warwickshire, 1901

Cyril Cactus Scott
Born Lewisham, London, 1909

Mitchell Big Tree
Born Chorlton, Lancashire, 1896

Sarabelle Tulip
Born St Marylebone, London, c.1850 (Rotherhithe, London, 1891 census)

Docitheus Twigg
Born np, c.1792; died Aston, Warwickshire, 1874

Chapter Seven

THE GOOD
THE BAD AND
THE UGLY

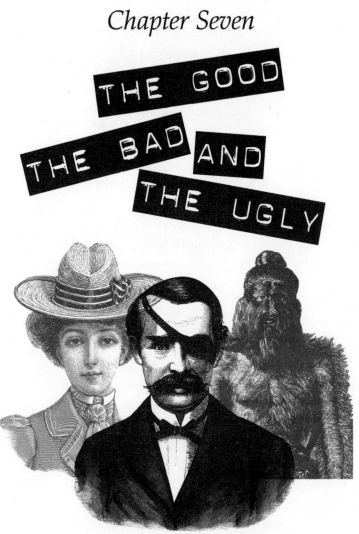

In which we meet a diverse array of people whose names are remarkable, baffling, uncategorizable, or just plain weird.

—A—

Alf Abbet
Born Teddington, Middlesex, c.1849 (Teddington, 1891 census)

George Sneezum Acock
Born Woolwich, London, 1873

Lettice Agree
Born Mottram, Cheshire, c.1866 (Ashton-under-Lyne, Lancashire, 1871 census)

Herbert Slap Aldhous
Born Islington, London, 1874

Agent Mildred Allsop
Born Barrow upon Soar, Leicestershire, 1904

Phil Ander
Born Westminster, London, c.1842
(St Martin-in-the-Fields, London, 1871 census)

Furious Andrews
(Female) Born Great Horwood, Buckinghamshire, c.1821
(Steeple Claydon, Buckinghamshire, 1881 census)

B. Ann Angel
(Female) Born Bedwelty, Monmouthshire, 1894

Elizabeth Comical Angel
Married Kingston upon Hull, Yorkshire, 1845

Onesiphorous Ankers
Married Blackburn, Lancashire, 1910

John Anonymous
Born np, c.1865; died West Ham, Essex, 1868

Rameses Arblaster
Born Cannock, Staffordshire, 1910

Ann Archy
Born Haslingden, Lancashire, 1886

Annie Argument
Born Durham, 1887

Wow Ashworth
(Female) Born np, Lancashire, c.1771
(Blackburn, Lancashire, 1841 census)

Herbert Abcdef Atkinson
Born Tynemouth, Northumberland, 1904

Betty Auckward
Baptized All Saints, Hereford, 6 June 1755

—B—

Fairest Babbett
Died Manchester, Lancashire, 1864

Eileen Back
Born Merthyr Tydfil, Glamorgan, 1908

Helen Back
Born Tiverton, Devon, 1849

Shepherdess Jane Backhoffner
Born St Marylebone, London, 1845 (St Marylebone, 1851 census)
Shepherdess was the daughter of George H. Backhoffner, Professor of Chemistry and Natural Philosophy and Registrar of Births & Deaths.

Ptolemy Tom Backholer
Born Sherborne, Dorset, 1872

Bedding Badding
Born Holborn, London, c.1889
(Lambeth, London, 1901 census)

Lilian Comforter Badman
Born West Ham, Essex, 1902

George Hand Bagguley
Born Stoke-on-Trent, Staffordshire, 1850

Earthly Emma Bailey
Born Mitford, Norfolk, 1879

Bertram Cannon Ball
Born Stourbridge, Worcestershire, 1875

Intercydonia M. Ball
(Female) Married James Jarvis, Wolstanton, Staffordshire, 1912

Mother Balmforth
Born Bramley, Yorkshire, 1866

Banger Balster
Married Manchester, Lancashire, 1855

Aberycusgentylis Balthropp
Baptized Iver, Buckinghamshire, 25 January 1648

Ed Banger
Baptized North Petherton, Somerset, 4 February 1635

Dimple H. Bangle
(Male) Born Barnstaple, Devon, c.1825 (Instow, Devon, 1871 census)

Piggy Banks
Born Kimmeridge, Dorset, c.1810 (East Stonehouse, Devon, 1851 census)

Robin Banks
Born Denton, Lancashire, c.1864 (Denton, 1901 census)

Fud Barbee
Born np, Scotland, c.1853 (on ship *Bride of the Nile*, Humber, 1871 census)

Ali Barber
Baptized Inveresk with Musselburgh, Midlothian, 29 August 1731

William Y. Barfly
Born Penmaenmar, Caernarvonshire, c.1864 (Leck, Lancashire, 1881 census)

Joseph XXX Barkass
Married Newcastle upon Tyne, Northumberland, 1855

Zerrubabel Barraclough
Born Keighley, Yorkshire, 1879

Faith Hope And Charity Barratt*
Born Exeter, Devon, 1846

Lilian Fluffy Barrett
Born Shoreditch, London, 1895

Thomas Honeybun Bartlett
Born Weymouth, Dorset, 1877

Monte Cristo T. Barton
Born Lambeth, London, 1898

Boadicea Basher
Baptized St Hilary, Cornwall, 13 January 1856

William Bashful
Born np, Staffordshire, c.1847 (Spitalfields, London, 1871 census)

Bertie Basin
Born Holborn, London, c.1891 (Clerkenwell, London, 1901 census)

Fancy Baskett
Married Steyning, Sussex, 1880

Sosthenes Bather
Died Colchester, Essex, 1847

Wholesome Bayliss
Born np, 27 January 1920; died np, Surrey, 1985

Thomas Grain Thought Bays
Married City of London, 1841

Sandy Beach
(Female) Born St George in the East, London, c.1899
(St George in the East, 1901 census)

New Year Beadle
(Female) Married James Theaker, Thorne, Lincolnshire, 1862

Mercy Beak
Married Bath, Somerset, 1870

One person

Hula Beanland
Born Burnley, Lancashire, 1871

Choo Ah Beano
Married Stepney, London, 1882

Astynax Beattle
Born Burghfield, Berkshire, c.1855 (Dorking, Surrey, 1871 census)

Harry Beatup
Born Eastbourne, Sussex, c.1878 (Eastbourne, 1881 census)

John Sidney Six Beckham
Born Norwich, Norfolk, 1860

Eleazer Bed
Born Whitechapel, London, 1871

John Goto Bed
Born London, c.1822 (Swanage, Dorset, 1861 census)

Gaylord Beebe
Born Ashton-under-Lyne, Lancashire, 1892

Sarah Pudentia Beeks
Married Bala, Merionethshire, 1868

Bess Befor
Baptized St Giles without Cripplegate, London, 26 July 1629

C. Below
Married John Howell, St Bride Fleet Street, London, 8 November 1808

Bozy Bench
Born Calverton, Nottinghamshire, c.1889 (Calverton, 1891 census)

May Snow Bennett
Born Plymouth, Devon, 1893

Thomas Churchreform Bennett
Married Faversham, Kent, 1858

Rob Bery
Born Whitechapel, London, 1857

Tunu Bibi
Born np, 1938; died St Albans, Hertfordshire, 1998
Tunu is said to be a Miwok Indian name meaning
'deer thinking about going to eat wild onions'.

Annice Bible
Born Wolstanton, Staffordshire, 1907

Uretha Jane Biddle
Born Nottingham, 1889

Betty Big
Baptized Rolvenden, Kent, 17 January 1762

Smallhope Biggs
(Male) Born Cranbrook, Kent, c.1556

Old Bill
Died Newcastle upon Tyne, Northumberland, 1906

Spanner Bing
Born Northwood, Isle of Wight, c.1822
(Newchurch, Hampshire, 1851 census)

Eliza Dribble Bingham
Married Chesterfield, Derbyshire, 1862

Beasley Bingo
(Male) Married Elizabeth Davies, Orleton, Herefordshire, 29 May 1681

Annie Primate Binnington
Married Sculcoates, Yorkshire, 1880

John Wheeler Binns
Born Wellington, Shropshire, 1874

Al Bino
Born St Marylebone, London, c.1860 (Southwark, London, 1871 census)

Parky Bishop
Died Pontypridd, Glamorgan, 1880

Simon Straight Bishop
Born np, c.1818; died St Columb, Cornwall, 1871

Loverly Biss
Born Sturminster Newton, Dorset, c.1825 (Bradford Abbas, Dorset, 1851 census)

Matt Black
Born Felling, Durham, c.1861 (Holmside, Durham, 1891 census)

Blandinah Blackhead
Baptized North Marston, Buckinghamshire, 6 July 1712

February Blacklog
Married Mary Harrison, All Saints, Shipdham, Norfolk, 1797

Thomas John Dosias Four Blackwell
Born Morpeth, Durham, 1842

Minnie Moon Blagg
Born Basford, Nottinghamshire, 1880

Billy Blah
Born np, Yorkshire, c.1807 (Huddersfield, Yorkshire, 1841 census)

Trueheart Blanchard
Died Spilsby, Lincolnshire, 1839

Marmaluke Bland
Married Spilsby, Lincolnshire, 1888

Stephen Bling
Married St Julian, Norwich, Norfolk, 3 August 1593

Silence Bliss
(Female) Born Woodend, Northamptonshire, c.1846
(Blakesley, Northamptonshire, 1871 census)

Strain Blogg
Born np, Norfolk, c.1773 (South Erpingham, Norfolk, 1841 census)

Emma Bloodisack
Born Rotherhithe, London, c.1858 (Hackney, 1881 census)

Phalliss Bloomer
Born Cradley, Worcestershire, c.1876 (Litchurch, Derbyshire, 1881 census)

Mary L. Blotto
Born Lambeth, London, 1911

Bill Board
Born Abergavenny, Monmouthshire, c.1890 (Abergavenny, 1891 Wales census)

Water Board
Born Axbridge, Somerset, 1853

Kiss Bobby
(Female) Born Diss, Norfolk, c.1853 (Fersfield, Norfolk, 1871 census)

Liar Bodwell
(Male) Born Manchester, Lancashire, c.1884
(Ince-in-Makerfield, Lancashire, 1901 census)

Annie Body
Born Plympton St Mary, Devon, 1866

Bold Bold
Married Salford, Lancashire, 1838

Nora Bone
Born South Stoneham, Hampshire, 1902

Fuku Nozwara Boogert
Born np, 1935; died Hammersmith, London, 1988

Risque Booth
Born Stockport, Cheshire, 1909

Julius Caesar K. Borgia
Born St Andrews, Middlesex, c.1867 (Holborn, London, 1871 census)

Friend Bottle
Born np, Middlesex, c.1816 (St Botolph, Aldersgate, London, 1841 census)

Pop Botts
(Male) Born np, Dorset, c.1878 (Bournemouth, Hampshire, 1891 census)

Bridget Bouncer
Baptized Dunchideock, Devon, 23 October 1659

Sarah Bouncy
Married Bishop's Stortford, Hertfordshire, 1876

Honour Bound
Buried St Pinnock, Cornwall, 1783

Spartacus Martial Bourdin
Born Hendon, Middlesex, 1890

He was a relative of French anarchist Martial Bourdin, who on
15 February 1894 blew himself up while attempting to detonate a bomb
at the Greenwich Observatory in Britain's first terrorist attack.

Faintnot Isaday Bourne
Born Rye, Sussex, 1878

Geronimo Bow
(Male) Married Cathe [sic] Williams, St George in the East, London, 1810

Charles Damp Bowden
Born Portsea Island, Hampshire, 1895

Utterly Bowles
Married Mary A. E. Hollier, Melton Mowbray, Leicestershire, 1918

Affability Box
Baptized St John Horsleydown, Bermondsey, London, 3 March 1822

Ima Box
Born Reading, Berkshire, c.1865 (Reading, 1871 census)

Teddy Boy
Born St Giles, London, 1902

Wallop Brabazon
Married Jane Du Pre, St Marylebone, London, 19 March 1796

Herbert Superbus Bradbury
Born Chorlton, Lancashire, 1908
His middle name is assumed to be 'Superb-us', as in Roman prefect
Marcus Superbus, rather than 'Super-bus'.

Amelia Disturnal Brassington
Born West Bromwich, Staffordshire, 1871

Susan Brasso
Baptized Wisborough Green, Sussex, 12 December 1602

Lettice Bray
Baptized Mobberley, Cheshire, 26 April 1807

Richard Clencher Brazier
Born Wolverhampton, Staffordshire, 1840

Freezer Breeze
Born Great Yarmouth, Norfolk, c.1839 (Great Yarmouth, 1851 census)

Eva Brick
(Female) Born np, Turkey c.1874 (Battersea, London, 1901 census)

Napoleon Lavoisier Voltaire Briggs
Married West Bromwich, Staffordshire, 1862

Jucy [*sic*] Ann Brocklebank
Born Bootle, Cumberland, 1871

Foetus Brocklehurst
Born Prestwich, Lancashire, 1877

Napkin Brooker
Married Mary Hawkins, St Michael, Lewes, 23 October 1799

Frederick National Broom
Born Islington, London, 1898

Rhoda Broom
Baptized St Matthew, Walsall, Staffordshire, 7 September 1795

Wack Broomhead
(Male) Born Over Haddon, Derbyshire, c.1848
(Haddon, Derbyshire, 1851 census)

Emily Pocohontas [*sic*] Brown
Born Gravesend, Kent, 1847
An appropriate middle name: native American princess
Pocahontas, wife of English colonist John Rolfe and eponymous star of the
Disney animated film, died in Gravesend 230 years earlier.

Irony Thomas Brown
Born Romford, Essex, 1843

James Skate Bubble
Baptized Pentridge, Dorset, 25 November 1876
The unfortunate son of James Skate Bubble.

Nimrod Buckett
Born Portsmouth, Hampshire, 1820

Content Increase Buckley
Born Oldham, Lancashire, 1860

Benito Mussolini Buckross
Born np, 1932; died Bradford, Yorkshire, 1997
What may have sounded like an interesting choice of first names when the
fascist dictator was allegedly making the Italian trains run on time perhaps
seemed less appealing ten years later.

Lovely Budge
Born Chard, Somerset, 1881

Alefounder Bugg
Born Brantham, Suffolk, 18 April 1817

Original Bugg
Born Lincoln, 1907

Bob Builder
Married Susanna Sproll, St Philip and St Jacob, Bristol,
Gloucestershire, 8 October 1778

Lamentation Bullivant
Born Spilsby, Lincolnshire, 1841

Rahartha Bung
(Female) Born Tiverton, Devon, c.1860 (Newton Abbot, Devon, 1861 census)

Philemon Bungy
Born Brighton, Sussex, c.1873 (Brighton, 1881 census)

Nylon S. Bunk
Married Trevor Cass, Grimsby, Yorkshire, 1987

Philadelphia Bunnyface
Laneast, Cornwall (will, 1722)

The inclusion of this name among those published by the Cornwall Record Office in its list of 'Silly Names' upset some people called Boniface, who believed the name to be a corruption of theirs.

Baby Bunting
(Female) Born Matlock, Derbyshire, c.1900 (Matlock, 1901 census)

Bounce E. Burbidge
(Female) Born Sheffield, Yorkshire, c.1856 (Sheffield, 1871 census)

Furry Jane Burbidge
Born Friskney, Lincolnshire, c.1847 (Friskney, 1871 census)

Rhoda Failing Burpee
Born Bucklow, Cheshire, 1905

Tim Burr
Born Watford, Hertfordshire, 1867

Ethelbert Bursting
Born Waterbeach, Cambridgeshire, c.1877 (Cambridge, 1901 census)

Judas Iscariot Burton
Born Stafford, 1882

Wealthy Buscomb
Buried St Breock, Cornwall, 1723

Florence May Bust
Born Nottingham, 1895

Thankful Butler
Born Hastings, Sussex, 1838

Providence Buttefant
(Female) Born np, c.1806 (Southwold, Suffolk, 1841 census)

Delight Butterworth
Born np, Massachusetts, USA, c.1856 (Droylsden, Lancashire, 1891 census)

Leviathan Buttress
Born Stevenage, Hertfordshire, c.1853 (Bartlow, Cambridgeshire, 1881 census)

Bob By
Born Battle, Sussex, c.1841 (Battle, 1841 census)
*Along with names such as Er and Up, By is one of a small
number of two-letter surnames in the UK.*

—C—

Harie Cabaret
Baptized London, 10 January 1628

T. Caddy
Born Beaminster, Somerset, 1841

Barry Cade
Married Jean M. Handley, Peterborough, Northamptonshire, 1995

William Snafu Cadman
Born St George, Southwark, London, 1853
*If correct, this would be a unique usage of 'Snafu' – better known as the
acronym for 'Situation Normal All Fucked Up' – as a name, but is more
probably a snafu by the Registrar, and is meant to be 'Snape'.*

Julia Caesar
Born Westminster, London, c.1832 (Lambeth, 1851 census)
Julia Caesar was the daughter of Octavius Caesar, a coachsmith.

Julius Caesar
Married Alice Dente, Mitcham, Surrey, 10 April 1596

Lurid Caldwell
(Male) Born np, Argyll, c.1857
(Greenock, Renfrewshire, 1871 Scotland census)

Rose Cann Cann
Born Barnstaple, Devon, 1867

Peculiar Cannon
(Female) Born Claypole, Lincolnshire, c.1876
(Hawton, Nottinghamshire, 1881 census)

Mephibosheth Capstack
(Male) Born Halifax, Yorkshire, 1869
(Northowram, Yorkshire, 1871 census)

Truly Carbon
Born Dorking, Surrey, c.1869
(Broadwater Down, Kent, 1901 census)

I. D. Card
(Female) Born Portsmouth, Hampshire, 1908

Valentine Card
(Male) Born np, 1913; died Chelmsford, Essex, 1993

Joseph Greenhouse Careless
Born Walsall, Staffordshire, 1874

John Lucknow Hidden Carpenter
Born Upton-upon-Severn, Worcestershire, 1859
*His name presumably commemorated the Siege of Lucknow,
India, two years earlier.*

Orson Carter
Born Llanelly, Monmouthshire, 1905

Clint Cartilige
Born Prescot, Lancashire, 1849

Splash Carver
Born np, 1913; died Romsey, Hampshire, 2001

George Frisky Cattermole
Born Depwade, Norfolk, 1896

Swill Baden Dentwyford Cawthorne
Born Leeds, Yorkshire, c.1900
(Chapel Allerton, Yorkshire, 1901 census)

Mary Celeste
Born np, Lancashire, c.1811 (Liverpool, Lancashire, 1841 census)
*A spookily prescient name – the mysterious case of the abandoned
ship* Mary Celeste *did not occur until 1872.*

Flora Sexburga Chambers
Born Durham, c.1874 (Altrincham, Cheshire, 1881 census)

Moon Chaplin
Died Norwich, Norfolk, 1844

Molesbury Vim Chapman
(Male) Born Helpston, Northamptonshire, c.1847
(Newborough, Northamptonshire, 1871 census)

Christian Charity
(Male) Baptized Hollesley, Suffolk, 19 December 1731

Eliza Kanbone Chegwidder
Baptized Feock, Cornwall, 28 May 1848

Alice Louisa Damp Child
Born Sandown, Hampshire, c.1877
(Portsea, Hampshire, 1891 census)

Pleasant Child
Buried St Dunstan, Canterbury, Kent, 21 December 1715

Charity Chilly
Baptized Menheniot, Cornwall, 24 November 1736

Emma Chiset
Born Brighton, Sussex, c.1828 (Brighton, 1851 census)

Ah Choo
Married Stepney, London, 1882

Jesus Christ
Born np, 1940; died Rotherham, Yorkshire, 2004

Eva Carol Christmas
Born np, 1919; died Corby, Northamptonshire, 2003

Merry Christmas
Born Midhurst, Sussex, 1874

Sabbath Church
(Male) Baptized Wybunbury, Cheshire, 3 March 1731

El Cid
(Female) Baptized St Paul, Norwich, Norfolk, 25 April 1686

Minnie Pudentiana Clague
Born West Derby, Lancashire, 1872

George Edward Short Clampit
Born Newton Abbot, Devon, 1848

Charlotte Clapsaddle
Born np, c.1796 (Rochdale, Lancashire, 1841 census)

Pussie Maude L. Clarke
Born Lexden, Essex, 1898

Argy Clatworthy
(Female) Born Exeter, Devon, 1876

Curvey Cleary
Born Newcastle upon Tyne, Northumberland, c.1846
(Paddington, London, 1891 census)

Minnehaha Clements
Born Wandsworth, London, 1874

Pubella Clements
(Female) Born np, Middlesex, c.1879
(Lambeth, London, 1881 census)

Hilda Clime
Born Brentford, Middlesex, c.1891 (Brentford, 1901 census)

Aureola Clinton
Born Battersea, London, c.1892 (Battersea, 1901 census)

Jelling Cluck
Baptized Bedlington, Northumberland, 17 December 1671

Jessie Clutterbuck Clutterbuck
Born Chepstow, Monmouthshire, 1845

Charles Cobweb
Baptized St James Roman Catholic Church, Winchester,
Hampshire, 12 February 1818

Mary Ann Cocaine
Born np, Derbyshire, c.1828
(Failsworth, Lancashire, 1901 census)

Earthy Cocksedge
Born Stowmarket, Suffolk, c.1899
(Stowmarket, 1901 census)

Christopher Cockshit
Baptized Clayton with Frickey, Yorkshire, 14 October 1771

Admonition Codd
Died Newton Abbot, Devon, 1842

Scissors C. S. R. Coker
Born Dartford, Kent, 1915

Not Wanted James Colvill
Born Lambeth, London, 1861

William Conqueror
Born Sunderland, Durham, 1862

Norman Conquest
Born Lewisham, London, 1904

Ellen Slow Cooch
Born Northampton, 1838

Chaste Cook
Born Birmingham, Warwickshire, 1878

Harry Tantrum Cook
Born Stockbridge, Hampshire, 1894

Sexy Cook
Died Bedminster, Somerset, 1848

William Henry Boke Cool
Baptized St Andrew by the Wardrobe, London, 5 April 1856

Honey Coombs
Born Stratford-upon-Avon, Warwickshire, 1880

Spicy Cooper
Born East Grinstead, Sussex, 1853

Richard Transvestent Copp
Born np, 1910; died Carlisle, Cumberland, 1995

Charles Crusher Corale
Born Leicester, 1844

Henry Porn Cordery
Born Petersfield, Hampshire, 1872

Bendy Corner
(Male) Born Stoke Damerel, Devon, 1892

Chunky Cornfield
Born np, 1931; died Birmingham, West Midlands, 2000

T. Cosy
(Male) Born South Molton, Devon, c.1820 (South Molton, 1881 census)

Rich Cousins
Died Epping, Essex, 1851

Flake Cox
(Female) Born np, Hampshire, c.1891 (Battersea, London, 1891 census)

Knickless J. Cox
(Male) Born Liverpool, Lancashire, c.1877 (Liverpool, 1881 census)

Lurking Crabb
Born Gosfield, Essex, c.1780 (West Hanningfield, Essex, 1861 census)

Charlotte Crack
Married John Amos, St Leonard, Shoreditch, London, 11 October 1846

Irene May Crack
Born Bury St Edmunds, Suffolk, 1913; died 1989

Patience Creep
Baptized Boyton, Cornwall, 3 October 1790

Peter Creeper
Baptized Tresmeer, Cornwall, 7 August 1768

Edmund Crisp Crick Crick
Born Loddon, Norfolk, 1842

Lusty Gladstone Cripps
Born Highworth, Wiltshire, 1894

Soapy Crooks
Married Bosmere, Suffolk, 1891

Apollo Croon
Born Epsom, Surrey, 1880

Chris Cross
Born Trull, Somerset, 1 November 1598

Orlando Furiosa Cross
Buried St Mary, Lichfield, Shropshire, 5 April 1621

Fuxilla Crowther
(Female) Born Facit, Lancashire, c.1829
(Whitworth, Lancashire, 1871 census)

Cosmo Crump
Born Pimlico, London, c.1863
(Islington, 1901 census)

Salome Cruncher
Born Stratford, Nottinghamshire, c.1841
(Newington, London, 1881 census)

Unseld Cruse
(Female) Born Marylebone, London, c.1842
(Westminster, London, 1871 census)

George Sidney Crush Crush
Born Chelmsford, Essex, 1845
and
George Sidney Crush Crush
Born Cheltenham, Gloucestershire, 1845
Both boys were born in the same year and given the same unusual combination of names.

Robinson Crusoe
Born np, Devon, c.1811 (Stoke Damerel, Devon, 1841 census)

Economy Joseph Cumpston
Born Brixworth, Northamptonshire, 1878

Ethel Nastina Cundick
Born Warminster, Wiltshire, 1877

Philliane Cunnilli
Born Birmingham, Warwickshire, 1905

T. Cupp
(Female) Born Beaminster, Dorset, 1876

Cornelius Curse
Baptized Leake, Lincolnshire, 19 May 1664

Annette Curtain
Married Mitchell Riley, Nottingham, 1985

Margaret Curvy
Baptized Rampton, Cambridge, 16 September 1627

—D—

Diddy Daddilums
(Female) Born np, Hertfordshire, c.1874
(St Albans, Hertfordshire, 1881 census)

Pubella Dalt
Born Stockport, Cheshire, c.1840 (Stockport, 1861 census)

Fan Dancer
Born Amersham, Buckinghamshire, 1844

Robert Morris Dancer
Born Prescot, Lancashire, 1903

Fuchny Mottieve Dangerfield
Married Newington, London, nd December 1850

Dann Dangle
Married Uxbridge, Middlesex, 1857

Admonish Daniel
(Female) Born Cramlington, Northumberland, c.1871
(Cramlington, 1881 census)

Dansey Dansey
(Male) Baptized St Helen's, Worcester, 18 September 1800

William Mikado Danvers
Born Liverpool, Lancashire, 1886
Gilbert & Sullivan's comic opera The Mikado *had opened
in London on 14 March 1885.*

Agnes Cigarette Danyow
Born Raglan, Monmouthshire, c.1865
(Tafolwern, Monmouthshire, 1891 Wales census)

William Cupid Dart
Born np, c.1843; died Bristol, Gloucestershire, 1903

Anita Date
Born Edmonton, Middlesex, 1893

Anchorite Peacock Davies
Born Ruthin, Denbighshire, 1837

Thomas Tricky Davies
Born np, c.1844; died St George Hanover Square, London, 1887

William Quack Dawson
Born Tynemouth, Northumberland, 1872

Name the Day

Any Day
Born Barningham, Suffolk, c.1857
(Crawshawbooth, Lancashire, 1871 census)

Christmas Day
(Male) Baptized Lowestoft, Suffolk, 27 December 1762

Godfrey Armistice Day
Born np, 11 November 1923*;
died Milton Keynes, Buckinghamshire, 2003

Juan Day
Rotherham, Yorkshire (phone book, 1946)

Lucky Day
Born Blything, Suffolk, 1859

May Day
Died Axbridge, Somerset, 1842

Selby Day
Born Ashton-under-Lyne, Lancashire, 1897

Species Day
(Female) Married John Hopkins, Christchurch,
Newgate Street, London, 1812

Time Of Day
(Male) Born Hoo, Kent, 1899

Valentine Day
Born Leeds, Yorkshire, 1842

Winter Day
Born Romsey, Hampshire, 1845

The fifth Armistice Day

Earwacker Deadman
Born Alton, Hampshire, 1849

Harry Oxo De Carte
Born Portsmouth, Hampshire, 1904

Erneburga De Flamville
Wife of Hugh De Hastings, born Bordwell, Leicestershire, 1109

Edmond Sufferrer De Mullett
Married Bolton, Lancashire, 1898

Mystic May Dent
Born Halifax, Yorkshire, 1894

Euphrasia De Spurtes
Born St Martin's, London, c.1838 (St Martin's, 1871 census)

Everleaner Dethick
Born np, Nottinghamshire, c.1825 (Nottingham, 1841 census)

Ziggy Thunderbird Deville
Born Bristol, Gloucestershire, 1986

Charles Glue Dibley
Born Westhampnett, Sussex, 1885

Lovely Selina Dickerson
Born Cosford, Suffolk, 1869

Pictorial Dickinson
(Male) Born Preston, Lancashire, c.1838 (Burnley, Lancashire, 1891 census)

Straddling Ernest E. Didot
Born Epsom, Surrey, 1900

Bill Ding
Baptized Easton-on-the-Hill, Northamptonshire, 22 September 1661

Ding Ding
Died Thanet, Kent, 30 April 1971

Warwick Giddy Dingle
Born np, c.1821; died Plymouth, Devon, 1877

Lula Dingledine
Born Widdrington, Northumberland, 24 February 1872

Delaviveve Discipline
Born Pakenham, Suffolk, 1737

Thomas Dodgem
Baptized Great Edstone, Yorkshire, 3 October 1774

Poofa Preeti Doll
Born Hillingdon, Middlesex, 1988

Wanna Dolly
(Male) Born Lambeth, London, c.1864 (Lambeth, 1901 census)

Melcom [*sic*] Garabed Donabed
Married Liverpool, Lancashire, 1906

All Done
Born Derby, 1898

Prudentia Doolittle
Born np, c.1852; died Ormskirk,
Lancashire, 1906

Ben Dover
Baptized St George in the East,
London, 10 March 1839

Eileen Dover
Born np, 1924; died Swindon,
Wiltshire, 1987

Win Dow
Born Maldon, Essex, 1886

Ida Down
Born Okehampton, Devon, 1894

Neale Down
Born 7 March 1823; baptized St Mary, St Marylebone Road, London, 2 April 1823

Abishag Doxey
(Female) Died Ashbourne, Derbyshire, 1854

Anonyma Drane
Born Dunmow, Essex, 1893

Frederick Hair Driver
Born Glanford Brigg, Lincolnshire, 1898

Lenaaser Duckass
Baptized St Giles, Willenhall, Staffordshire, 22 November 1829

Mesmer Dumbrell
Born Brighton, Sussex, 1871

Domingo Dumdum
Baptized Kirk Merrington, Durham, 4 September 1706

Dinah Dump
Born Whitechapel, London, 1897

Trulove Dunk
Born Sheffield, Yorkshire, 1 January 1870

Hugh Dunnet
Born np, Scotland c.1836 ('attendant to the insane',
Dinsdale Asylum, Dinsdale, Durham, 1861 census)

I. Dunnit
(Female) Born Paisley, Renfrewshire, 9 October 1812

No More Durrant
Born Risbridge, Suffolk, 1899

James Brook Dust Dust
Born St Pancras, London, 1841

Uriah Dust
Married Anne Comely, Kingston St Michael, Wiltshire, 8 October 1772

Barb Dwyer
Baptized Sacred Heart and English Martyrs, Thornley,
Durham, 7 January 1877

Sexbus Dyball
Born Ludlow, Shropshire, c.1832; died Reigate, Surrey, 1898

Alfred Arthur Forsaken Dymock
Born Croydon, Surrey, 1862

—E—

Emmeline Nirvana Eaborn
Born Wrexham, Denbighshire, 1902

Gladys Rose Early
Born Wandsworth, London, 1899

Archibald Earthman
Born np, Dumfriesshire, c.1840 (Lochmaben, Dumfriesshire, 1841 Scotland census)

Epenetus Earwaker
Born St Saviour, Southwark, London, 1871

Epaphreditus Eatty
(Male) Born St Luke, Middlesex, c.1830 (St Luke, 1881 census)

Cliff Edge
Born Haslingden, Lancashire, 1903

Oracabessa Edge
Baptized Little Ryburgh, Norfolk, 10 November 1862

Esther Egg
Married Glanford Brigg, Lincolnshire, 1863

National Elder
Born South Shields, Durham, c.1864 (South Shields, 1881 census)

Finale Eldridge
Born Wharfedale, Yorkshire, 1893

Kate Breeder Elliott
Born Playden, Sussex, c.1854 (Rye, Sussex, 1861 census)

Alice Nut Brown Emmett
Born Leeds, Yorkshire, 1864

Albina Gubbing Enticknap
Baptized Chertsey, Surrey, 20 January 1833

Ann Eraser
Married John Mackie, Aberdeen, 13 May 1831

Augustus Caesar Evans
Born Bedwelty, Monmouthshire, 1874

F. Ewe
(Male) Married St Pancras, London, 1899

Anna Expert
Married John J. Coen, Kingston, Surrey, 1918

Worthy Extra
Married Malmesbury, Wiltshire, 1865

—F—

Job Fab
(Male) Married Elizabeth Banyard, Teversham,
Cambridgeshire, 6 April 1713

Eva Faithfull
Born Winchester, Hampshire, 1895

Fourteen E. Falconer
Married Clyde M. Wright, Milton Keynes, Buckinghamshire, 1986

Alice May Fall
Born Shoreditch, London, 1894

Madora Fankboner
(Female) Born np, Wales, c.1861 (Claines, Worcestershire, 1861 census)

Woolf Fanlight
Born np, Russia, c.1869 (Whitechapel, London, 1901 census)

Ancient Fanthorpe
(Male) Born Lincoln, 1843 (Kingston upon Hull, Yorkshire, 1881 census)

Sidney Hilarious Farrow
Born St Marylebone, London, 1877

Drusilla National Fear
Born Axbridge, Somerset, 1896

Jemima Lottery Fearman
Born Holborn, London, 1852

Orgie B. Feast
(Female) Born Fareham, Hampshire, c.1879 (Fareham, 1881 census)

Wave Feather
(Male) Born Windsor, Berkshire, c.1825 (Hampton, Middlesex, 1851 census)

Munday February
Born St Pancras, London, 1848

Obediencia Feck
Baptized Poundstock, Cornwall, 12 March 1642

Low Fee
Married Chorlton, Cheshire, 1908

Number Seven Fell
Born Alton, Hampshire, 1879

Ethel Congress Few
Born Chesterton, Cambridgeshire, 1904

Ffaithfull Ffillips
Married Lanreath, Cornwall, 29 November 1660

Fickess Fickess
Born Chesterton, Cambridgeshire, 1844

Fried Field
Married East Preston, West Sussex, 1890

Paddy Fields
Born West Derby, Lancashire, 1908

Benny Fitt
Born Shoreditch, London, 1876

Sarah Ann Flapper
Born Gateshead, Durham, c.1876 (Gateshead, 1881 census)

Joseph Flicker Flicker
Born Dartford, Kent, 1844

Egesta M. Flopsey
(Female) Born Romford, Essex, c.1870 (Romford, 1871 census)

Albert Fluck Fluck
Born Westbury-on-Severn, Gloucestershire, 1893

Adelaide Fluff
Born St Pancras, London, c.1867 (St Pancras, 1881 census)

Fanetta Annie Fluke
Born Melksham, Wiltshire, 1867

Gail Force
Married Raymond W. Bowler, Colchester, Essex, 1984

Wonderful George Forsdyke
Born Bosmere, Suffolk, 1886

Sally Forth
Born Eye, Northamptonshire, c.1847 (Eye, 1881 census)

Ellen Step Forward
Born East Stonehouse, Devon, 1846; died Penzance, Cornwall, 1848

George Tweet Foster
Born Mattingley, Hampshire, c.1870 (Heckfield, Hampshire, 1891 census)

Victor Frankenstein
Born Whitechapel, London, 1884
*The 1891 census reveals a family of 10 Frankensteins in Whitechapel,
headed by Polish-born Simon.*

Scott Free
Born Bethnal Green, London, 1901

Al Fresco
Born St Giles, London, 1853

Dresden China Fretwell
Born Wortley, Yorkshire, 1880

Gladys Friday
Born np, 1900; died Brent, Middlesex, 1987

Catherine Frisky
Born np, c.1826; died Uppingham, Rutland, 1907

Hopton Frothingham
Baptized St Andrew, Holborn, London, 14 January 1657

William Gubb Fry Fry
Born Barnstaple, Devon, 1852

Adolph Fuhrer
Born np, Germany, c.1868 (Ystradyfodwg, Glamorgan, 1901 Wales census)
Fuhrer's son Leo Adolph Fuhrer was born in Pontypridd, Glamorgan, in 1898, but died in infancy, thus avoiding problems he might have encountered with his name in his forties.

Bathiah Fumble
Married John Miller, St Katherine by the Tower, London, 16 November 1729

Strongman Fussell
Born Rochester, Kent, c.1821 (Newington, London, 1881 census)

Sweetie Winifred Futter
Born Blofield, Norfolk, 1898

Truthful Futty
Born Stockton-on-Tees, Durham, 1867

—G—

Christina Rebecca Gagging
Born St George, Southwark, London, 1862

Isabella Blows Gale
Born Greenwich, Kent, 1837

Opportune Ganwit
(Female) Born np, France, c.1842 (Shirburn, Oxfordshire, 1871 census)

Phil Gapp
Married Forehoe, Norfolk, 1859

Medium Matilda Garlick
Born Melksham, Wiltshire, 1860

Pearly Gates
Married Kevin M. Cadle, Westminster, London, 1996

Fartune Gathercole
(Female) Born np, Norfolk, c.1766 (Mattishall, Mitford, Norfolk, 1841 census)

A. Certain Gaze
Born np, c.1788; died Norwich, Norfolk, 1871

Skimpool Gealy
Born Leeds, Yorkshire, c.1880 (Armley, Yorkshire, 1901 census)

Forget-me-not Geeves
Born Hertford, 1898

Ann Clown Gentleman
Married St Pancras, London, 1880

Big George
Died Guisborough, Yorkshire, 1871

Dan Ger
Born np, Devon, c.1796 (Roborough, Devon, 1841 census)

Lolita Stuckey Gifford
Born Llandilofawr, Carmarthenshire, 1882

John Giggler
Born Luton, Bedfordshire, c.1826 (Biggleswade, 1861 census)

John Farmer Giles
Born np, c.1881; died Witney, Oxfordshire, 1904

Glamour Girl
Married Robert H. Travers, Edmonton, London, 1960

Peter Gloob
Married Elizabeth Natters, Chester-le-Street, Durham, 23 June 1716

Fynae Glue
Baptized Pateley Bridge, Yorkshire, 16 April 1634

Margaret Glug
Baptized Brechin, Angus, 20 May 1756

Goodchild Gobbett
(Male) Baptized Earl Soham, Suffolk, 13 March 1686

George Goblin
Married Maria Boot, Whorlton, Yorkshire, 11 June 1805

Blastus Godley
Married Alicia Seabrooke, St Stephens, St Albans, Hertfordshire,
21 November 1609

Herman Goering
Born Birmingham, Warwickshire, 1882

Peter Herman Goering
Born Birmingham, Warwickshire, 18 May 1915
*The son of the above, during World War II Goering junior changed his name
to Peter Howard Girling; he died in Towcester, Northamptonshire, in 1991.*

Will Gofar
Baptized Howden, Yorkshire, 15 January 1632

Lactarias Golley
Born Caerhays, Cornwall, c.1846 (Caerhays, 1851 census)

Finess Gollop
Born Poole, Dorset, 1857

Alexander Gonk
Baptized Arbroath, Angus, 18 June 1810

Simeon Goo
Baptized St Michael, Ashton-under-Lyne, Lancashire, 24 August 1828

Rhoda Goodsheep
Married Dudley, Staffordshire, 1874

Old England Goodson
Born Aylesbury, Buckinghamshire, 1875

Alonzo Goody Goody
Born Sudbury, Suffolk, 1856

Mary Strip Gordon
Born Poplar, London, 1864

Manly Gore
Born Brighton, Sussex, c.1863 (Portsea, Hampshire, 1871 census)

Susannah L. Gorgeous
Married Dominic T. J. Carter, Hackney, London, 2003

Gertrude May Gotobed
Born Wandsworth, London, 1900

Waxwax Goughe
Baptized Burrington, Herefordshire, 23 January 1561

One Too Many Gouldstone
Born West Ham, Essex, 1870

Isobel Gowdielock
Married James Dunn, Peebles, 25 September 1756

Anna Gram
Born np, c.1811
(Ambrosden, Oxfordshire, 1841 census)

Errata Grant
Born Sheffield, Yorkshire, 1844

Jane Trafalgar Grapes
Born Newport, Isle of Wight, 1805
*One of the children of John and Hannah Grapes, who were all given
middle names that related to the Napoleonic Wars, including
William Nile Grapes (1815), Charlotte Waterloo Grapes (1815)
and Charles Wellington Grapes (1811).*

George Grassmuck
Born Littlehampton, Sussex, c.1840 (Littlehampton, 1851 census)

Emma Gration
Baptized Birstall, Yorkshire, 25 December 1831

Ann Gravity
Married Daniel Arnold, St Dunstan, Stepney, London,
28 September 1788

Contents Increase Greatorix
(Female) Born Oldham, Lancashire, 1872

Greatwichnellie May Greatwich
Born Ashton-under-Lyne, Lancashire, 1910

Brown Green
(Male) Born Gressenhall, Norfolk, c.1851
(Norwich, Norfolk, 1861 census)

Ever Green
(Female) Born Lexden, Essex, 1847

Pea Green
Born Halifax, Yorkshire, 1856

Barbary Groat
Baptized Westray, Orkney, 30 May 1808

Hephzibah Gromit
Married Boston, Lincolnshire, 1855

Ice Groom
Born Stockton-on-Tees, Durham, 1871

Sarah Grunge
Born St Marylebone, London, c.1818
(St George Hanover Square, London, 1851 census)

Hugh Grunt
Born Colchester, Essex, c.1875 (Hampstead, London, 1881 census)

Tommy Gun
Born Evesham, Worcestershire, 1838

Fried Gunly
Born Lincoln, 1838

—H—

Caractacus L. Habakkuk
Born np, c.1857 (Peterstone Super Montern, Glamorgan, 1881 Wales census)

Angel Hackabout
(Male) Baptized St Luke, Old Street, Finsbury, London, 20 September 1752

Kink Hailagman
Married Liverpool, Lancashire, 1878

Gabriel Hairbottle
Baptized St Andrew by the Wardrobe, London, 20 August 1721

John Halloween
Baptized St Nicholas, Liverpool, Lancashire, 13 June 1852

Trannie Percy Hampshire
Born Chertsey, Surrey, c.1897 (Chertsey, 1901 census)

Peter Handsomebody
Baptized St Andrew, Holborn, London, 19 February 1758

Rifle Handworker
Born np, Russia, c.1851 (Leeds, Yorkshire, 1891 census)

Beniventrus Hanky
'Drowned while bathing at Le Posterne', Chester, 6 August 1586
(Chester Coroners' Inquests)

Robert Jackson Hardcore
Born Long Preston, Yorkshire, c.1842
(Henllan, Denbighshire, 1881 Wales census)

Abort Hardman
Born Oldham, Lancashire, c.1860 (Oldham, 1861 census)

Bartelmowe Hardup
Married Margaret Sewell, Smallburgh, Norfolk, 15 November 1601

Hannah Harmless
Married James Eston, Byford, Herefordshire, 13 October 1829

William No. 1 Harris
Married Islington, London, 1896

William No. 2 Harris
Married Maria A. Trent, Islington, London, 1913

Phil Harrup
Born Royston, Hertfordshire, 1839

Tom Dick Harry
Born Carmarthen, 1890

Sweet Hart
Died St Mary Newington, London, 1837

Beaten Shakerley Harvey
Married Penzance, Cornwall, 1854

Mary Ann Haste
Married Edward Robert Pomprey, St Clements, Hastings, Sussex, 22 April 1871

Henry Hatful
Died Holborn, London, 1908

B. Have
Born 26 August 1787; baptized St Mary's Independent,
Glossop, Derbyshire, nd September 1787

Tom A. Hawk
Born St Dennis, Cornwall, c.1890 (St Dennis, 1891 census)

Lunabella S. Heagorty
Born Cork, Ireland, c.1870 (Limehouse, London, 1881 census)
She was the daughter of Lunabella C. Heagorty.

Neglected Heaks
Baptized St Mary's, Aylesbury, Buckinghamshire, 3 February 1627
*The parish record also states: '1627 – Buried Neglected,
the daughter of Jeffrey Heaks, the 11th of February, and she was
so named because she had no God father or God mother
prepared at the time of Baptizing.'*

Fluffy Heaver
Born np, 1901; died Kensington and Chelsea, London, 1998

O. Heck
(Male) Born Leeds, c.1836 (Headingley cum Burley, Yorkshire, 1901 census)

T. Hee
(Male) Born Nafferton, Yorkshire, c.1891 (Great Driffield, Yorkshire, 1901 census)

O. Hell
(Male) Baptized Old Meeting Gaol Street Presbyterian, Great Yarmouth,
Norfolk, 24 February 1709

Snobia Hemp
(Female) Born Merther, Cornwall, c.1839 (Merther, 1851 census)

Agnes Skid Henderson
Born np, Scotland, c.1831 (Earsdon, Northumberland, 1881 census)

Squidge Hewer
Born np, 1930; died Bristol, Gloucestershire, 2000

Alpha and Omega Heydinrych
(Twins) Born Wandsworth, London, 1886

Xpopher Hic
Baptized Snaith, Yorkshire, 19 January 1607

Radium Hickie
Born Wandsworth, London, 1904

Exodus Hickling
(Female) Born Ripley, Derbyshire, c.1791 (Shillington, Yorkshire, 1861 census)

Thomas Antique Hicks
Born Cardiff, Glamorgan, 1852

Miles High
Born Ulverston, Cumberland, 1860

Heinrich Himmler
Born np, 1942; died Durham, 1990

Girly Hind
Born Southwell, Nottinghamshire, 1873

James Desperate Hines
Born Samford, Suffolk, 1885

Abraham and Joe Hitler
(Twins) Born Prestwich, Lancashire, 1901

A. Hitman
Baptized St George in the East, London, 12 November 1775

Adolf Hitt
Born np, Germany, c.1871 (Willesden, London, 1901 census)

B. Hive
Married Thomas Redding, Stepney, London, 17 August 1656

Gulielinus Hobbit
(Male) Married Margaretam [sic] Rayer, Swindon,
Gloucestershire, 22 July 1607

Police Hogg
(Male) Born np, c.1881
(Newcastle upon Tyne, Northumberland, 1901 census)

Vage Hoke
(Male) Born Lettaford, Devon, c.1836 (Bridgwater, Somerset, 1901 census)

Doug Hole
Born Farnham, Surrey, 1924

Happy Holiday
(Female) Born Hardingham, Norfolk, c.1829
(Wymondham, Norfolk, 1851 census)

May Holiday
Born Westminster, London, 1878

Glossy Agnes Holland
Born Wooton St Lawrence, Hampshire, 1891

X.Y.Z. Holyland
(Female) Born np, c.1851 (Thurlaston, Leicestershire, 1851 census)

Mary Perpetual Homer
Born Blandford, Dorset, 1853

Honesty Honesty
(Male) Born Greenwich, Kent, c.1849 (Dover, Kent, 1891 census)

James Riding Hood
Married Clifton, Gloucestershire, 1875

Harriet Fecund Hooper
Born Bethnal Green, London, 1848

Abacuck Hoore
Married Joan Wallpoole, Bury St Edmunds, Suffolk, 1575

Mary Crack Hopkins
Born Cardiff, Glamorgan, 1841

Jeronimo Hornblow
Married Mary Mew, Upton-cum-Chalvey,
Buckinghamshire, 1 October 1743

Adeline Louisa Maria Horsey de Horsey
Born London, 24 December 1824;
died Corby, Northamptonshire, 25 May 1915

Hugh Gentleman Horspole
Born Wisbech, Cambridgeshire, 1900

Chastity Ellen Hosegood
Born St George, Southwark, London, 1844

Cautious House
Born Farnborough, Hampshire, 1859

Happy Helen Hovel
Born Flegg, Norfolk, 1851

Annie How
Born Ecclesfield, Yorkshire, 1843

Ernest William Gnash Hoyle
Born St Mary le Wigford, Lincoln, c.1872
(Lincoln, 1881 census)

Caiusillarcius Coriolanus Hubble
Married Lewisham, London, 1863

Pontius Pilate Hughes
Born Dewsbury, Yorkshire, 1872

Sexas Huish
Born Axbridge, Somerset, 1888

Penitent Humphreys
Married Manchester, Lancashire, 1850

Alice Man Hunter
Born Stepney, London, c.1850 (Stepney, 1851 census)

Pleasure Hunter
(Female) Born Shipdham, Norfolk, c.1840
(Shipdham, 1851 census)

Ben Hur
Born np, Wales, c.1816
(Bedwelty, Monmouthshire, 1841 Wales census)

Napoleon Austin Lucas Hymen Hurry
Born Linton, Cambridgeshire, 1844

Alice Surprise Hutchinson
Born Islington, London, 1883

George Execellent [sic] Sargent Banning Hyne
Born Stoke Damerel, Devon, 1843

—I—

Dorothea Mary A. E. Iceberg
Born City of London, 1873

Gabriel Incarnation
Married St George Hanover Square, London, 1855

Ann Inch
Baptized St Kew, Cornwall, 16 February 1713

F. Ing
(Male) Baptized Blean, Kent, 21 June 1829

F. Ingood
Born Tutbury, Staffordshire, c.1851 (Burton upon Trent, Staffordshire, 1861 census)

Kissey Inwards
Born Woburn, Bedfordshire, 1873

Cadwalader Ish
Born Llanbeblig, Caernarvonshire, c.1851 (Llanbeblig, 1851 Wales census)

—J—

Frothy Jackson
(Female) Born Markington, Yorkshire, c.1831 (Potternewton, Yorkshire, 1901 census)

Question James
Born Williton, Somerset, 1880

Adolphus Shaft Jarman
Born Westminster, London, 1849

Offspring Jeeves
Married Sophia Dear, Arlesey, Bedfordshire, 21 January 1854
*'Offspring' is occasionally encountered where a newborn baby is recorded
before it has been named, but it appears to have been widely used as
a first name among several generations of the Jeeves, Dear and
Webb families of Arlesey.*

Thomas Jellyblood
Of Easton in Gordano, Somerset (will, 1590)

Prodigal Robert Jennings
Born Battersea, London, 1858 (Battersea, 1861 census)

Tom Jerry
Born Walsall, Staffordshire, c.1875 (Walsall, 1901 census)

Jane Jiffy
Died South Shields, Durham, 1857

Bob A. Job
Born Sunderland, Durham, c.1878 (Sunderland, 1901 census)

Rarely John
(Male) Born Cardiff, Glamorgan, c.1852 (Cardiff, 1861 Wales census)

Miracle Johnson
(Female) Married Andrew Pratt, Hertford, c.1558

Elizabeth Jollyblood
Of Exeter, Devon (will, 1583)

Keeping up with the Joneses

Decimal Jones
Born Corwen, Denbighshire, 1889

Frederick Alphabet Jones
Born Kendal, Westmorland, 1873

Lama Dana Jones
(Female) Born Cemmes, Montgomeryshire, c.1859
(Brynuchel, Montgomeryshire, 1861 Wales census)

Robert Meteor Jones
Born Camberwell, London, 1857

Youthful Jones
Baptized St Andrew, Enfield, Middlesex, 29 May 1776

Starbuck Jordan
Born Market Bosworth, Leicestershire, 1874

Thankful Joy
(Female) Born Arundel, Sussex, 4 November 1816

Marathon Mary Judge
Born np, 1909; died Chiltern, Buckinghamshire, 1999

Thomas Highfield Jump
Born Chorley, Lancashire, 1902

—K—

Wong Kee
(Female) Born np, China, c.1874
(aboard ship *Glenlochy*, Middlesbrough, Yorkshire, 1901 census)

Christmas Evan Keel
Married Toxteth Park, Lancashire, 1894

Joseph B. Keeper
Born Bethnal Green, London, 1921

Sargassa Zulu Kerrison
Born np, c.1874; died Colchester, Essex, 1879

Indiana Kettle
Born Dudley, Staffordshire, 1854

Lydia Kettle
Born Marylebone, London, 1839

Molly Kewell
Born Westhampnett, Sussex, 1911

Alan Key
Born Poole, Dorset, 1900

Edwin King Key
Born np, Warwickshire, c.1869 (Congleton, Cheshire, 1881 census)

Kings Rule

Ada Waste King
Born Worcester, c.1860 (Lewisham, London, 1901 census)

Dirty King
Died Hatfield, Hertfordshire, 1863

Fay King
Born np, 1922; died Bromley, Kent, 1998

Hopeful King
Born Norwich, Norfolk, 1866

Joe King
Married Alice Adams, North Mimms, Hertfordshire, 15 April 1668
*He probably really enjoyed people constantly remarking,
'You must be Joe King . . .'*

Lea King
(Female) Born Chard, Somerset, c.1777
(North Wraxall, Wiltshire, 1861 census)

Matilda Handsomebody King
Married Barton Regis, Gloucestershire, 1893

Royal King
Born Portsmouth, Hampshire, 1902

Win King
(Female) Born np, Lancashire, c.1839
(Manchester, Lancashire, 1841 census)

Harriet Circus Kirby
Born Skipton, Yorkshire, 1904

Annette Kirton
Baptized Manea, Cambridgeshire, 15 August 1862

Edmund Stanley Knife
Born City of London, 1892

Pleasant Knight
(Female) Born Blaxhall, Suffolk, c.1781 (Blaxhall, 1861 census)

Tamara Knight
Born np, c.1882; died Aston, Warwickshire, 1892

Shirley Knott
Born Edmonton, Middlesex, 1902

Mary Immaculate Knox
Born Merthyr Tydfil, Glamorgan, 1909

Industrious Kubb
Born Chelsea, London, c.1806 (Wandsworth, London, 1881 census)

Pock Kum
Born np, c.1854; died Holyhead, Anglesey, 1894

—L—

Easter Ladle
Married John Spalding, St Augustine, Norwich, Norfolk, 31 March 1793

Appolonia Lallas
(Female) Born np, c.1801 (Powick, Worcestershire, 1841 census)

Panter Lambert
Married Wellingborough, Northamptonshire, 1912

Dowsabell Lambole
(Female) Married William Boles, St Swithun over Kingsgate, Winchester, Hampshire, 19 July 1624

Leonard Level Land
Born Wisbech, Cambridgeshire, 1900

Bona Large
Died Freebridge Lynn, Norfolk, 1850

Fishy Larkar
Born np, Kent, c.1815 (Greenwich, Kent, 1851 census)

Alice Lashings
Born Brighton, Sussex, c.1833 (Brighton, 1881 census)

Henery Zaphnath La Small
Born Dover, Kent, c.1822 (Carlby, Lincolnshire, 1851 census)

Laura Lather
Born Shardlow, Derbyshire, 1893

Ernest Laughter
Born Bromsgrove, Worcestershire, c.1880 (Bromsgrove, 1881 census)

Carnage Laverack
Born Selby, Yorkshire, 1877

Aymyn Electric R. Lawrence
Born Pontypridd, Glamorgan, 1908

Fling Lazewody
(Female) Born Stoke Fleming, Devon, c.1879 (Stoke Fleming, 1901 census)

Manish Leather
Born Walthamstow, Essex, c.1890 (Shirley, Hampshire, 1901 census)

Mabel Jubi Lee
Born Peterborough, Northamptonshire, 1897
*Named as a patriotic tribute to Queen Victoria, who celebrated
her Diamond Jubilee in this year.*

Anaesthesia Leech
Born np, 1903; died Hartlepool, Durham, 1903

Starlight D.V. Le Garde
Married William H. Jones, Llanrwst, Denbighshire, 1913

Lucinda Legassick Legassick
Born Penzance, Cornwall, 1874

Modern Leggo
Born Penzance, Cornwall, 1859

Magdalene Tramp Leisure
Married Plymouth, Devon, 1838

A. Level
Baptized Sudbury, Suffolk, 19 January 1792

I. Level
Born Hutchesontown, Glasgow, 10 December 1859

Hyacinth Cleopatra Licorish
Born np, 8 July 1917; died Lambeth, London, 2004

Dee Light
Born np, 1964; died Hackney, London, 2004

Fan Light
Baptized West Wittering, Sussex, 20 February 1760

Medium Light
Died Henley, Oxfordshire, 1849

Joseph Lightowlers Lightowlers
Born Bradford, Yorkshire, 1878

Hephzibah Lillycrap
Married Lesnewth, Cornwall, 22 September 1768

Phil Ling
Born St Olave, Southwark, London, 1882

Strange Livings
(Male) Born Little Hallingbury, Essex, c.1863 (Little Hallingbury, 1871 census)

Cautious Constance Lock
Born Binstead, Hampshire, c.1871 (Binstead, 1891 census)

Jim Locker
Married Stoke-on-Trent, Staffordshire, 1864

Miles Long
Born Sleaford, Lincolnshire, 2 January 1661

Noah Lott
Baptized Hipswell, Yorkshire, 16 August 1843

True Love
Born Newington, London, 1848

Young Love
(Male) Born Donegal, Ireland, 29 March 1788;
died Pike, Ohio, USA, 20 May 1845

George Conk Lovibond
Born East Chinnock, Somerset, c.1811 (East Chinnock, 1861 census)

Bea Lowe
Baptized Winwick, Lancashire, 18 October 1706

Thanks Luck
(Male) Born London, c.1890 (South Weald, Essex, 1891 census)

Epiphany Lullaby
Married Veryan, Cornwall, 3 January 1767

Skimer Lunce
Born Tonbridge, Kent, c.1869 (Wandsworth, London, 1891 census)

Copernicus Mephibosheth Lynam
Born Basford, Nottinghamshire, 1898

—M—

Charlotte Grease MacDonald
Born West Derby, Lancashire, 1877

Beaky Mace
Born np, 1929; died np, Surrey, 2001

Elizabeth Drizzle MacLean
Died St Luke, London, 1858

Veneril Virtue Maggs
Married Clifton, Gloucestershire, 1865

Major Major
Born Islington, London, 1871

Breezy Majors
Born np, 8 March 1954; died Chorley, Lancashire, 2001

Arthur Phosphor Mallam
Born Headington, Oxfordshire, 1872

Frou-Frou Mallett
Born np, c.1904; died St Pancras, London, 1907

Dinonysius Mancarter
Married St Endellion, Cornwall, 30 July 1748

Prism Manchip
(Female) Born Bridgwater, Somerset, c.1810 (Bridgwater, 1851 census)

Charity Mangle
Baptized Chesterfield, Derbyshire, 28 January 1834

Phoebe Manhole
Married John Clarke, Peatling Magna, Leicestershire, 16 November 1835

Handy Mann
Died Croydon, Surrey, 1860

Knowledge Mann
Born Kenn, Devon, c.1863 (Dawlish, Devon, 1881 census)

Armageddon Danbury Margerum
Born East Stonehouse, Devon, 1875
(Raunds, Northamptonshire, 1881 census)

Zaphnaphpanth Marker
(Male) Born Nottingham, c.1811 (Greasley, Nottinghamshire, 1841 census)

Thats Marshall
Born Walkeringham, Nottinghamshire, c.1881
(Normanby, Lincolnshire, 1901 census)

Polyphemus Ann Martin
Born Medway, Kent, 1903

Thomas Alias Christ Martin
Born np, Wiltshire, c.1811 (Warminster, Wiltshire, 1841 census)

Panting Mary
(Female) Born Crockley, Wiltshire, c.1842 (Paddington, London, 1901 census)

Martha Masculine
Married Robert Marsh, St Katherine by the Tower, London, 18 November 1675

Hannah Mattress
Died Bishop Auckland, Durham, 1859

Patience Mayhem
Married William Vigian, Maidstone, Kent, 19 January 1596

Preserved McDonald
(Female) Born Elgin, Moray, c.1810 (Elgin, 1851 Scotland census)

Zaiboon McDoom
Born np, 11 November 1916; died Waltham Forest, London, 2003

Mercy Mee
(Female) Born Loughborough, Leicestershire, 1880

Minnie Mee
Born Derby, 1873

Y. Mee
Born np, 1936; died Stoke-on-Trent, Staffordshire, 1997

A. Men
(Male) Born np, Cornwall, c.1840 (Camborne, Cornwall, 1841 census)

O. Men
(Male) Born Blackfriars, London, c.1870 (Southwark, London, 1881 census)

Mary Mermaid
Baptized St Martin-in-the-Fields, London, 30 May 1690

Mildew Michaels
(Female) Born London, c.1874 (Kensington, London, 1901 census)

Egbert Stark Midlane
Born Newport, Isle of Wight, 1849 (Newport, 1901 census)

Prima Donna Charlotte Mildren
Baptized St Mawes, Cornwall, 11 April 1870

George Washington Milkman
Married Chorlton, Lancashire, 1888

Jane Whip Miller
Born Tynemouth, Northumberland, 1891

Arthur Mind
Born Poplar, London, 1907

Solomon Mines
Married Bath, Somerset, 1874
A curiously coincidental name – H. Rider Haggard's popular adventure novel
King Solomon's Mines *was not published until 1885.*

Arthur Minute
Born Hastings, Sussex, 1882

Foam Mitchell
(Female) Born Tottenham, London, c.1866
(Hackney, London, 1891 census)

Lowdy Moan
Baptized Tywardreath, Cornwall, 4 November 1666

Harriet Moans
Baptized Enniskillen, Fermanagh, Ireland, 20 March 1865

Faithfull Mock
(Male) Married Elizabeth Cullis, Roche, Cornwall,
5 May 1702

Minnie Mouse Mollinson
Born Chelsea, London, 1859

Owen Money
Born Headington, Oxfordshire, 1884

Hitler Hindi Mongon
Born np, 1937; died Stockton-on-Tees, Durham, 2002

Nelly Monk Monk
Born Bedwelty, Monmouthshire, 1886

Nelson Monument
Born Mitford, Norfolk, 1872

Phases of the Moon

Cyril Centurion Moon
Born np, 1922; died Chippenham, Wiltshire, 1985

Mary Moon Moon
Born Clutton, Somerset, 1882

Nehemiah Epaphrodites Moon
Born Frome, Somerset, 23 February 1828

Robert Howling Moon
Born np, c.1878; died Pickering, Yorkshire, 1882

Trash Moon
Born np, Kent, c.1787
(Tenterden, Kent, 1851 census)

Zebulon Moon
Born Dudley, Staffordshire, 1860

Zipporah Moonshine
Born Mile End Old Town, London, 1908

Les Moore
Born np, 1935; died Enfield, Middlesex, 2000

Lean Twister Morgan
Born Rhyl, Flintshire, c.1862
(Pensarn, Denbighshire, 1871 Wales census)

Professor Hydropath Mort
Born Birmingham, Warwickshire, 1868
'Professor' was his first name, not his academic title.

Charlotte Freezer Mortimer
Born Saffron Walden, Essex, 1879

Helen Naughty Morton
Born np, 1906; died Hitchin, Hertfordshire, 1998

Libertine Moss
Married Ashton-under-Lyne, Lancashire, 1855

Reveille Naorose R. Motabhoy
Married Croydon, Surrey, 1892

Doris Large Mothers
Born Leicester, 1899

Rocco Motto
Born np, Italy, c.1854 (St Pancras, London, 1881 census)

Salome Mud
Born Mile End, London, c.1876 (Bethnal Green, London, 1891 census)

Henrietta Mug
Born Whitechapel, London, 1874

Margaret Muggle
Married William Prosser, St Mary Somerset, London,
21 January 1627

Zealous Farraginous Mullard
Born Bedwelty, Monmouthshire, 1892

Ellis Wallis Mumpower
Born Wandsworth, London, c.1889 (Wandsworth, 1891 census)

Anne Muppet
Baptized St Nicholas, Brighton, Sussex, 12 October 1799

Magic Muxworthy
Born Doncaster, Yorkshire, 1889

—N—

Nancy Nappy
Baptized Hemingbrough, Yorkshire, 24 July 1785

Fish Pool Neville
Died Ongar, Essex, 1837

James Noose Newcomb
Born Newport, Monmouthshire, 1861

Martha Thunder Nipp
Born Hull, Yorkshire, c.1821 (Hull, 1851 census)

Alfred Nix Nix
Born Faversham, Kent, 1881

Munte Cum Bernet Nixon
Died Brampton, Cumberland, 1859

Hades Nobbs
(Female) Born Southampton, Hampshire, c.1895 (Southampton, 1901 census)

Harry Nobody
Born np, c.1901; died Mile End Old Town, London, 1905

Hi Noon
(Male) Born Radford, Nottinghamshire, 1878

Zachary Noseworthy
Married Alice Dudeny, Dunchideock, Devon, 19 November 1699

Y. Nott
(Female) Born np, 1930; died Tunbridge Wells, Kent, 2002

Rachell Nude
Married Stephen Smith, Caister-on-Sea, Norfolk, 20 November 1572

Ada Nudy
Married Harry Bott, Ecclesall Bierlow, Yorkshire, 1913

Priscilla Nuke
Married Edward Martyn, Cathedral Church of St Thomas of Canterbury,
Portsmouth, Hampshire, 18 April 1704

Uranus Nussey
Married Dewsbury, Yorkshire, 1890

Strop Willy Nutall
Born Higher Booths, Lancashire, c.1841 (Newchurch, Lancashire, 1861 census)

Nellie Hinge Nutt
Born Kensington, London, 1900

—O—

F. Off
(Male) Baptized Ampthill, Bedfordshire, 14 February 1875

Driphena Old
Born Stepney, London, 1849

Harold Snarl Oliphant
Born Salford, Lancashire, 1886

Andrea Opening
Married Andrew Davies, Yeovil, Somerset, 1990

John Opium
Baptized St Andrew, Holborn, London, 5 May 1764

Rick O'Shea
Married Kennington, London, 1864

Ann Other
Died Leyburn, Yorkshire, 1899

Ephraim Very Ott
Born Plumstead, London, c.1879 (Plumstead, 1881 census)

George Special Ottaway
Born West Ham, Essex, 1873

Pluto Oulton
Born Manchester, Lancashire, 1871

Zechariah Outrage
Baptized Ryarsh, Kent, 6 August 1780

Gladys Over
Born Foleshill, Warwickshire, 1898

Fanny Overland
Born Wisbech, Cambridgeshire, 1876

Crispy Ann Overton
Born np, Lincolnshire, c.1876 (Wainfleet St Thomas, Orby, Lincolnshire, 1841 census)

—P—

Benigna Scholastica M. Pain
Born Thanet, Kent, 1867

Knob Hill Palmer
Born Uppingham, Rutland, 1905

Matilda Panter-Downes
Died Bristol, Gloucestershire, 1901

Wal Paper
Born Greenwich, Kent, c.1864 (Greenwich, 1901 census)

Agape Parker
(Female) Born Oxford, c.1875 (Oxford, 1891 census)

Blandina Parody
Born Bedwelty, Monmouthshire, 1875

Edwin Titanic Pascoe
Born np, 1912; died Penzance, Cornwall, 1996
He was born twelve days before the Titanic *disaster, but presumably named to commemorate its launch.*

Emily Odd Paste
Married West Ham, Essex, 1882

George Yokel Pavett
Born Leighton Buzzard, Bedfordshire, c.1874
(on ship *Pembroke*, Chatham, Kent, 1901 census)

Scunt Pazney
(Male) Born np, Kent, c.1803 (Stone, Kent, 1841 census)

Faith Hope Charity Peace
Born Ashby-de-la-Zouch, Leicestershire, 1864

Joseph Green Peace
Born Huddersfield, Yorkshire, 1868

Ann Shakes Peare
Born Wrexham, Denbighshire, c.1849 (Wrexham 1901 Wales census)

Easy Pease
Died Billericay, Essex, 1889

Nimby Pedder
Born West Derby, Lancashire, 1875

Acts Apostles Pegden
Born Dunkirk, Kent, c.1796 (Canterbury, Kent, 1851 census)

University Diana Pembrook
Born St Pancras, London, 1898

Cuthbert Penix
Born Mile End, London, c.1865 (Mile End, 1891 census)

Enid Reverie G. Pennefather
Born np, 1902; died Worthing, West Sussex, 1998

Sexaple [*sic*] Pennell
Born np, Surrey, c.1847 (Leamington Spa, Warwickshire, 1871 census)

Barbara Penthouse
Born Kirkby Malzead, Yorkshire, 5 October 1600

Talitha-Cumi People
Married Andover, Hampshire, 1852

Martha Ann Nark Perfect
Died Yarmouth, Norfolk, 1859

Perfect Perfect
Born Chatham, Kent, c.1887
(Chatham, 1891 census)

Boileta Perks
Born Birmingham, Warwickshire, 1843

Sue Perman
Born np, Wiltshire, c.1791
(Downton, Wiltshire, 1841 census)

Sue Perrior
Married David Yeatman, Downton,
Wiltshire, 6 October 1755

Polly Hankey Phantom
Baptized St Nicholas, Liverpool, Lancashire, 31 January 1779

Sydgestermondayer Phillips
Married Thomas Jones, Shrewsbury, Shropshire, 1864
*She was born in Shrewsbury in 1844 and said to have been
baptized Sigismunda Phillips, but when it came to her wedding no one,
including the bride, knew how to spell her name, so her marriage
was registered with this approximate phonetic version.*

Sanspareil Audacious T. Philpott
Born Faversham, Kent, 1892

Frances Listerine Phipps
Born np, 1940; died Birmingham, Warwickshire, 1991

Hannah Grime Pickup
Born Oldham, Lancashire, 1860

Thomas Strangeways Pigg-Strangeways
Married Emily Dorothy Beck, Cambridge, 1902

Zankey Pilch
Married Mary Chapman, East Rudham, Norfolk, 7 January 1768

Narcissus Pinch
Born Shoreditch, London, 1860

Jane Curvey Pink
Born Bishop's Waltham, Hampshire, c.1835 (Bishop's Waltham, 1891 census)

Arthur Pint
Born Portsmouth, Hampshire, c.1797 ('brewer', Portsea, 1851 census)

Darth Pish
Born Stoke-next-Guildford, Surrey, c.1844
(Stoke-next-Guildford, 1851 census)

Frankensteine Pitt
Married Barton Regis, Gloucestershire, 1885

William Plank A. Plank
Born Poole, Dorset, 1886

Emma Nickers Platt
(Female) Born Hurst, Lancashire, c.1869 (Levenshulme, Lancashire, 1901 census)

Snowflake George Pledger
Born Hampstead, London, 1877

Howard Junie Ploof
Born np, Nottinghamshire, c.1878 (Nottingham, 1891 census)

Richard Mayhem Pogson
Died Wisbech, Cambridgeshire, 1839

Lew Pole
Born Pontypridd, Glamorgan, 1898

May Pole
Born Leicester, 1904

Caesar Policarp
Nantwich, Cheshire (will, 1692)

Elias Pollymounter
Baptized St Stephen-in-Brannel, Cornwall, 14 March 1830
*At the time of the 1851 census, there were fifteen Pollymounters,
all residing in the same parish; by 1871, there were four, all in
St Columb Major, Cornwall; now there are none.*

Hannah Pong
Baptized Upton-cum-Chalvey, Buckinghamshire, 15 February 1818

Frayton Poocock
Born Laughton, Sussex, c.1825 (Chiddingly, Sussex, 1891 census)

Jean Pool
Born np, c.1841; died West Derby, Lancashire, 1899

Posh Pope
(Male) Born np, c.1811 (Brixton, London, 1841 census)

Harry Sequin Portch
Born Farnham, Hampshire, 1877

Wee Girlie Potter
Born Risbridge, Suffolk, 1906

John Pottyblank
Born Devonport, Devon, c.1811 (Stoke Damerel, Devon, 1871 census)

Cush Powderhill
Born Winchcombe, Gloucestershire, 1839

Josephine Valkyrie A. Powell
Born Cardiff, Glamorgan, 1889
Wagner's Die Walküre *had been first performed in London in 1882.*

Obesience Powell
(Female) Born Northfield, Worcestershire, c.1828
(Oldbury, Worcestershire, 1891 census)

Max Power
Born Tredegar Park, Newport, Monmouthshire, c.1856
(Newport, 1881 Wales census)

Tesco Power
(Female) Born np, Warwickshire, c.1807 (Birmingham, Warwickshire, 1841 census)

Will Power
Baptized Rye, Sussex, 27 February 1545

Burpee P. H. Preensides
(Male) Born Stallington, Lincolnshire, c.1864
(Middlesbrough, Yorkshire, 1871 census)

George Pregnant
Born np, c.1830 (East Stonehouse, Devon, 1871 census)

Ono Prescott
(Male) Born Wigan, Lancashire, 1887

Purify Press
Baptized St Matthew Friday Street, London, 22 November 1584

Final Edwin Preston
(Male) Born Market Bosworth, Leicestershire, 1892
Final was, they hoped, the last-born of the six children of Lot and Amy Preston.

Alfred Pretty Pretty
Born Leicester, 1877

The Price is Wright

High Price
Married Presteigne, Herefordshire, 1861

John Lower Price
Born Wolverhampton, Staffordshire, 1844

Mad Price
(Male) Born Bishop Auckland, Durham, c.1865
(Bishop Auckland, 1891 census)

Over Price
(Male) Born np, c.1812
(Merthyr Tydfil, Glamorgan, 1841 Wales census)

Silly Price
(Female) Born Sheffield, Yorkshire, c.1855 (Sheffield, 1891 census)

Worthy Price
Born Malmesbury, Wiltshire, 1857

Wright Price
Born Louth, Ireland, c.1868 (Watford, Hertfordshire, 1871 census)

Quim Prim
Married Zaneta Vaskova, Westminster, London, 2002

George Bambusy Primate
Baptized St Matthew, Bethnal Green, London, 17 October 1819

Jiggy Proper
(Female) Born Dowlais, Glamorgan, c.1840 (Dowlais, 1851 Wales census)

Arsenal Berriball Prout
Born Tavistock, Cornwall, 1845

Floppy Pryor
Died Ashton-under-Lyne, Lancashire, 1885

Joseph Ghost Puddephal
Born Coventry, Warwickshire, 1861

Bolthazer Puffparker
Baptized Crossthwaite, Cumberland, 29 January 1603

Fartumalus Purdger
(Male) Born np, Kent, c.1829 (Margate, Kent, 1841 census)

Wonky Purdom
(Female) Born Hoxton, London, c.1879
(Hemel Hempstead, Hertfordshire, 1891 census)

Globelle W. E. S. Puxley
(Male) Born Catworth, Huntingdonshire, c.1877
(Kessingland, Suffolk, 1891 census)

—Q—

Edwin Mowgwong Quack
Married St Pancras, London, 1861

Pythagoras Quarry
Baptized St Pancras Old Church, London, 2 May 1847

B. Quick
(Female) Born np, Ireland, c.1822 (Tower Hamlets, London, 1881 census)

Maude Quick Quick
Born Helston, Cornwall, 1878

—R—

Wacks Racke
(Male) Born np, Yorkshire, c.1899 (Barnsley, Yorkshire, 1901 census)

Virgin Rackstraw
Died Wycombe, Buckinghamshire, 1896

Hiram Brown Rainwater
Born St Merryn, Cornwall, 9 October 1881

Thomas Thing Ramplin
Born Cosford, Suffolk, 1847

Nathaniel Ratcatcher
Married Amye Wright, Stoke-by-Nayland, Suffolk, 23 July 1622

Nora Rawbone
Born Kenysham, Somerset, 1904

Love Reading
Baptized Rickmansworth, Hertfordshire, 20 November 1768

Eva Ready
Born Halifax, Yorkshire, 1896

Violence Reason
Born Buckden, Huntingdonshire, c.1893 (Buckden, 1901 census)

Ethel Red
Born Kentish Town, London, c.1900 (St Pancras, London, 1901 census)

Sensitive Redhead
(Female) Born Bridlington, Yorkshire, 1873

Goblin Reeves
Born Orsett, Essex, 1848

John Estuary Register
Married Hastings, Sussex, 1874

Hughe Relief
Born Stackpole Elidor, Pembrokeshire, c.1579

Charlotte Rentfree
Born np, c.1828; died Portsea Island, Hampshire, 1871

Francis Respect
Baptized Kirk Rushen, Isle of Man, 26 May 1793

Au Revoir
(Male) Born St Giles, London, 1887

August Revolt
Born np, c.1836; died Northwich, Cheshire, 1894

Dusty Rhodes
Born np, 1940; died Wigan, Lancashire, 1999

Yeah Rich
Born np, Devon, c.1821 (Kingskerswell, Devon, 1841 census)

Irene Joy Riding
Born Preston, Lancashire, 1910

Isabel Ringer
Born Hartismere, Suffolk, 1911

Digory Ripper
Born Truro, Cornwall, 1870

Mike Robe
Baptized Kilsyth, Stirling, 15 May 1743

Marie Antoinette L. Robust
Married St Marylebone, London, 1905

High Rockett
Married Bridport, Dorset, 1856

Roger Roger
Baptized Moreton, Shropshire, 7 February 1587

Heavy Roots
Born Ryarsh, Kent, c.1823 (Cheshunt, Hertfordshire, 1871 census)

John Tight Roper
Born Guisborough, Yorkshire, 1898

Wooloomooloo Roscoe
(Male) Born Oldham, Lancashire, 1876

Tommy Rot
Born Shoreditch, London, 1871

Fice Rotondo
Born Sunderland, Durham, c.1876 (Sunderland, 1901 census)

Susan Rottengoose
Baptized Hemsby, Norfolk, 10 July 1636

Roderick Random Round
Born np, c.1814; died Blackburn, Lancashire, 1889

Catherine Roundabout
Married John Cook, St Martin, Birmingham, Warwickshire, 29 December 1735

Dick Rubber
Born Bristol, Gloucestershire, 1838

Sudden Rusher
Born Keighley, Yorkshire, c.1847 (Keighley, 1851 census)

Grease Ellen Rushgrove
Born Gloucester, 1861

Kenneth Creamy Russell
Born Lewisham, London, 1909

—S—

Calculus Sage
Born Foleshill, Warwickshire, 1901

Alexandra Fluorine L. St Bernard
Born Westminster, London, December 1986

Pete Sake
Born np, Cheshire, c.1840 (Macclesfield, Cheshire, 1841 census)

Gusty Sandbag
Born np, c.1853; died Thornbury, Gloucestershire, 1902

Caroline Hangman Saunders
Born Honiton, Devon, 1840

William Waterloo Napoleon Saunders
Born Sutton Courtney, Berkshire, c.1868 (Brighton, Sussex, 1881 census)
*William Waterloo Napoleon Saunders was the elder brother
of Pius Romulus Saunders.*

Photo Gilbert Scales
Born Hartlepool, Durham, 1866

Susannah Scandal
Married James Musgove, Holy Trinity, Gosport, Hampshire, 26 December 1778

John Scared
Married Chester, Cheshire, 1892

Pigge Scattergutt
(Female) Born np, Derbyshire, c.1767 (Chesterfield, Derbyshire, 1841 census)

Eliza Scavenger
Died Stepney, London, 1839

Hepsa Scoggins
(Female) Born np, Suffolk, c.1830 (Badingham, Suffolk, 1841 census)

Zilpah Scotchedge
Baptized Rickmansworth, Hertfordshire, 20 June 1773

Timosin Scrag
Married James Oliver, Leek, Staffordshire, 25 October 1748

Isobella Scream
Baptized Paisley Abbey, Renfrewshire, 23 May 1824

Aaron Screech
Married Catherine Tippett, Saltash, Cornwall, 20 October 1746

Cordelia Goneril Scrivens
Born np, 1914; died Bury, Lancashire, 1988
Her parents were presumably fans of King Lear.

Totty Seeds
Born St Olave, Southwark, London, 1885

C. Senor
(Male) Born np, Middlesex, c.1831 (Clerkenwell, London, 1841 census)

Marmaduke Sewer
Married Mary Goulsbrough, St Paul, Lincoln, 11 June 1629

Huge Shakeshaft
Born Buerton, Cheshire, 1871 (Buerton, 1871 census)

Samuel Squelch Shakespeare
Born Ashby-de-la-Zouch, Leicestershire, 1841

Bertha Innerarity Shallcross
Born Wirral, Cheshire, 1877

Maria Shampoo
Baptized St Martin-in-the-Fields, London, 7 January 1664

Rick Shaw
Born Romford, Essex, c.1857 (Tottenham, London, 1881 census)

Nehemiah Shed
Born Rochford, Essex, 1852

Florry Shegog
Born Wolverhampton, Staffordshire, 1877

Loveless Shepherd
Died Thornbury, Gloucestershire, 1863

Maude Ship
Born London, c.1866 (Hackney, London, 1901 census)
She had a daughter, another Maude Ship, born c.1892.

Methuselah Shonk
Died Romford, Essex, 1902

Mary Winkle Shufflebotham
Born Macclesfield, Cheshire, 1843

Hannah Quick Shugg
Born Penzance, Cornwall, 1852

I. Sickle
(Female) Born Newcastle upon Tyne, Northumberland, c.1857
(Washington, Durham, 1871 census)

C. Side
(Female) Born St Saviour, Southwark, London, 1841

I. Sight
(Female) Born Shirley, Hampshire, c.1895 (Shirley, 1901 census)

V. Sign
Born Lewisham, London, 1895

George Slaberdash
Born Bath, Somerset, c.1791 ('worm destroyer', Hereford, 1871 census)

Nutty Slack
Born np, Italy, c.1864 (Islington, London, 1881 census)

Jacob Slader
Born np, Devon, c.1796 (Tor Morham, Devon, 1841 census)

James Scanty Slingsby
Born Hull, Yorkshire, 1840

Budgel Slop
Married John Mitchell, Bishops Cannings, Wiltshire, 18 June 1608

Tiny Slurd
(Male) Born Plymouth, Devon (Everton, Lancashire, 1881 census)

Sinderella [*sic*] Small
(Female) Born np, Cornwall, c.1853 (Newton Abbot, Devon, 1881 census)

Bonaparte Smallbone
Born Guildford, Surrey, 1861

Didimus Smalley
Born Lincoln, 1886

C. Letterquist Smither
(Male) Born Newington, Surrey, c.1839 (Greenwich, Kent, 1851 census)

George Zellweger Sneezum
Born Edinburgh, Midlothian, 4 July 1866

Selina Snip
Born West Ashford, Kent, 1846

Harry Snitch
Born St Neots, Huntingdonshire, 1898

Mary Snogglegrass
Born Fife, c.1862 (St Giles-in-the-Fields, London, 1881 census)

Hargood Snooke
Married Ann Foote, Stoke Damerel, Devon, 11 April 1780

Arabella Snoot
Married Shaftesbury, Dorset, 1838

Eli Messiah Snutch
Born Birmingham, Warwickshire, 1878

Yetta Sofa
Born St George in the East, London, 1886

Sing Song
Died Liverpool, Lancashire, 1847

Zsuzsanna M. Sooty
Married Ferenc Liscsey, Hammersmith, London, 1988

Mud Sowersby
Born Driffield, Yorkshire, 1879

Zenas Spaceman
Born Chesterton, Cambridgeshire, 1861

Shaga Spagatner
Died Holborn, London, 1907

Sarah Mary Tumble Spargo
Born Newton Abbot, Devon, 1853

Ann Billion Sparkes
Married Shrewsbury, Shropshire, 1841

Ellinor Oil Spartalis
Born Tenby, Pembrokeshire, c.1870 (Tenby, 1871 Wales census)

Agabus Spendlove
Born Belper, Derbyshire, 1885

Spark Spinks
Born Thetford, Norfolk, 1840

Wilhelmina Tiffin Spirit
Born Hexham, Northumberland, 1901

Sidwella Splat
Married William Small, Chagford, Devon, 21 June 1613

John Spong Spong
Born Maidstone, Kent, 1842

Samuel Spoon
Married Anna Maria Aldred, St Peter Mancroft, Norwich, Norfolk, 28 August 1858

Icy Constance Spragg
Born Fulham, London, 1904

Lettice Spray
Baptized Greasley, Nottinghamshire, 23 April 1633

Martin Spreadeagle
Married Elizabeth Pitcher, St Mary in the Marsh, Norwich, Norfolk, 22 July 1672

Lezetta Stacker
Born Tynemouth, Northumberland, 1861

Focks Stain
(Male) Born Histon, Cambridgeshire, c.1807
(Great Gransden, Huntingdonshire, 1851 census)

Matilda Sperman Staines
Born Kensington, London, 1860

Silence Starbuck
Married Bingham, Nottinghamshire, 1841
The surname 'Starbuck' is more commonly found in
Derbyshire and Leicestershire. Over 1,300 are currently recorded.

Even Stephens
Born Llanwrthwl, Breconshire, c.1856 (Aberdare, Glamorgan, 1891 Wales census)

Grissell Stick
Married Hendrie Thomsoun [sic], South Leith, Midlothian, 8 July 1615

Joss Stick
Born Ulverston, Lancashire, 1887

Cornelius Sticky
Born np, Ireland, c.1828 (Stepney, London, 1851 census)

Pharoah Stingemore
Born Axbridge, Somerset, 1875

Flint Stone
(Male) Baptized Marsham, Norfolk, 12 September 1790

Rosetta Stone
Baptized St Giles without Cripplegate, London, 3 August 1828
The Rosetta Stone was acquired by the British Museum in 1802.

William Short Story
Born Newcastle upon Tyne, Northumberland, 1846

Meleor Strangewidge
Buried Breage, Cornwall, 16 July 1620

Nicholas Streaker
Baptized St Oswald, Durham, 27 October 1747

Acheron Strench
Born np, Ireland, c.1801 (Liverpool, Lancashire, 1841 census)
In Greek mythology, Acheron is one of five rivers of Hades.

Flossy May Strike
Born Aylsham, Norfolk, 1890

Peculiar Stringer
Born np, c.1803; died Wolverhampton, Staffordshire, 1882

Jane Strips
Born Portsea Island, Hampshire, 1845

Hercules Stuffing
Baptized Pleasley, Derbyshire, 1 December 1564

Heinrich Stumpy
Born St George in the East, London, 1878

Alicia Sucbich
Buried Clyst St George, Devon, 20 January 1637

Dude Sugarberg
Born Mile End, London, c.1895 (Mile End, 1901 census)

Pubice Sula
(Female) Born Smethwick, Staffordshire, c.1816
(Harborne, Staffordshire, 1861 census)

Low Sum
Died Cardiff, Glamorgan, 1909

Martha Kitchen Sunshine
Born West Ham, Essex, 1868

Christian Sustenance
Baptized Attleborough, Norfolk, 10 January 1742

Er Sutcliffe
Born np, Lancashire, c.1834 (Whalley, Lancashire, 1841 census)

Nanki Poo Sutton
(Male) Born Bristol, Gloucestershire, c.1887 (Bristol, 1891 census)
Another child whose parents had seen Gilbert & Sullivan's The Mikado.

Mary Quato Swindle
Born Newcastle upon Tyne, Northumberland, 1902

Alphabeta Swithinbank
Died Hunslet, Yorkshire, 1849

Bamlet Neptune Switzer
Married Ada Charlotte Prince, Uckfield, East Sussex, 1890
Bamlet Neptune Switzer, later curate of Crowborough, Sussex,
was born at sea, hence his apt middle name.

Blender Swock
(Female) Born Dickleburgh, Norfolk, c.1832 (Diss, Norfolk, 1871 census)

Fare-well Sykes
Born Honley, Yorkshire, 1842
One of the four sons of Sydney and Betty Sykes, Fare-well – who drowned in
1865 – was the brother of Live-well, Do-well and Die-well Sykes.

Fortune Symons
(Female) Buried Hammersmith, London, 8 April 1723
She was claimed to be 111 years old.

—T—

Noah Tall
Baptized Antony, Cornwall, 21 April 1783

Mary Ann Lickerish Tandy
Born Warwick, 1847

Ada Tantrum
Born Ludlow, Shropshire, 1875

Confucius Tarry
Born Leicester, 1872

Dick Tater
Married Elizabeth Wayman, Elmore, Gloucester, 23 April 1621

Francis Levi Tation
Born np, 1922; died Stoke-on-Trent, Staffordshire, 1995

Ann Teak
Ann, *née* Morley, married William Teak, Rothwell, Yorkshire, 22 May 1722

Thomas Teehee
Born Bilston, Staffordshire, c.1830 (Darlaston, Staffordshire, 1871 census)

James Deboo Teflon
Born Huntingdon, 1875

Hannah Velocity Tempest
Born np, c.1834; died Shoreditch, London, 1886

Fannasibilla Temple
Baptized Sibbeston, Leicestershire, 24 May 1602

Penny Tent
Licence to marry Nathaniel Crew, 2 December 1691

Iris Tew
Born np, 1922; died Chester and Ellesmere Port, Cheshire, 1985

Tamper Tharth
Born Durham, c.1838 (Bishop Wearmouth, Durham, 1841 census)

Hate Thatcher
Born Hungerford, Berkshire, 1848

Dick Thickbroom
Baptized Church Gresley, Derbyshire, 27 July 1718

A Few of My Favourite Things

Annie Thing
Born Broughton, Buckinghamshire, c.1870 (Broughton, 1891 census)
'Thing' is predominantly a Norfolk and Suffolk surname.

John Thomas Thing
Died Stow, Suffolk, 1872

Minnie Thing
Born Steeple Langford, Wiltshire, c.1888 (Steeple Langford, 1891 census)

Pleasance Thing
Born np, c.1792; died Stow, Suffolk, 1869

Violet Thing
Born Ipswich, Suffolk, 1896

Silly Things
Born Stowmarket, Suffolk, c.1892 (Ipswich, Suffolk, 1901 census)

William Thingy
Born Matlock, Derbyshire, c.1784 (Matlock, 1851 census)

James Bomb Third
Born Dundee, Forfarshire, c.1844 (Dundee, 1861 Scotland census)

Creamaleanouss Thompson
Married Liverpool, Lancashire, 1874

Old Book Thomspilie
Born Congleton, Cheshire, c.1863 (Hulme, Lancashire, 1871 census)

Nut Cell Nude Thorne
(Female) Born Ilminster, Somerset, c.1863 (Ilminster, 1901 census)

Albert Throbby
Born Leicester, 1866

Polly Throttle
Born Lincoln, c.1886 (Lincoln, 1901 census)

Hubert Revelation Thrower
Born Worksop, Nottinghamshire, 1905

Abraham Thunderwolff
Married Abigail Thomas, St Just-in-Roseland, Cornwall, 1813

Fran Tick
Married Shoreditch, London, 1877

Polly Tickle
Born Clifton, Lancashire, c.1876 (Swinton, Lancashire, 1901 census)

Sarah Tight Tight
Born Blofield, Norfolk, 1850

Frou-Frou Tilley
Born Bristol, Gloucestershire, c.1874
(Clifton, Gloucestershire, 1881 census)

T. Time
Married Anne Delloe, Furneaux Pelham, Hertfordshire, 26 April 1618

Will Ting
Born Aldgate, London, c.1838 (City of London, 1891 census)

Experience Tingle
Married Thomas Meek, Walford, Herefordshire, 4 June 1689

Veginia [sic] Tiplady
Born Salford, Lancashire, c.1828 (Hulme, Lancashire, 1881 census)

Joseph Stalin Tipple
Born np, 1942; died Dewsbury, Yorkshire, 1999

Minnie Haha Tipple
Married Thanet, Kent, 1890

Ella L. Toadvine
Born Ryde, Isle of Wight, c.1882 (Surbiton, Surrey, 1901 census)

Thomas Toaster
Died Birmingham, Warwickshire, 1905

Sweeny Todd
Born Marylebone, London, c.1845 (St George in the East, London, 1881 census)
Since he described himself as a barber, (Sweeney Todd, the Barber of Fleet Street had premiered in London in 1865) and other inhabitants in his lodging house included Dick Turpin and Dutch-born Thomas Treacle, this may be an example of a census spoof.

Vitruvius Palladio Toft
Married Alice Tatham, Barton-upon-Irwell, Lancashire, 1874

Extravaganza Muriel M. Tomkyns-Grafton
Born Ulverston, Lancashire, 1871

Beatrice Jester Toon
Born Chorlton, Lancashire, 1909

Onysephoris Toop
Married Christian Whisker, Seaton and Beer, Devon, 1 June 1708

Science Tootle
Married Liverpool, Lancashire, 1877

Fanny Topless
Born Ashby-de-la-Zouch, Leicestershire, 1851

Vic Tory
Born Bedford, 1908

Robert Ludolphus Davis Tosswill Tosswill
Born Newton Abbot, Devon, 1840

Andy Tover
Born np, Warwickshire, c.1821
(Birmingham, Warwickshire, 1841 census)

T. Towel
Married Deborah Handsley, Freiston, Lincolnshire, 13 May 1783

Clammy Townend
Born Pontefract, Yorkshire, c.1877 (Golcar, Yorkshire, 1891 census)

Martha Snowflake Tozer
Born Holywell, Flintshire, 21 January 1892

Benoni Trampleasure
Born Kingsbridge, Devon, 14 February 1815

Kate Trembler
Married Chorlton, Lancashire, 1892

Lucy Mysterious Trigg
Born Kensington, London, 1852

Halloween Lucy Troddan
Born Lanchester, Durham, 1899

Vera Horsey Trott
Born Weymouth, Dorset, 1901

Misty Tuffin
Born np, Dorset, c.1791 (Fontmell Magna, Dorset, 1841 census)

Ada Tugnutt
Born Steyning, Sussex, 1879

Merab Emily K. Jane Austen Tumber
Born Sheppey, Kent, 1860

Fridget Tumilty
Born Durham, 1909

Elizabeth Head Turner
Born np, c.1837; died Stroud, Gloucestershire, 1897

Page Turner
Born Axminster, Devon, 1865

Thomas Tweet
Died Tiverton, Devon, 1852

Mary Ann Twinkle
Baptized All Saints, Worcester, 26 December 1807

What Tyler
Born Halsted, Essex, 1864

—U—

Fred Umbrella
Born np, Essex, c.1875 (Danbury, Essex, 1881 census)

Elizabeth Underlay
Married Robert Baston, East Teignmouth, Devon, 10 February 1669

Volantine Unthank
Baptized Gateshead, Durham, 10 March 1717

Sapiens Upright
Married John Shergall, St Dunstan, Stepney, London,
9 April 1667

Alice Desideratum D. Upstill
Born Taunton, Somerset, 1869

Rose Upward
Born Iwerne, Dorset, c.1847 (Motcombe, Dorset, 1871 census)

—V—

Rosetta Vaculine
Born Hornchurch, Essex, c.1840 (Hornchurch, 1861 census)

Crucifix Valente
Died Sunderland, Durham, 1900

Elle Vator
Born Newhaven, Sussex, c.1858 (Brighton, Sussex, 1881 census)

Maximum Velocity
Married Teresa N. Hanks, Coventry, Warwickshire, 1999

Nicholas Virgin
Born Guisborough, Yorkshire, 1875

Love Rake Vizard
Born Thornbury, Gloucestershire, 1892

German Voice
(Male) Married Elizabeth Watkins, Abbey Dore, Herefordshire,
27 December 1731

John Volcano
Married Debra D. Beasley, Islington, London, 1995

Robert Blackadder Vuncombe
Born Chirnside, Berwickshire, c.1821
(Plumstead, London, 1881 census)

—W—

Gwendolen De Blois Wack
Born St Pancras, London, 1900

Xpofer Wad
Married Grace Murgatruid, Halifax, Yorkshire, 13 February 1552

Agrippa Wadge
Baptized Callington, Cornwall, 5 October 1750

Charles Druid Waine
Born Lambeth, London, 1879

Charles was the son of nightwatchman Charles W. and Emma Waine and the elder brother of twins Bessie and Rebecca Druid Waine (born 1881) and Emma Druid Waine (born 1884) – strangely, one of two born that year, she in Kingston, Surrey, the other in King's Lynn, Norfolk.

Never Wait
Born Manchester, Lancashire, c.1834
(Warrington, Lancashire, 1891 census)

Isa Wake
(Female) Born North Shields, Durham, c.1863
(Gateshead, Durham, 1891 census)

Book Waks
Born Kirkby Bain, Lincolnshire, c.1860
(Kirkby Bain, 1861 census)

Baby Walkers

Comfort Walker
(Female) Baptized Holbeck, Yorkshire, 29 June 1735

Jay Walker
(Female) Born Battersea, London, c.1889
(Hackney, London, 1901 census)

Pubus Walker
Born Bedale, Yorkshire, 1847

Risky Walker
Born Harrington, Cumberland, c.1880
(Parton, Cumberland, 1880 census)

Slack Walker
Born Wigton, Cumberland, 1840

Archibald Walkingstick
Born Midlothian, c.1831 (Crichton, Midlothian, 1841 Scotland census)

Baxter Wall
Born West Ham, Essex, 1906

Bendy Wall
Born Yarmouth, Norfolk, c.1851 (Great Yarmouth, 1861 census)

Walter Wall
Born Witney, Oxfordshire, 1840

Violent [*sic*] Irene Wallis
Born Barton Regis, Gloucestershire, 1883

Mary Bath Walters
Born Kingsbridge, Devon, 1854

Amos Rolex Walwands
Died Ipswich, Suffolk, 1998

Batman Wanless
Married Tynemouth, Northumberland, 1871

Energy Ward
Born Sculcoates, Yorkshire, 1839

B. Ware
(Male) Born Pontypool, Monmouthshire, 1911

Luke Warm
(Female) Born Ely, Cambridgeshire, c.1891 (Ely, 1901 census)

Regula Warning
(Female) Born Middlesex, c.1781
(St Mary Magdalen, Old Fish Street, London, 1841 census)

Libra Waterfall
(Female) Born Foleshill, Warwickshire, c.1803 (Foleshill, 1861 census)

Mary Blessed Waterfall
Born Holbeach, Lincolnshire, 1882

U. Watt
(Male) Married Castle Ward, Northumberland, 1900

Milky Wax
Born np, Yorkshire, c.1806 (Wilberfoss, Yorkshire, 1841 census)

Ally Way
Born Saddleton, Surrey, 1961

Harriet Moist Way
Born Newton Abbot, Devon, 1873

Olive Hyder Way
Born Woolwich, London, 1893

Mary Mallarkey Wealleans
Born Newcastle upon Tyne, Northumberland, 1904

Samuel Weatherwax
Born np, Devon, c.1823 (St Sidwell, Devon, 1841 census)

Windebank Webb
Married Lambert Coot, St Margaret, Westminster, London, 30 July 1668

Marvellous Webster
Married Todmorden, Yorkshire, 1861

June Sucky Winter Weeden
Born Uxbridge, Middlesex, 1846

George String West
Born Stepney, London, 1856

Socrates Demosthenes Westmoreland
Born Knaresborough, Yorkshire, 1853

Occupye Wet
Born Otley, Yorkshire, c.1540

Adeline Wetnight
Born np, c.1821
(St George Hanover Square, London, 1841 census)

Theseus Adonis Wexham
Born St George Hanover Square, London, 1883

Jonah Whalebelly
Born Saham Toney, Norfolk, c.1818
(Saham Toney, 1891 census)

Catherine Wheel
Born Auckland, Durham, 1867

Ferris Wheeler
(Male) Born Melksham, Wiltshire, 1860
He predates the invention of the Ferris wheel (named after its inventor George Washington Gale Ferris) by thirty-three years.

Harriet Trickle Wheway
Married Nuneaton, Warwickshire, 1875

Christian Whinge
Baptized Great Barrington, Gloucestershire, 19 April 1590

Noah Whirligig
Buried Abdon, Herefordshire, 18 November 1813

Whiter than White

Albino White
Married Hackney, London, 1907

George Seamen White
Born Clifton, Gloucestershire, 1853

Nothing Henry White
Born Stoke-on-Trent, Staffordshire, 1852

Pearl E. White
Born Gravesend, Kent, 1908

Thomas Snow White
Born Frome, Somerset, 1882

Shirtliff Whitehead
Born Thorne, Yorkshire, 1904

Skyrack Whitham
Born Burnley, Lancashire, 1847

Rev Cornelius Whur
Born Pulham Market, Norfolk, 1782; died Loddon, Norfolk 1853
*In addition to his unusual name, Whur was regarded as one of the worst
poets of all time, penning verses with titles that included
'The Cheerful Invalid', 'The Diseased Legs' and 'The Armless Artist',
containing such immortal phrases as 'throbbing bosom' and 'whizzing balls'.*

Benjamin Loose Wick
Born Walsingham, Norfolk, 1846

Hanky Wick
(Male) Born Trowbridge, Wiltshire, c.1833 (Bristol, Gloucestershire, 1851 census)

Selina World Wigger
Died Marylebone, Middlesex, 1860

Ralph Heavysides Wigham
Born np, c.1844; died Teesdale, Durham, 1895

Lapidoth Stratton Wigley
(Female) Born Wallingford, Berkshire, 1846
Lapidoth was the sister of Keturah, Philetus, Philiplus, Theophilius,
Tryphena and Tryphosa Wigley.

Jackanaias Wild
Born Oldham, Lancashire, 1853

Franklin Addenda Wilkins
Born Liversedge, Yorkshire, 1878
(Wellingborough, Northamptonshire, 1891 census)

Happy Always Wilkins
Born Dursley, Gloucestershire, 1849

George Sudden Willderspin
Born St Ives, Huntingdonshire, 1838

Something Willis
(Male) Born np, Ireland, c.1801 (Glamorgan, 1851 Wales census)

Betsy Supple Wilson
Born Nottingham, 1842

Moses Windibank
Born Bentley, Hampshire, c.1850 (Binstead, Hampshire, 1861 census)

Richard Edwards Windup
Born Burton upon Trent, Staffordshire, 1882

Ebenezer Hanshaw Winkie Winter
Born Norwich, Norfolk, 1841

Ernest Frosty Winter
Born Leeds, Yorkshire, 1878

Walter Spring Winter
Born Romford, Essex, 1885

Oval Henry Winterflood
Born np, c.1865; died Islington, London, 1900

Barb Wire
Born West Ham, Essex, 1912

Head Wise
Born Newbury, Berkshire, 1843

Scholastica Wise
Born Dudley, Staffordshire, 1910

G. Wiss
(Male) Born Whitechapel, London, 1865

Betsy Witch Witch
Baptized Ringwood, Hampshire, 1 September 1772

Lovelace Bigg Wither
(Male) Born Wymering, Hampshire, c.1806
(Wooton St Lawrence, Hampshire, 1841 census)

Careless Withers
Born Dudley, Staffordshire, 1859

Minnie Woman
Born Caistor, Lincolnshire, 1891

Ernest Womble Womble
Born Chesterfield, Derbyshire, 1908

Chip Wood
Born Huddersfield, Yorkshire, 1867

Juggler Woodhouse
Married Runcorn, Cheshire, 1884

Frederick Slick Woof
Born Kendal, Westmorland, 1885

Regina Woog
Born St Giles, London, 1868

Elkanah Wookey
Born Burrington, Somerset, c.1854 (Burrington, 1861 census)

Henry Clotworthy Woolcook
Born Penzance, Cornwall, 1859

William Absolute Wordsworth
Born Ecclesfield, Yorkshire, 1846

Ice Worker
(Female) Born Langwith, Derbyshire, c.1896 (Bolsover, Derbyshire, 1901 census)

Mary Bare Workman
Born Liverpool, Lancashire, c.1869 (Liverpool, 1871 census)

Christian World
Baptized Hilton, Dorset, 6 May 1726

Sinister Worrall
Married Letty Nield, Ashton-under-Lyne, Lancashire, 1919

Hot Mary Worth
Born Tavistock, Devon, 1867

Elizabeth Wrench Wrench
Born Ampthill, Bedfordshire, 1842

Olive Quatorzieme Wright
Born Stoke Damerel, Devon, 1897

Zownds Wright
Born np, Bedfordshire, c.1781 (Harrold, Bedfordshire, 1841 census)

Liza Wrong
Baptized St Margaret, Westminster, London, 11 February 1618

Win Wynn
Born Prescot, Lancashire, 1889

G. Wyss
Born np, Switzerland, c.1852 (St Pancras, London, 1901 census)

Human Wythers
Born Newmarket, Cambridgeshire, 1862

Mary Xmas
Baptized Petworth, Sussex, 10 December 1759

—Y—

Humphredo Yallop
Baptized Hargham, Norfolk, 26 August 1672

Neilly Yarr Yarr
Born np, 1925; died Hillingdon, Middlesex, 1988

Matthew Yellow Yellow
Born Thirsk, Yorkshire, 1862

Winifred Kate Yob
Baptized St Mary, Bristol, Gloucestershire, 26 May 1891

B. Yond
(Male) Born Prescot, Lancashire, 1905

Arden Thicknesse V. Yonge
Born Nantwich, Cheshire, 1868

Sue You
Born Saint Helena, c.1862 (British subject aboard
Royal Navy ship *Flora*, Ascension, 1881 census)

Virdie Youngblood
Born Gainford, Durham, 24 September 1879

—Z—

Canute Zane
Born St Thomas, Devon, 1870

Charles Zebedee Zebedee
Born Alderbury, Wiltshire, 1877

Thomas Zillion
Born Kippax, Yorkshire, c.1822 (Allerton Bywater, Yorkshire, 1851 census)

Maggie Zine
Born Kensington, London, c.1871 (Willesden, Middlesex, 1891 census)

Chapter Eight

BY ACCIDENT

OR DESIGN

SIGN HERE, PLEASE (IF THERE'S ROOM)

◆

Ded Jarvis Blue Adams Handcock Amesbury
Died Bridgwater, Somerset, 1859

Xenophilus Epaphreditus Baycock Calvert
Died Huddersfield, Yorkshire, 1842

Zaphnathpaaneah Isaiah Obededom Nicodemus Francis Edward Clarke
Baptized Beccles, Suffolk, 14 October 1804

Only Francis Edward would fit in the parish register, so the other names were added as a footnote. In 1877 it was reported that 'Mr Zaphnath-Paaneah Isaiah Obed-Edom Nicodemus Francis Edward Clarke, a bloater merchant at Lowestoft, has been poisoned by taking a lotion in mistake for a draught.'

La Rhennee Le Veghonora Jannette Betsey Restall De Louth
Born Midhurst, Hampshire, 1850

Gilbert Edward George Lariston Elliot-Murray-Kynynmound
6th Earl of Minto, 1928–2005

Alaric Fetherstonhaugh-Frampton
Born Kensington, London, 1900

On its own, Fetherstonhaugh is claimed to be the longest unhyphenated English surname. In 1781 Sir Harry Fetherstonhaugh (1754–1846) had as his mistress Emma Hart, later to achieve fame as Emma Hamilton.

Shadrach Meshach Abednego Daniel Goldsmith
Died Stow, Suffolk, 1849

Albrecht Franz Joseph Carl Friedrich Georg Hubert Maria Hapsburg-Lothingen
Archduke of Austria, Prince of Hungary, married Irene Dora Rudnay, Brighton, East Sussex, 16 August 1930

Amy Elizabeth Ezeerd Copah Cash Macintosh
Born Dover, Kent, c.1891 (Shoeburyness, Essex, 1891 census)

Xenia Marelina Veronique Caroline Sophia Murray Moore

Born Richmond, Surrey, 1888

Thomas Hill Joseph Napoleon Horatio Bonaparte Swindlehurst Nelson

Born Preston, Lancashire, 1839

Tracy Mariclaire Lisa Tammy Samantha Christine Alexandra Candy Bonnie Ursula Zoe Nichola Patricia Lynda Kate Jean Sandra Karren Julie Jane Elizabeth Felicity Gabriella Jackie Corina Constance Arabella Clara Honor Geraldine Giona Erika Fillippa Anabel Elsie Amanda Cheryl Alanna Louise Angie Beth Crystal Dawn Debbie Eileen Grace Susan Rebecca Valerie Kay Lena Margaret Anna Amy Carol Bella Avril Ava Audry Andrea Daphne Donna Cynthia Cassie Christable Vivien Wendy Moira Jennifer Abbie Adelaide Carissa Clara Anne Astrid Barbara Clarissa Catalina Bonny Dee Hazel Iris Anthea Clarinda Bernadette Cara Alison Carrie Angela Beryl Caroline Emma Dana Vanessa Zara Violet Lynn Maggie Pamela Rosemary Ruth Cathlene Alexandrina Annette Hilary Diana Angelina Carrinna Victoria Sara Mandy Annabella Beverley Bridget Cecilia Catherine Brenda Jessica Isabella Delilah Camila Candice Helen Connie Charmaine Dorothy Melinda Nancy Marian Vicki Selina Miriam Norma Pauline Toni Penny Shari Zsa Zsa Queenie Nelson

Born Chesterfield, Derbyshire, 31 December 1985

Maria de los Dolores Petrona Ramona Juana Nepomucena Josefa Cayetana Beatriz de la Santisima Trinidad North

Born np, c.1811; died Lambeth, London, 1890

Ann Bertha Cecilia Diana Emily Fanny Gertrude Hypatia Inez Jane Kate Louisa Maud Nora Ophelia Quince Rebecca Starkey Teresa Ulysis Venus Winifred Xenophen Yetty Zeus Pepper

Born West Derby, Lancashire, 19 December 1882

She was given a name for each letter of the alphabet, except that of her surname, in alphabetical order.

The Honourable Sir Reginald Aylmer Ranfurly Plunkett-Ernle-Erle-Drax

Born London, 28 August 1880; died Poole, Dorset, 16 October 1967

Charles Caractacus Ostorius Maximillian Gustavus Adolphus Stone

Baptized Burbage, Wiltshire, 29 April 1781

Mahershalalhashbaz Sturgeon

Born Hessett, Suffolk, c.1857 (Hessett, 1881 census)

Mahershalalhashbaz is the longest personal name in the Bible.

Richard Plantagenet Campbell Temple-Nugent-Brydges-Chandos-Grenville

Born np, 10 September 1823; died London, 26 March 1882

The 3rd Duke and 4th Marquis of Buckingham;
after him the title became extinct.

TOLLEMACHE-TOLLEMACHE

The Reverend Ralph William Lyonel Tollemache (1826–1895)
was rector of South Wytham, near Grantham, Lincolnshire.
His first wife was his cousin Caroline Tollemache (1828–1867),
with whom he had five children:

Lyonel Felix Carteret Eugene Tollemache (1854–1952)

Florence Caroline Artemisia Hume Tollemache (1855–1935)

Evelyne Clementina Wentworth Cornelia Maude
Tollemache (1856–1919)

Granville Gray Marchmont Manners Plantagenet
Tollemache (1858–1891)

Marchmont Murray Reginald Grasett Stanhope
Plantagenet Tollemache (1860–1898)

*Following the death of his first wife, in 1869 he married Dora Cleopatra
Maria Lorenza de Orellana y Revest (c.1847–1929) and got into his
naming stride with their ten children:*

Dora Viola Gertrude Irenez de Orellana Dysart
Plantagenet Tollemache-Tollemache (1869–1874)

Mabel Helmingham Ethel Huntingtower Beatrice
Blazonberrie Evangeline Vise de Lou de Orellana
Plantagenet Saxon Toedmag Tollemache-Tollemache
(1872–1955)

Lyonesse Matilda Dora Ida Agne Ernestine Curson Paulet
Wilbraham Joyce Eugénie Bentley Saxonia Dysart
Plantagenet Tollemache-Tollemache (1874–1944)

Lyulph Ydwallo Odin Nestor Egbert Lyonel Toedmag
Hugh Erchenwyne Saxon Esa Cromwell Orma Nevill
Dysart Plantagenet Tollemache-Tollemache (1876–1961)

The initial letters of his first names spell 'Lyonel the Second'.

Lyona Decima Veronica Esyth Undine Cyssa Hylda
Rowena Viola Adela Thyra Ursula Ysabel Blanche Lelias
Dysart Plantagenet Tollemache-Tollemache (1878–1962)

Leo Quintus Tollemache-Tollemache de Orellana
Plantagenet Tollemache-Tollemache (1879–1914)

*In 1908 he renounced all but the first and last of his extravagant
names by deed poll.*

Lyonella Fredegunda Cuthberga Ethelswytha Ideth
Ysabel Grace Monica de Orellana Plantagenet
Tollemache-Tollemache (1882–1952)

**Leone Sextus Denys Oswolf Fraudatifilius
Tollemache-Tollemache de Orellana Plantagenet
Tollemache-Tollemache (1884–1917)**

**Lyonetta Edith Regina Valentine Myra Polwarth
Avelina Philippa Violantha de Orellana Plantagenet
Tollemache-Tollemache (1887–1951)**

**Lynonulph Cospatrick Bruce Berkeley Jermyn
Tullibardine Petersham de Orellana Dysart Plantagenet
Tollemache-Tollemache (1892–1966)**

Henry Edward Montague Dorington
Clotworthy Upton

Born Kensington, London, 1853

On the death of his uncle in 1890, he became Viscount Templeton.

Kiscernotta Corniella Sling Kend Whittaker

Born np, Netherlands, British subject, c.1864

(Poulton-le-Fylde, Lancashire, 1901 census)

Dancell Dallphebo Marc Antony Dallery
Gallery Caesar Williams

Baptized Old Swinford, Worcestershire, 28 January 1676

*Son of Dancell Dallphebo Marc Antony
Dallery Gallery Caesar Williams.*

Puritan Names

Even biblical names were not considered sufficiently pure by Puritan extremists, so they gave their children 'virtue' names such as Humiliation and Mercy, or slogans (Fly-fornication, Seek-wisdom, et al). They were especially prevalent in Kent, Sussex and Northamptonshire. Among Sussex Puritans, in the parish of Warbleton, almost half the children baptized between 1570 and 1600 received such names. A few girls' names, including Felicity, Joy and Prudence, have survived in the British name stock, but most have not.

Fly-fornication Andrewes
Baptized Waldron, Sussex, 17 December 1609
'Bastard son of Catren Andrewes.'

Nicholas If-Jesus-Christ-Had-Not-Died-For-Thee-Thou-Hadst-Been-Damned Barebon
Born London, c.1640; died Osterley, Middlesex, 1698
Son of Praise-God Barbon (after whom the 'Barebones Parliament' was named) and, following the Great Fire of London in 1666, inventor of fire insurance. He used the name Nicholas Barbon.

Magnify Beard
Baptized Warbleton, Sussex, 17 September 1587

Lament Bible
Married Nicholas Hussher, Ticehurst, Sussex, 9 September 1640

Mercye Bike
Baptized Thornhill by Dewsbury, Yorkshire, 9 February 1651

Fear Brewster
Born Scrooby, Nottinghamshire, c.1586

Fear and her siblings Patience, Love and Wrestling were among the
'Pilgrim Fathers' who emigrated to America in 1620 aboard the Mayflower.
She died in Massachussetts on 12 December 1634. US President Zachary
Taylor was a descendant of Fear. The Little Women *author,*
Louisa May Alcott, the singer Bing Crosby and the actress
Katharine Hepburn were all Brewster descendants.

Repent Champney
Baptized Warbleton, Sussex, 14 August 1608
'A bastard.'

Clemency Chawncey
Buried St Dionis Backchurch, London, 27 August 1625

Be-Courteous Cole
Born Pevensey, Sussex, 1570

Changed Collins
(Female) Born Brightling, Sussex, 1 January 1598
She was the sister of:

Increased Collins
Born Brightling, Sussex, 30 March 1604

Redeemed Compton
Born Battle, Sussex, 1588

Diligence Constant
Buried St Peter upon Cornhill, London, 1 November 1724

God-help Cooper
Baptized Weybridge, Surrey, 12 June 1628

Sorry-for-sin Coupard
Baptized Warbleton, Sussex, 25 January 1589

Abuse-not Ellis
Baptized Warbleton, Sussex, 17 September 1592

Preserved Emms
(Female) Died St Nicholas, Yarmouth, 17 November 1712

More-fruit Fenner
Baptized Cranbrook, Kent, 22 December 1583

Dudley Fenner (c.1558–1587), preacher of Romford, Essex, was accused of baptizing children with such names as Joy-again and From-above, but defended himself by pointing out that he had given his own daughters the names More-fruit, Faint-not and Dust.

Replenish French
Baptized Warbleton, Sussex, 13 May 1660

Accepted Frewen
Baptized Northiam, Sussex, 26 May 1588; died 28 March 1664

Accepted Frewen, brother of Thankfull Frewen (born Northiam, Sussex, 1591; died 1656), became Archbishop of York.

Joy-in-sorrow Godman
Married Joseph Baysie, All Saints, Lewes, Sussex, 20 May 1614

Hate-evil Greenhill
Baptized Banbury, Oxfordshire, 15 April 1660

Sin-deny Hely
(Female) Married William Swane, Burwash, Sussex, 4 September 1621

Humiliation Hinde
Married Elizabeth Phillips, St Peter upon Cornhill, London,
24 January 1629

Safe-on-high Hopkinson
Baptized Salehurst, Sussex, 28 February 1591

Job-rakt-out-of-the-asshes [*sic*]
(Foundling) Baptized St Helen, Bishopsgate, London,
1 September 1611

First-borne and Sadness Luffe
(Female twins) Baptized Aylesbury, Buckinghamshire, 2 September 1656

Free-gift and Fear-not Lulham
(Male twins) Baptized Warbleton, Sussex, 12 October 1589

Aydonhigh Mutlow
(Male) Baptized Bosbury, Herefordshire, 22 November 1601
The brother of Comfort and Truth Mutlow.

Abstinence Pougher
(Male) Baptized St Nicholas, Leicester, 30 June 1672

More-fruit Stone
(Male) Baptized Alfriston, Sussex, 6 June 1587
The father of:

Zealous Stone
(Male) Baptized Hellingley, Sussex, 8 March 1612

No-merit Vynall
(Female) Baptized Warbleton, Sussex, 28 September 1589

Continent Walker
(Female) Baptized Alfriston, Sussex, 22 December 1594

Discretion Watkinson
Married Elizabeth Wild, South Muskham, Nottinghamshire,
17 November 1659

Restored Weekes
Married Constant Sumar, Chiddingly, Sussex, 27 August 1618

Faint-not Wood
Married William Clarke, Laughton, Sussex, 24 December 1618

Repentance Wrath
(Male) Baptized Elham, Kent, 26 March 1612

Rejoice Wratten
(Female) Baptized Warbleton, Sussex, 18 October 1679

THICKIES, BASTARDS AND BITCHES

Many of the names in this book are bad enough, but imagine having to live with one that is, or sounds as if it might be, pejorative or downright insulting.

Blooming Alexander
Born Plymouth, Devon, c.1816 (Plymouth, 1851 census)

Nosy Allen
Born St Clement, Oxford, c.1883 (St Clement, 1891 census)

B. Astard
(Male) Born Staffordshire, c.1826
(West Bromwich, Staffordshire, 1841 census)

Fatty Atkinson
(Male) Born Hull, Yorkshire, c.1868
(Kingston upon Hull, Yorkshire, 1881 census)

Elizabeth Awkward
Married Bury, Lancashire, 1866

Bag Carolin [*sic*] Bagley
Married Southampton, Hampshire, 1861

Hannah Banal
Born np, c.1806
(Clifton, Derbyshire, 1851 census)

Africa Bastard
(Male) Born Bromley, Kent, 1870

Ellen Ferran Bastard Bastard
Born Walsingham, Norfolk, 1846

Ellen U. Bastard
Born Cley next the Sea, Norfolk, 1866

Friendless Baxter
Born Holbeck, Yorkshire, 1871

Benjamin Beastly
Baptized Buckland, Berkshire, 13 February 1774

Shouvaveva J. Berk
Died Bromley, Kent, 1910

Xpoferus Berk
(Male) Married Aliciam Browne, Gillingham, Dorset, 18 November 1661

Patrick Bighead
Died Chorlton, Lancashire, 1864

Maryan Bitch
Married Taunton, Somerset, 1840

A. Blob
(Female) Born np, Yorkshire, c.1827 (Snaith, Yorkshire, 1841 census)

Philip Percy Bonehead
Married Bedminster, Somerset, 1895

David Twitty Boocock
Born Adlington, Cheshire, 1855

Fiend Boothroyd
Born Huddersfield, Yorkshire, 1850

Mary Boring
Born West Derby, Lancashire, 1857

P. George Hopeless Bradbury
Born Sheffield, Yorkshire, 1874

Dick Brain
Born Stoke-on-Trent, Staffordshire, 1871

John Brainless
Born Durham, c.1863 (Durham, 1891 census)

Porker Braybrook
Died Sudbury, Suffolk, 1845

James Crummy Brewis
Married Tynemouth, Northumberland, 1842

Frightful Brown
Born np, c.1886 (Attercliffe, Yorkshire, 1871 census)

John Dull Brown
Born West Derby, Lancashire, 1888

Hannah Buffoon
Born np, c.1793; died Stockton-on-Tees, Durham, 1872

Thick Burke
Born np, Ireland, c.1791 (Manchester, Lancashire, 1841 census)

Lousy Butler
Born Bradford, Yorkshire, 1885

Eleanor Misery Charlotte
Born Stepney, London, 1873

Thomas Chav
Married Jane Parkinson, St John's, Preston, Lancashire, 30 January 1867

Charles Daffy Child
Born Dewsbury, Yorkshire, 1899

Louise Emma Clot
Married Westminster, London, 1903

Nasty Clough
(Male) Born np, Yorkshire, c.1786 (Bowdon, Cheshire, 1861 census)

Rancid R. Clow
Born Wisbech, Cambridgeshire, 1912

George James Cockhead Cockhead
Born St George in the East, London, 1860

George Cokehead
Married Ware, Hertfordshire, 1839

Thomas Creep Collingwood
Born Islington, London, c.1852 (Kensington, London, 1871 census)

Seedy Mary Cooper
Born Llanelli, Monmouthshire, 1901

Wanton Coward
(Male) Born Warminster, Wiltshire, c.1863 (Warminster, 1871 census)

Cruel John Crane
Born np, Shropshire, c.1885 (Shifnal, Shropshire, 1891 census)

Henry Craphome
Born Paddington, London, c.1866 (Deptford, London, 1901 census)

Sophia Crappy
Baptized Maker, Cornwall, 17 January 1802

Justa Crook
(Female) Born London, c.1855 (Mile End, London, 1901 census)

Fanny Crud
Born St Marylebone, London, c.1855 (Rotherhithe, London, 1881 census)

Evil Dennis
Born Llanelli, Carmarthenshire, 1884

Blanche Despot
Born St Marylebone, London, c.1867 (Willesden, Middlesex, 1901 census)

Mary Dirty
Baptized St Martin-in-the-Fields, London, 8 November 1685

Charles Dismal
Born Greenwich, Kent, 1858

Thomas Dizzy
Married Elizabeth Wright, St Giles, Reading, Berkshire, 19 October 1740
She thus became Lizzie Dizzy.

Lucy Drip
Baptized Shirley, Warwickshire, 10 November 1833

Richard Drivel
Baptized St Botolph, Aldersgate, London, 28 October 1666

Hubert Drunk
Born Chelsea, London, c.1835
(Stretford, Lancashire, 1861 census)

Reginald Daisy Dull
Born St George Hanover Square, London, 1878

Hanora Dummy
Born Cork, Ireland, 13 May 1878

Dora Dunce
Born Chertsey, Surrey, 1877

Goon Eccles
(Male) Born Pimlico, London, c.1841
(Chelsea, 1891 census)

Weakly Ekins
Inquisition of Lunacy, London, 6 July 1697

Hopeless Evans
Born Stoke-on-Trent, Staffordshire, 1880

Dick Face
Baptized Ridgmont, Bedfordshire, 14 July 1551

Will Fail
Baptized Dunblane, Perthshire, 21 March 1708

Martha Fat
Married Richard Chalkwright, Cathedral Church of St Thomas of Canterbury, Portsmouth, Hampshire, 16 June 1703

George Fatman
Born Broadbottom, Cheshire, c.1893 (Harefield, Middlesex, 1901 census)

Hugh Fatty
Born Flint, c.1790 (Leadbrook Major, Flintshire, 1851 Wales census)

Fanny Fecker
Born np, Suffolk, c.1841 (Bardwell, Suffolk, 1841 census)

Harriet Mann Fiend
Baptized St John the Baptist, Shoreditch, London, 24 March 1839

Pedor File
(Male) Born Glasgow, Lanarkshire, c.1864
(Barrhead, Renfrewshire, 1871 Scotland census)

Charles Filth
Baptized Putney, London, 3 August 1737

Thomas Flop
Married Martha Burges, Wells, Somerset, 25 October 1632

Rich Fool
Married Isabella Dicconson, Chorley, Lancashire, 24 December 1703

Dolt Fretwell
Born Wortley, Yorkshire, 1890

Fanny Fright
Married Faversham, Kent, 1859

A. Frump
Born North Petherton, Somerset, c.1841 (North Petherton, 1851 census)

Henry Small Fry
Born Bloxworth, Dorset, 1862 (Bloxworth, 1881 census)

George Garbage
Baptized St Thomas, Dudley, Worcestershire, 7 December 1823

William Nicholas Geek
Born Tavistock, Cornwall, 1848

Richard Gibberish
Married Sarah Manninghe, Poling, Sussex, 22 November 1678

George Gimp
Baptized Axminster, Devon, 26 February 1769

Augusta S. Git
Born Finsbury, London, c.1811 (Islington, 1881 census)

Herbert Blasted Grace
Born Romsey, Hampshire, 1879

Louisa Greatbitch
Born Longton, Staffordshire, c.1816 (Longton, 1861 census)

John Pest Grimshaw
Born Preston, Lancashire, 1885

Hannah Grubby
Married Thomas Lenn, St Mary Magdalene, Lincoln, 20 May 1787

William Henry Grunge
Born np, 17 May 1731; baptized St Martin-in-the-Fields, London, 24 May 1731

Herman Gunge
Died St George in the East, London, 1867

Barbary Hag
(Female) Baptized Haddington, East Lothian, 13 October 1667

Nasty Elizabeth Halsey
Born Berkhamsted, Hertfordshire, 1882

Lazy Harris
Born West Derby, Lancashire, 1903

Dick Head
Born Wandsworth, London, 1890

Odious Heaton
Died Halifax, Yorkshire, 1888

Abraham Mouldy Herman
Born Wallingford, Berkshire, 1864

Bother Hislop
(Female) Born Midlothian, c.1806
(Edinburgh, 1841 Scotland census)

Clotworthy Hoare
Born np, Kent, c.1837 (Blackheath, Kent, 1841 census)

Spoilt Eliza Hobbs
Born Huntingdon, 1871

Dork Holmes
Born Huddersfield, Yorkshire, 1905

James Greasy Holmes
Died Hoxne, Suffolk, 1856

Dorothy Horrible
Married Jeremiah Ford, Fleet Prison, London, 20 May 1733

Nelly Horrid
Baptized Fawley, Hampshire, 29 April 1786

Immanuel Horror
Baptized Acklam, Yorkshire, 4 June 1826

Berk Hunt
Born St Pancras, London, c.1898 (St Pancras, 1901 census)

Rock Idle
Born Dewsbury, Yorkshire, 1873

Eliza Inane
Baptized St Margaret's, Leicester, 2 February 1820

George Joyless
Baptized Manchester Cathedral, Manchester, Lancashire, 7 June 1795

Friggin Lawer
Married Freebridge Lynn, Norfolk, 1838

Vanity Lawrence
Born Chipping Sodbury, Gloucestershire, 1845

Grace Less
Married William Gifford, Taunton, Somerset, 8 September 1738

John Liar
Married Kesia Pryer, St Olave, Southwark, London,
18 October 1765

Scary Looker
(Female) Born Warrington, Lancashire, c.1841
(Warrington, 1851 census)

Niphena Loser
Born np, c.1816 (Zeal Monachorum, Devon, 1841 census)

Jeremiah Lousy
Born Boherboy, Cork, Ireland, 25 April 1866

Martha Manky
Married William Waterhouse, Calverley, Yorkshire, 8 February 1798

Vandal Mason
Born Wirral, Cheshire, 1895

Sarah McNasty
Died Carlisle, Cumbria, 1847

Dim McTavish
Born Argyll, c.1849 (Argyll, 1851 Scotland census)

S. Melly
Born Liverpool, Lancashire, 1871

Grace Banshee Merchant
Born Elham, Kent, 1888

Gustavus Berk Middleditch
Born Bury St Edmunds, Suffolk, 1876

Ditsy Millard
(Female) Born Land's End, Cornwall, c.1876
(West Moors, Dorset, 1901 census)

Strange Milliner
(Male) Married Emma Moore, Faversham, Kent, 1859

Fanny Minger
Born Fishersgate, Sussex, c.1881 (Fishersgate, 1891 census)

Stephen Molester
Born np, c.1895 (St John, Hackney, London, 1841 census)
Stephen and Hannah Molester are recorded in the census along with their five children, including one just three days old and as-yet unnamed who is unfortunately listed as 'Infant Molester'.

Marget [*sic*] Morose
Married Thomas Slacke, Belchamp Walter, Essex, 23 September 1610

Gwen Sod Mortimer
Born St Saviour, Southwark, London, 1845

Libertine Moss
Married Ashton-under-Lyne, Lancashire, 1855

Bannastes Naff
(Male) Born np, Lancashire, c.1821 (Blackburn, Lancashire, 1841 census)

Charles Henry Nerd
Baptized St Nicholas, Gloucester, 1 May 1831

Betty Nit
Married Robert Hooper, Westbury, Wiltshire, 9 July 1764

Young Nogood
(Female) Born Newbury, Berkshire, c.1838 (St Giles, London, 1861 census)

Rude Nolan
Married Gravesend, Kent, 1857

Lonely Jack Overton
Born Bosmere, Suffolk, 1903

James Royal Payne
Married Braintree, Essex, 1897

Margaret Perve
Born Kelvedon, Colchester, Essex, c.1519

A. Pervert
(Female) Married George Kelway, Yeovil, Somerset, 15 April 1816

Harry Terrible Phillips
Born St Pancras, London, 1899

Fred Pillock
Baptized Eastrington, Yorkshire, 2 February 1862

Philip Plonker
Baptized Shalford, Surrey, 3 June 1632

Pedro Ponce
Baptized Mitford, Northumberland, 22 August 1885

A Bunch of Pratts

Alfred Pratt Pratt
Born Chipping Norton, Oxfordshire, 1908

Arkless Pratt
(Male) Born Haswell, Durham, c.1863
(Haswell, 1881 census)

Emo Pratt
(Female) Born Lamorlaye, Oise, France, c.1869
(Newmarket, Suffolk, 1871 census)

Favourete Pratt
Born Felling, Durham, c.1891
(Felling, 1901 census)

Horace Jealous Pratt
Born Huntingdon, 1883

John Gash Pratt
Born Lincoln, 1874

Mystery Pratt
Born np, c.1856; died Dewsbury, Yorkshire, 1893

Oswald Beagle Pratt
Born Great Yarmouth, Norfolk, 1879

Failure Radley
Born Lambeth, London, 1864

Whalebelly Robert
Born Saham Toney, Norfolk, c.1818 (Saham Toney, 1861 census)

Robert Rubbish
Baptized St Olave, Southwark, Surrey, 23 August 1702

Fanny Scum
Baptized Calstock, Cornwall, 1805

Dorothy Villain Seymour
Born Islington, London, 1903

Harris Shifty
Born np, Russia, c.1875 (Mile End, London, 1901 census)

Elizabeth Bastard Silly
Born Totnes, Devon, 1846

Maggie Skankey
Married West Derby, Lancashire, 1895

Susannah Slattern
Baptized Bourne, Lincolnshire, 29 August 1725

R. Slicker
(Male) Died Bradford, Yorkshire, 1876

Charlotte Slob
Baptized St Mary the Virgin, Dover, Kent, 12 July 1805

Mary J. Sloppy
Born Stithians, Cornwall, c.1839 (Falmouth, Cornwall, 1861 census)

Nancy Sluggard
Married William Stoneman, Stoke Damerel, Devon, 10 June 1807

Elizabeth Frump Smeath
Married Exeter, Devon, 1841

Constance Smell
Born Witham, Essex, c.1878 (Witham, 1901 census)

Susanna Smelly
Baptized Cambusnethan, Lanarkshire, 15 September 1695

John Minging Smith
Born Marylebone, London, 1865

Inane Barker Smithson
Born Guisborough, Yorkshire, 1879

Samuel Sod
Baptized Bourn, Cambridgeshire, 6 March 1836

William Sodoff
Married Christine Naylor, St Thomas, Dudley, Staffordshire, 3 April 1848

Silly Staryroom
(Female) Born Whissonsett, Norfolk, c.1877
(Hindolveston, Norfolk, 1901 census)

Susannah Rotten Stevens
Married Newton Abbot, Devon, 1876

Melior Strangeman
Baptized Shapwick, Dorset, 2 April 1739

Mary Ann Stupid
Born np, Middlesex, c.1821 (St Dunstan-in-the-West, London, 1841 census)

Feeble Sutcliffe
(Female) Born Erringden, Yorkshire, c.1880 (Erringden, 1881 census)

Richard Pillock Sutton
Born Dover, Kent, 1840

Thomas Tacky
Born Loughborough, Leicestershire, 1860

John Dullard Taylor
Born Bethnal Green, London, 1891

Kate Terrible
Married Charles Henry Kerry, White Notley, Essex, 16 June 1872

Mary Terror
Born Merthyr Tydfil, Glamorgan, 1856

Laurance [*sic*] Thicky
Born Staines, Middlesex, 1855

Filthy Thiele
Born np, *c.*1879, German subject (Hampstead, London, 1901 census)

David Wino Thomas
Born Aberayron, Cardiganshire, 1896

Mary Drippy Tilley
Married Spalding, Lincolnshire, 1847

William James Bitch Tolhurst
Born Lambeth, London, 1841

Silly Trollope
(Female) Born Doncaster, Yorkshire, *c.*1894 (Doncaster, 1901 census)

Thomas Trouble
Married Wincanton, Somerset, 1861

Violet Porteous Twaddle
Born Stonehouse, Lanarkshire, 30 March 1856

Janam Twit
Married Thomas Newton, Wrawby, Lincolnshire, 1606

Frida Mary Ugly
Married Holborn, London, 1907

William Tippen Useless
Baptized Tewkesbury, Gloucestershire, 3 May 1772

Freak Ustick
Buried Egloshayle, Cornwall, 1730

D. Viant
(Male) Born Stoke Damerel, Devon, 1857

E. Vil
(Female) Born Hermitage, Staffordshire, *c.*1864 (Nottingham, 1881 census)

Oceans Vile
Married Langport, Somerset, 1871

Mamelia Vulgar
Married Dartford, Kent, 1903

Louisa Dippy Walker
Born Hitchin, Hertfordshire, 1841

Theodosia Wally
Died Chepstow, Monmouthshire, 1856

Ephraim Uriah Weird
Born South Shields, Durham, 1902

James Wells Tawdry Wells
Born Newton Abbot, Devon, 1849

Prickhead Whelan
Born St Helens, Lancashire, c.1858 (Widnes, Lancashire, 1861 census)

Sarah Gobby Whipp
Born Greenwich, Kent, 1856

Elsutt Wicked
Married Roger Crossman, St Maurice, Plympton, Devon, 1663

Drunke Widegans
(Male) Born np, Romania, c.1856
(St George Hanover Square, London, 1891 census)

Dumbo Willans
Born np, 1918; died Truro, Cornwall, 2004

Urseley Wimp
Baptized Husthwaite, Yorkshire, 26 June 1755

Mary Jane Hutchcome Wino
Married Plymouth, Devon, 1850

Henry Wuss
Married St Pancras, London, 1902

Phebe Yuck
Baptized Brougham Street Primitive Methodist Chapel,
West Hartlepool, Durham, 20 January 1876

THE ONOMASTIC ORCHESTRA

◆

Hannah Harmonic Barrowcliff
Married Mansfield, Nottinghamshire, 1873

Burt Bass
Married Elizabeth Stapleton, Marston Mortayne, Bedfordshire, 19 May 1757

Andrew White Baton
Baptized Milton, Glasgow, Lanarkshire, 15 September 1873

Isabella Bugle
Baptized Christ Church, Tynemouth,
Northumberland, 18 July 1790

Loudy Cello
Baptized Tywardreath, Cornwall,
2 October 1672

Johannes Cymbal
Baptized St Martin-in-the-Fields, London,
16 March 1667

Honor Drum
Married Edmond Horele, London,
16 December 1720

Abba Funk
Born St George in the East, London, 1900

John Gong
Baptized St George the Martyr,
Southwark, London, 9 November 1823

Elias Guitar
Married Susanna Jeanmorann, St Dunstan, Stepney, London, 5 October 1713

Harriet Harp
Born Stoke-on-Trent, Staffordshire, 1861

Violet Horn
Born Alloah, Clackmannanshire, 27 October 1863

Johann Sebastian Jagger
Born Whitehaven, Cumberland, 1889

Epiphany Lullaby
Married Veryan, Cornwall, 3 January 1767

Mary Music
Married Joseph Woods, Biggleswade, Bedfordshire, 15 March 1824

Robert Oboe
Married Ann Wigg, Bobbing, Kent, 16 July 1801

Mel Oddy
Born Halifax, Yorkshire, 1886

Oboe Oglesby
(Female) Born Seaham, Durham, c.1899 (Seaham, 1901 census)

Carrie Oke
Born Bideford, Devon, 1864

Lo-Ruhamah Organ
Baptized North Nibley, Gloucestershire, 6 November 1785

Nudina Harriet Organ
Born Cheltenham, Gloucestershire, 1846

Servina Piano
Baptized Escomb, Durham, 31 August 1879

Violin Prigg
(Female) Born Bury St Edmunds, Suffolk, c.1887
(Bury St Edmunds, 1891 census)

Samuel Rapper Scrutton
Married Dewsbury, Yorkshire, 1910

Barbara Seville
Born Birkenhead, Cheshire, c.1882 (Birkenhead, 1901 census)

Topsy Sharp
Born Bristol, Gloucestershire, 1862

Mike Stand
Born Durham, c.1844 (Newcastle upon Tyne, Northumberland, 1851 census)

Banjo Thomas
(Male) Born Dudley, Worcestershire, c.1836 (Walsall, Staffordshire, 1871 census)

Tom Tom
Born Bristol, Gloucestershire, c.1862
(Barton Regis, Gloucestershire, 1891 census)

Priscilla Trumpet
Baptized Tipton, Staffordshire, 19 August 1832

John Tuba
Married Sarah Chenery, St Margaret's, Lowestoft, Suffolk, 16 January 1774

I. Tunes
(Female) Married Durham, 1874

Roger Viola
Baptized St Mary Whitechapel, Stepney, London, 4 April 1604

Mary Violin
Married John Pearce, St Mary Soho, Westminster, London, 23 August 1870

Concettina [*sic*] Lucia Wilfart
Born np, 1928; died Bradford, Yorkshire, 1992

TRANSPORTS OF DELIGHT

Ivan Austin
Born Hastings, Sussex, 1883

Submarine Miners Banacks
Born Kingston upon Hull, Yorkshire, c.1837 (Kingston upon Hull, 1891 census)

Mac Maximilian Bike
Born Shoreditch, London, c.1847
(St Mary Aldermanbury, London, 1861 census)

Rhoda Boat
Born Rogate, Hampshire, c.1813 (Graffham, Sussex, 1861 census)

Driver Bus

(Male) Born np, Somerset, c.1879 (Leeds, Yorkshire, 1901 census)

Julia Matilda Trike Cable

Born Stoke Damerel, Devon, 1851

Ford Carr

Born Newcastle upon Tyne, Northumberland, c.1863
(Newcastle upon Tyne, 1871 census)

John Bump Carr

Born Sedgehill, Northumberland, c.1846
(Chirton, Northumberland, 1891 census)

Cycle Cockwell

Born Plymouth, Devon, c.1888 (Plymouth, 1891 census)

Mercedes Conga

Born np, Brazil, c.1856 (Sunninghill, Berkshire, 1881 census)

Biking Cooper

(Female) Born Wellington, Shropshire, c.1830
(Wellington, 1851 census)

Minnie Cooper

Born Spalding, Lincolnshire, 1859

Leicester Railway Cope

Born Leicester, 1864

Bountiful Coupe

Born Bolsover, Derbyshire, 1844

Harley Davidson

Born Cainham, Shropshire c.1879 (Cainham, 1881 census)

Driver Driver

Born Trawden, Lancashire, c.1868
(Colne, Lancashire, 1901 census)

Laurie Driver

Born np, 1895; died np, Surrey, 1990

Morris Driver
Born Whitechapel, London, 1859

Julia Penny Farthing
Born Midhurst, Sussex, 1876

Tranquilline Ferrari
Born Holborn, London, 1895

Zed Flying
Born Portsmouth, Hampshire, c.1884 (West Ham, Essex, 1901 census)

Iva Ford
Born Blything, Suffolk, 1882

Philadelphia Fuel
Baptized Denham, Buckinghamshire, 15 November 1840

Georgiana Top Gear
Born Wambrook, Somerset, c.1862 (Tarrant Hinton, Dorset, 1891 census)

Hy Geers
(Male) Baptized Bridge Sollers, Herefordshire, 26 January 1681

Jane Hardtop
Married John Cheshire, Runcorn, Cheshire, 7 February 1836

Aeronaut Hayes
Born Lincoln, c.1865 (Lincoln, 1881 census)

Thomas Tank Hotten
Born Bodmin, Cornwall, 1887

Frederick Petroleum Hughes
Married Islington, London, 1873

Garage Hulse
Born Great Boughton, Cheshire, 1860

Charles Aston Martin
Born St Pancras, London, 1864

Mary Zeppelin Matthewman
Born np, 1916; died Rotherham, Yorkshire, 2000

Christ Metro
Born Caithness, c.1838 (Wick, Caithness, 1841 Scotland census)

Minnie Minor
Born Bristol, Gloucestershire, 1889

Mary Moped
Born np, c.1816 (Barton Regis, Gloucestershire, 1841 census)

Lada Morgan
(Female) Born Colorado, USA, c.1853 (Kensington, London, 1881 census)

Jane Ada Motorhead
Born Great Broughton, Cumberland, c.1874 (Great Broughton, 1881 census)

Messy Parker
(Female) Born np, Kent, c.1839 (Chiddingstone, Kent, 1841 census)

Tram Plant
Married Stourbridge, Worcestershire, 1855

L. Plate
(Female) Born np, Sussex, c.1811 (Warminghurst, Sussex, 1841 census)

Noel Plate
Born Binfield, Buckinghamshire, c.1847 (Hendon, Middlesex, 1891 census)

Rover Rolls
Born Cookham, Berkshire, 1891

Sarah Roundabout
Born Sutton, Warwickshire, c.1828 (Kingsbury, Warwickshire, 1851 census)

Hugh Scooter
Married Margaret Kerr, Dalry, Ayrshire, 5 September 1829

John Skoda
Born Glastonbury, Somerset, c.1827 (Evercreech, Somerset, 1871 census)

Bob Sleigh
Baptized Edinburgh, Midlothian, 6 November 1608

George Quick Sloman
Died Okehampton, Devon, 1858

Thomas Silly Speed
Born Newark, Nottinghamshire, 1843

Wacke Speed
(Male) Born Bradford, Yorkshire, c.1861 (Bradford, 1881 census)

Anthony Speedo
Married Margaret Barker, Nayland, Suffolk, 25 October 1562

Mary Petrol Swanson
Born Bridgend, Glamorgan, 1901

John Turbo Tapper
Married Birmingham, Warwickshire, 1879

Pilot Tidd
Died Houghton-le-Spring, Durham, 1882

William Tooslow
Baptized Topsham, Devon, 6 April 1652

Funily Tram
Born Newcastle upon Tyne, Northumberland, c.1848
(Newcastle upon Tyne, 1881 census)

Minnie Wheels
Born Chelsea, London, c.1857 (Bermondsey, London, 1881 census)

Gasoline McKenzie Yeats
Born Manchester, Lancashire, 1845

OUT OF THE CLOSET

◆

Nellie Knickerbocker Beach
Married Paddington, London, 1907

Freeston Blazer
(Female) Married Thomas James, West Bradenham, Norfolk,
6 December 1756

Sarah Bloomers
Baptized St Leonard, New Malton, Yorkshire, 1 March 1792

Jack Boot
Born Uxbridge, Middlesex, 1899

Wellington Boot
Born Linton, Cambridgeshire, 1869

Cashmere Boss
Born Louth, Lincolnshire, 1849

Bellah Bottoms
Born Skipton, Yorkshire, c.1803
(Bingley, Yorkshire, 1851 census)

Thomas Bowtie
Married Agnes Myller, St Andrew, Plymouth,
Devon, 25 January 1613

John Bra
Born Hardwick, Devon, c.1851
('draper's assistant', City of London, 1881 census)

Sarah Braces
Born Wandsworth, London, 1841

Pinkus Brief
Born Whitechapel, London, 1911

Zipper Brotherwood
Born Uckfield, Sussex, 1885

William Brownhat
Married Elizabeth Jordan, St John the Baptist,
Croydon, Surrey, 7 September 1813

Lively Busby
(Male) Born np, c.1832; died Chertsey, Surrey, 1907

Pearl Button
Born Hollingbourne, Kent, 1903

Fanny Cap
Married Charles Panton, Hemingbrough, Yorkshire, 7 September 1876

Sophia Clothes
Born Ashton-under-Lyne, Lancashire, 1843

Hattie Coates
Married Middlesbrough, Yorkshire, 1895

Panty Coppola
Married Rose Johnson, St Pancras, London, 1918

Agnea Corset
Born Ulverston, Lancashire, 1875

and

Agnea Winship Corset
Born Tynemouth, Northumberland, 1875
Only two Agnea Corsets are recorded, both of them born in the same year.

Lapel Davies
(Female) Born Lambeth, London, c.1890
(St George the Martyr, London, 1891 census)

Edward Drawers
Baptized Haydor, Lincolnshire, 18 February 1576

Polly Esther
Born Bradford, Yorkshire, c.1870 (Manningham, Yorkshire, 1871 census)

Maggie Shirt Fidler
Born Chapel-en-le-Frith, Derbyshire, 1897

Mary Gestring
Born np, Shropshire, c.1830 (Shifnal, Shropshire, 1841 census)

Brown Hatt
Born Bury, Lancashire, c.1842 (Musbury, Lancashire, 1871 census)

Topsy Hatter
Born Rye, East Sussex, 1898

Girdle Headley
(Male) Born Great Ouseburn, Yorkshire, 1886

Jean Jacket
Born np, Ireland, c.1837 (Paisley, Renfrewshire, 1841 Scotland census)

Levi Jeans
Baptized Stalbridge, Dorset, 24 February 1811

Hugh Knicker
Born np, Ireland, c.1866 (Maryhill, Lanarkshire, 1871 Scotland census)

Flares Moore
(Female) Born Birmingham, Warwickshire, c.1856
(Handsworth, Staffordshire, 1871 census)

Jacket Nicholson
(Male) Born Hawkshead, Lancashire, c.1841
(Satterthwaite, Lancashire, 1871 census)

Elizabeth Nylon
Died Lambeth, London, 1853

Jemima Panties
Born Poplar, London, c.1846 (Poplar, 1861 census)

Elizabeth Pantoff
Married William Hutt, St Botolph without Bishopsgate, London,
17 September 1751

Mary Panty
Baptized Glatton, Huntingdonshire, 1 September 1751

George Clap Plimsoll
Married Bristol, Gloucestershire, 1875

Anna Rack
Married St George in the East, London, 1881

Pants Schubert
(Male) Born Chiswick, Middlesex, c.1898
(Chiswick, 1901 census)

T. Shirt
(Male) Born Ecclesfield, Yorkshire, 1843

Jim Shoe
Married Bawdrip, Somerset, 28 February 1602

Sadie Shorts
Born West Derby, Lancashire, 1901

Minnie Skirt
Baptized St Mary's, Sandwich, Kent, 17 July 1777

Jim Slip
Born Bath, Somerset, 1856

Mary Bra Small
Born Newcastle, Northumberland, c.1861
(Westgate, Northumberland, 1861 census)

Elizabeth Snickers
Married Robert Musgrave, Burneston, Yorkshire,
20 December 1751

Emmaretta Snood
Married Lexden, Essex, 1881

Martha Socks
Married John Truman, Stapleford, Nottinghamshire, 27 June 1762

Archibald Sporran
Born Cambeltown, Argyll, 21 January 1855

Nanny G. String
Born Gateshead, Durham, c.1859 (Gateshead, 1861 census)

Ana Sweater
Married Michael Pollard, Halifax, Yorkshire, 18 July 1670

Original Walker John Bedford Thong
Died Huntingdon, 1858

Maud Camelia Tights
Born Cambridge, 1876

Florenett Trousers
(Female) Born Walsall, Staffordshire, c.1852
(Paddington, London, 1881 census)

Violet Trunks
Born Williton, Somerset, 1898

Rebecca Vest
Born Ludlow, Shropshire, 1844

Frock Watton
Born Solihull, Warwickshire, 1860

Trainers Wheatfield
(Male) Born St Luke, London, c.1850 (St Luke, 1861 census)

Felty Wooley
(Female) Born Radford, Nottinghamshire, c.1889
(Bulwell, Nottinghamshire, 1891 census)

Glad Wragg
Born Bakewell, Derbyshire, 1894

Collar Zacks
Born Riga, Russia, c.1870 (St George in the East, London, 1891 census)

Matthias Zip
Baptized Heworth, Durham, 23 September 1705

GOOD SPORTS

Batty Ball
(Female) Born North Meols, Lancashire, c.1797 (North Meols, 1871 census)

Mary Bowley Ball
Born np, USA, c.1850 (Loughborough, Leicestershire, 1891 census)

Spinner Ball
Born Wanstead, Essex, c.1900 (Wanstead, 1901 census)

Mark Foot Balls
Born South Shields, Durham, 1890

Olympic Bell
Born Lanchester, Durham, 1889

Tom Bola
Born Sheffield, Yorkshire, c.1841 (Sheffield, 1851 census)

Tennis Bust
Born Stonebroom, Derbyshire, c.1897 (Shirland, Derbyshire, 1901 census)

Bartholemew Cricket
Baptized St John, Margate, Kent, 25 April 1755

Cricket Crisp
(Female) Born Bath, Somerset, c.1838 (Walcot, Somerset, 1851 census)

Francois Croquet
Baptized French Huguenot Church, Threadneedle Street, London, 28 November 1744

Dan Darts
Born Biggleswade, Bedfordshire, 1874

Sarah Bounce P. Frisby
Born Leicester, 1878

Fanny Golf
Married George Rolph, Cardiff, Glamorgan, 1915

Sarah Googly
Married Henry Cork, St John the Evangelist, Limehouse, London, 9 August 1859

Sporty Gray
Born Alton, Hampshire, 1897

Hannah Hurdles
Born Reading, Berkshire, 1883

Frisby Lightfoot
Born Luton, Bedfordshire, 1873

Jim Locker
Married Stoke-on-Trent, Staffordshire, 1864

Marathon Beatrice Pearson
Born Warwick 1889

Jack Potts
Born Wolstanton, Staffordshire, 1902

Wrestle Raynsford
Born Guildford, Surrey, 1873

Thomas Rodeo
Baptized St Margaret's, Durham, 17 April 1808

Lavinia Roulette
Married Lambeth, London, 1859

C. Saw
(Male) Born Edmonton, Middlesex, 1879

William Snooker
Married Ann Kerwood, Bosham, Sussex, 25 September 1775

Gladys Badminton Sweett
Born Devonport, Devon, 1903

Thomas Tenpin
Born Plymouth, Devon, c.1837
(Rattery, Devon, 1901 census)

Lot Terry
Born Prestwich, Lancashire, 1884

Rugby Thrower
Died King's Lynn, Norfolk, 1895

Urban Wicket
Born Sheviock, Cornwall, c.1633

Uncommon Smiths

The most recent estimate of the number of people in England and Wales with the surname 'Smith' was 652,563. And forget all those 'Mcs' – Smith is by a long margin the most common surname in Scotland as well. About twelve people out of every thousand in the UK are called Smith. In the period 1837–2007, some 62,070 babies were given the archetypal name 'John Smith', and there are 12,793 of them currently on the National Health Service Register. If you happen to be called Smith there is therefore a clear temptation to elevate your child above the commonplace by coming up with a first name that is a little different.

Abishag Martha Smith
Born Thraptson, Northamptonshire, 1876

Amorous Smith
Born Bury, Lancashire, 1858

Anonymous Smith
Married Eleanor Carlisle, Leckhampton, Buckinghamshire, 17 May 1604

Blondina Smith
Born np, c.1826; died Hemel Hempstead, Hertfordshire, 1893

Bonus Smith
Born Skipton, Yorkshire, 1843

Brick Smith
Died York, 1851

Cleopatra Smith
Born Newington, London, 1860

Cock Smith
Born np, Yorkshire, c.1839 (Kirk Burton, Yorkshire, 1841 census)

Cockshott Smith Smith
Born Keighley, Yorkshire, 1845

Cuckoo Smith
Born Brimpton, Berkshire, c.1877 (Brimpton, 1881 census)

Cupid Aaron T. Smith
Born Wandsworth, London, 1870

Despair Smith
Born Ely, Cambridgeshire, 1856

Devil Smith
(Female) Born np, c.1816 (St Pancras, London, 1841 census)

Dorothy Rubbery Smith
Born West Bromwich, Staffordshire, 1900

Dozer Smith
Born Kettering Northamptonshire, 1893

Dripper Smith
(Female) Born Whaplode, Lincolnshire, c.1882 (Whaplode, 1901 census)

Elizabeth Utterly Smith
Married Glanford Brigg, Lincolnshire, 1865

Elsie Penile Smith
Died Barton Regis, Gloucestershire, 1894

Exuperius Smith
(Male) Baptized Whitford, Flintshire, 18 October 1818

Fang Smith
(Female) Born Hopesay, Shropshire, c.1848
(Woolston, Shropshire, 1851 census)

Fortunate Hortensius Smith
Married Reading, Berkshire, 1884

Frank Walrus Smith
Born Portsea Island, Hampshire, 1880

George Wackerbarth Smith
Born Wirral, Cheshire, 1851

Gladys Passion Smith
Born Bristol, Gloucestershire, 1904

Goliath Smith
Born Buckingham, 1844

Goon Smith
Born np, Surrey, c.1854 (London, 1871 census)

Hairy Smith
Born Keighley, Yorkshire, c.1877 (Keighley, 1881 census)

Hannah Booby Smith
Born Cirencester, Gloucestershire, 1842

Hannibal Smith
Born Houghton-le-Spring, Durham, 1862

Harry Two Smith
Married Derby, Derbyshire, 1900

Henry Waste Smith
Born Nuneaton, Warwickshire, 1901

Hiawatha Smith
Born Islington, London, 1890

Indiana Smith
Born Colchester, Essex, 1852

Ink Smith
Married Whitby, Yorkshire, 1857

Jesus Smith
Born np, Angus, c.1823 (Brechin, Angus, 1841 Scotland census)

John Philosopher Smith
Born Aston, Warwickshire, 1879

Julius Caesar Smith
Born Leverington, Cambridgeshire, c.1821 (Kirton, Lincolnshire, 1851 census)

Kaiser Smith
Born Warwick, 1873

Lewis Unexpected Smith
Born Medway, Kent, 1899

Lichen M. J. Smith
(Female) Born Birmingham, c.1848 (Aston, Warwickshire, 1871 census)

Lizzie Muffin Smith
Born Burton upon Trent, Staffordshire, 1898

Lustrous Luke Smith
Married Ipswich, Suffolk, 1858

Mango Smith
(Male) Born np, Scotland, c.1804 (Litchurch, Derbyshire, 1871 census)

Maudlin Smith
Born Durham, 1864

Messiah Smith
Born Sheffield, Yorkshire, 1848

Mice Smith
(Female) Born Cradley, Herefordshire, c.1867
(Suckley, Worcestershire, 1871 census)

Minge Smith
Born Crich, Derbyshire, c.1860 (Holbeck, Nottinghamshire, 1891 census)

Minniehaha Smith
Born Gravesend, Kent, nd (Gravesend, 1881 census)

Murder John Smith
Born St George Hanover Square, London, 1878

Mystic Smith
Born South Stoneham, Hampshire, 1855

Nebuchadnezzar Smith
Born Hollingbourne, Kent, 1882

Perpugilliam Smith
Born West Bromwich, Staffordshire, 1847

Perseverance Smith
Born Fulham, London, 1876

Pickles Smith
Born Burnley, Lancashire, 1863

Plato Smith
Born Blything, Suffolk, 1880

Ponce Smith
(Male) Born Hellington, Shropshire, c.1833
(Chorlton-cum-Hardy, Lancashire, 1891 census)

President Percy Smith
Born Poplar, London, 1882

Queen Victoria Smith
Born Rochford, Essex, 1901

Rap Smith
Born Doncaster, Yorkshire, 1900

Semen Smith
Born Burrough on the Hill, Leicestershire, c.1834
(Burton upon Trent, Staffordshire, 1861 census)

Sexey Jane Smith
Born np, c.1842; died Amesbury, Wiltshire, 1898

Shed Smith
Born Hoxne, Yorkshire, 1885

Speedy Smith
(Female) Born St Helens, Lancashire, c.1885 (Lockwood, Yorkshire, 1891 census)

Streaker Smith
(Male) Born Easington, Durham, 1845

Submit Smith
(Female) Born Hatfield, Hertfordshire, c.1736

Suckey Smith
(Female) Born np, Gloucestershire, c.1868
(Little Rissington, Gloucestershire, 1881 census)

Susannah Ink Smith
Married Manchester, Lancashire, 1863

Tilgathpilneser Smith
Born Newmarket, Suffolk, 1861
After Mahershalalhashbaz, Tilgathpilneser is one of the longest personal names in the Bible.

Tin Smith
Born np, c.1876; died Sleaford, Lincolnshire, 1884

Uz Smith
Born Hoxne, Yorkshire, 1892

Vaulter Smith
(Male) Born Thurne, Norfolk, c.1855 (Thurne, 1861 census)

Warp Smith
(Male) Born Manchester, Lancashire, c.1846 (Manchester, 1891 census)

William Whynot Smith
Born Ipswich, Suffolk, 1861

Wonderful Smith
Born Blything, Suffolk, 1893

DYSLEXIA RULES, KO

Misspeled names

There are a number of examples of clumsiness that are clearly attributable to parents who are either trying to be original or simply cannot spell, among them:

English Channels
In the period 1984–2007, perhaps as a homage to French designer Coco Chanel, over 5,000 British girls were given the first name Chanel – along with over 600 who received the name Channel, almost 400 Chanells, and 100 Channells.

Era Error
In the period around the millennium, 1999–2000, some 23 children were called 'Millenium', but only six with it spelled correctly.

'I am Sparticus'

Some 19 boys were so-called in 1994–2007 – almost as many as with the correct spelling, Spartacus.

Then there are those resulting from transcription errors, such as:

Horrible mistake

The Honourable Alexander William Crawford Lindsay, who married at St George Hanover Square, London, in 1846, appears in the register abbreviated as 'The Hon'ble' which has duly been transcribed as 'The Horrible'.

Glad to be Alive?

Alive Annie Andress, born in Bridport, Dorset, in 1901, is one of over 60 women appearing in birth registers in the period 1837–1983 who were actually named 'Olive', but whose names have been transcribed as 'Alive'.

Martha and the vandals

Martha Dobbs, the five-year-old daughter of Martha Dobbs, is in the 1851 England census as 'Masher'.

Like it or lump it

Hugh Lamplugh Brookshank, on the training ship Torewall, *moored in the Thames at the time of the 1891 census, is listed as Hugh Lump Loza Brockbank.*

Finally, these are examples of apparent errors in the original records – which leads one to speculate whether they were deliberate or accidental, and did their bearers go through life with misspelled names?

Jmaes Butters

Born Swaffham, Norfolk, 1838

Jhon Cap

Married, Salford, Lancashire, 1882

Samuel Brain Churchill

Born Clifton, Gloucestershire, 1874

Geroge Gibbons

Born Lincoln, 1864

Atrhur Hancock

Born Torrington, Devon, 1909

Rcihard Morris
Born Whitechapel, London, 1864

Dnaiel Smart
Born Otley, Yorkshire, 1860

Maud Smiht
Born Hull, Yorkshire, 1911

Mray Snare
Married Thetford, Norfolk, 1882

Jsoeph Trunks
Married Annie Harding, Islington, London, 1915

◆

ANAGRAMS

Names where the first name and surname are anagrams of each other.

Mary Army
Married Aron [*sic*] Memory, St Andrew, Plymouth, Devon, 6 October 1663

Ronald Arnold
Born Bedford, 1885

Abel Bale
Born Market Harborough, Leicestershire, 1844

Albert Bartel
Born Battersea, London, *c.*1889 (Lambeth, London, 1891 census)

Bertha Bather
Born Peover, Cheshire, *c.*1880 (Chelford, Cheshire, 1901 census)

Brian Brain
Born np, 1942; died Worcester, 1997

Clare Clear
Born Stepney, London, 1896

Lydia Daily
Baptized St John de Sepulchre, Norwich, Norfolk, 25 May 1748

Edna Dean
Baptized Stalybridge, Cheshire, 5 November 1797

Denis Dines
Born np, 1923; died Tower Hamlets, London, 1991

Gary Gray
Born np, Suffolk, c.1827 (Durham, 1851 census)

Thelma Hamlet
Born Aston, Warwickshire, 1909

Ruth Hurt
Baptized Alfreton, Derbyshire, 29 August 1731

Jane Jean
Baptized Stoke Climsland, Cornwall, 7 February 1830

Charles Larches
Born Bethnal Green, London, c.1890 (Bethnal Green, 1891 census)

Ann Nan
Born Bradford, Yorkshire, 1868

Ernest Nester
Born West Ham, Essex, 1895

Mary Ramy
Born Stepney, London, c.1838 (Willesden, London, 1871 census)

Eric Rice
Born Bromley, Kent, 1901

Eros Rose
Born Amesbury, Wiltshire, 1884

Rosa Soar
Born Ticknall, Derbyshire, c.1858 (Ticknall, 1861 census)

Rose Sore
Born Stowmarket, Suffolk, c.1867 (Bradford, Yorkshire, 1901 census)

Andrew Wander

Married Jane Little, Wamphray, Dumfries, 19 July 1835

Lewis Wiles

Born 21 May 1839; baptized St Peter Mancroft, Norwich,
Norfolk, 25 September 1839

◆

PALINDROMIC FIRST AND SURNAMES

Names where both the first name and surname are palindromic . . .

Anna Malam

Born Legsby, Lincolnshire, c.1844 (West Rasen, Lincolnshire, 1861 census)

Bob Notton

Married Anne Burden, Chirton, Wiltshire, 9 February 1673

Hannah Tippitt

Baptized Sheffield Cathedral, 12 March 1756

. . . and others where the entire name is a palindrome:

Abba Abba

Born np, Leicestershire, 1987

Ada Ada

Born Stone, Staffordshire, c.1855 (Longton, Staffordshire, 1901 census)

Nell Allen

Born Leeds, Yorkshire, 1884

Nella Allen

Born Doncaster, Yorkshire, 1908

Anna Anna
Born Bradford, Yorkshire, c.1850
(Birkenhead, Cheshire, 1851 census)

Mary Byram
Baptized Pontefract, Yorkshire, 5 August 1631

Anna D'Anna
Born np, 1925; died Aylesbury, Buckinghamshire, 2001

Enid Dine
Born Edmonton, Middlesex, 1900
Her mother Ada also had a palindromic first name.

Elle G. Elle
Born Dover, Kent, c.1900 (Dover, 1901 census)

Eve Eve
Born np, Essex, c.1828
(High Easter, Essex, 1841 census)

Hannah Hannah
Born Erpingham, Norfolk, 1846

Noel Leon
Married Julia Stevens, Salisbury, Wiltshire, 2003

Tom Mot
Born np, 1906; died Colchester, Essex, 1990

Leon Noel
Born Warrington, Cheshire, 1984

Revilo Oliver
Born Beaminster, Dorset, 1851

Otto Otto
Born Berne, Switzerland, c.1879
(St Pancras, London, 1901 census)

Yendis Sidney
Born West Ham, Essex, 1900

BACKWARD PEOPLE – ANANYMS

◆

Most British people are familiar with the confectionery company Trebor, named after Trebor Villas, where the company started in Forest Gate, London, in 1906. Trebor was also coincidentally the ananym (reverse spelling) of the name of the company's co-founder, Robert Robertson (with William Woodcock – it was originally called Robertson and Woodcock). They were in partnership with Sydney Marks and Thomas King, none of whose names work backwards (although Skram is not without its appeal). Beyond commerce, such somewhat contrived names are encountered as first names. Some may be coincidences: Floda, a place in Sweden, existed as a name long before it was identified as an ananym of Adolf. Often, the ananym is a cunning way of giving a girl the name of a male family member, or vice versa, such as Leinad William, daughter of Daniel William.

Samot Barker
(Female) Born Manchester, Lancashire, c.1856 (Beswick, Lancashire, 1891 census)

Divad Bean
(Male) Born Fife, c.1838 (Fife, 1841 Scotland census)

Alleb Billard
(Female) Born np, Nottinghamshire, c.1822
(Warsop, Nottinghamshire, 1841 census)

Semaj Bovingdon
Born Brentford, Middlesex, 1899

Rednaxela Brown
(Female) Born Cambuslang, Lanarkshire, c.1888
(Cambuslang, 1891 Scotland census)

Floda Bumson
(Female) Born Kilmington, Somerset, c.1843 (Kilmington, 1851 census)

Azile Edith De Gruchy
Born Lewisham, London, 1901

Nomis F. Dickinson
(Male) Born Welton, Lincolnshire, c.1867 (Welton, 1881 census)

Yendor Gordon
Married Lee J. Bellamy, Surrey, 1994

Ecila Gore
(Female) Born Taunton, Somerset, 1904

Amron Hardill
Married Pontefract, Yorkshire, 1898

Yram K. O. Hoare
(Female) Born Ballygarrett, Wexford, Ireland, c.1857
(Liverpool, Lancashire, 1891 census)

Legin Ignacy
Born np, 1892; died Oldham, Lancashire, 1987

Cire Douglas W. Jehnke
Born Bath, Avon, 1901

Senga Jepsen
Born Falmouth, Cornwall, 1879

Nivek Kerley
Born Bournemouth, Hampshire, 1987

Regor Kirsup
(Male) Born Durham, c.1829 (Durham, 1841 census)

Aniles Martin
(Female) Born np, Tasmania, Australia (Marylebone, London, 1881 census)

William Nitram Martyn
Born Brockham, Surrey, c.1848 (Croydon, Surrey, 1881 census)

Airam Mason
Married Abergavenny, Monmouthshire, 1845

Enaid Price
Born Crickhowell, Brecon, 1899

Allegin Reymond
(Male) Born np, Italy, c.1871 (Dumbarton, 1901 Scotland census)

Trebor Roberts
Born St Asaph, Denbighshire, 1912

Luap Amo Snowball
(Female) Born Keighley, Yorkshire, c.1849 (Hunslet, Yorkshire, 1891 census)

Mailliw Toop
(Female) Born Lambeth, London, 1842

Ronaele Mary E. Walbrand-Evans
Born Kensington, London, 1904

Leinad William
(Female) Born Cardiff, Glamorgan, c.1860
(Canton, Glamorgan, 1871 Wales census)

———◆———

REVERSE NAMES

*These are names where placing the surname first (in the form Smith, John)
changes the meaning, sometimes making the innocuous noxious . . .*

Charlotte Apple
Born np, Germany, c.1847 (Kingston upon Hull, Yorkshire, 1851 census)

Fanny Bare
Baptized Milton Damerel, Devon, 31 December 1826

Willy Big
Married Rachel Haselwood, Dartford, Kent, 5 October 1626

William Job Blow
Born Lincoln, 1887

Dick Chew
Born np, 1912; died Blackburn, Lancashire, 2003

Eve Christmas
Died Stockport, Cheshire, 1859

Comfort Close
Born Ross, Herefordshire, 1869

Feel Copper
Born Rochdale, Lancashire, 1850 (Rochdale, 1851 census)

Fanny Damp
Born Chard, Devon, 1844

Kate Forni
Born np, Austria, c.1865 (St Martin-in-the-Fields, London, 1891 census)

Dick Hard
Baptized Alford, Lincolnshire, 24 August 1652

Dick Huge
Born np, Wales, c.1865 (Marsden, Yorkshire, 1891 census)

Fanny Huge
Born Kenwyn, Cornwall, c.1807 (Kenwyn, 1851 census)

Roger Jolly
Baptized Parham, Suffolk, 15 April 1549

Dick Longest
Baptized Bletchworth, Surrey, 18 July 1602

Fanny Loose
Born Peterborough, Northamptonshire, 1863

Fanny Lovely
Born Stogursey, Somerset, c.1883 (Stogursey, 1891 census)

Christmas Merry
Born Williton, Somerset, 1885

Dick Moby
Born Woodstock, Oxfordshire, 1876

Fanny Moist
Born Newton Abbot, Devon, 1850

Dick Nice
Baptized All Saints, Sudbury, Suffolk, 31 July 1778

Fanny Nice
Born Sheffield, Yorkshire, 1904

Dick Pink
Baptized Hambledon, Hampshire, 20 August 1647

Fanny Pink
Born Malling, Kent, 1853

Jane Plain
Married John Rogers, Shernborne, Norfolk, 11 October 1757

Crusoe Robinson
Born Wortley, Yorkshire, 1888

Fanny Shaves
Born Doncaster, Yorkshire, c.1860 (Doncaster, 1871 census)

Billy Silly
Baptized Markfield, Leicestershire, 13 September 1603

Dick Slippery
Married Anne Gipson, St Dunstan, Stepney, London,
21 December 1675

Argument Small
Born Guisborough, Yorkshire, 1853

Dick Stiff
Born St Luke, London, 1846

Fanny Tight
Born Ware, Hertfordshire, 1847

Christmas White
Born Boston, Lincolnshire, 1858

Fanny Wide
Married Cardiff, Glamorgan, 1900

Enough Wright
(Male) Born np, Shropshire, c.1835
(Wellington, Shropshire, 1841 census)

BEST SPOONERISM NAMES

Joe Blobs

Married Sarah Smith, Sedgley, Staffordshire, 11 September 1803

Fanny Cucker

Born Sutton, Surrey, c.1857 (Sutton, 1871 census)

Harry Punt Cunnington

Born Lutterworth, Leicestershire, 1875

Pat Fenis

Born np, Ireland, c.1841 (Greenwich, London, 1881 census)

Kate Grunt

Born np, Scotland, c.1842 (Camberwell, London, 1881 census)

Mary Hinge

Born Clutton, Somerset, 1846

Carey Hunt

Born March, Cambridge, c.1896 (March, 1901 census)

Kurt Hunt

Born Liverpool, Lancashire, 1985

Kenny Lunt

Born West Derby, Lancashire, 1910

Betty Swall

Married Auckland, Durham, 1860

RHYMES WITHOUT REASON

Mabel Abel

Born Norwich, Norfolk, c.1895 (Norwich, 1901 census)

Sally Alley

Born np, Yorkshire, c.1825 (Halifax, Yorkshire, 1841 census)

Paul Ball
Baptized Bath Abbey, Somerset, 7 February 1599

Anna Banner
Born Liverpool, Lancashire, 1879

Charley Barley
Born New Cross, Kent, c.1857 (Croydon, Surrey, 1861 census)

Harry Barry
Born Frome, Somerset, 1842

Peter Beater
Baptized West Teignmouth, Devon, 17 August 1809

Ethel Bethel
Born Stockport, Cheshire, 1905

Ruth Booth
Baptized St Bartholemew Exchange, London, 18 June 1580

Fred Bread
Born np, c.1818; died Halifax, Yorkshire, 1875

John Nooks Brooks
Married Lambeth, London, 1862

Lizzie Busy
Baptized Modbury, Devon, 18 July 1632

Mary Canary
Born Prescot, Lancashire, 1859

Harry Carry
Born Folkestone, Kent, c.1901 (Folkestone, 1901 census)

Agnise Chemise
Married Alexander Biggar, Canongate,
Edinburgh, Midlothian, 27 October 1566

Hester Chester
Born Blackburn, Lancashire, 1862

Nancy Clancy
Born Brent, Devon, c.1847 (Brent, 1871 census)

Beverley Cleveley
Married Stephen Reynolds, Solihull, West Midlands, 2000

Shirley Curley
Born np, 1940; died Greenwich, London, 2002

Mary Dairy
Married John Homes, Whitgift, Yorkshire, 10 January 1809

Sam Dam
Born Stoke Prior, Herefordshire, c.1795
(Kingsland, Herefordshire, 1851 census)

Andy Dandy
Baptized St Stephen Walbrook, London, 28 May 1712

Mark Dark
Born Keynsham, Somerset, 1867

Fred Dead
Born Donhead St Mary, Wiltshire, c.1900 (Donhead St Mary, 1901 census)

Cow Dow
Married Grantham, Lincolnshire, 1858

Peter Eater
Born np, Cheshire, c.1781 (Great Budworth, Cheshire, 1841 census)

Mary Fairy
Baptized Ringstead, Northamptonshire, 16 June 1763

Nancy Fancy
Born np, 1928; died np, Surrey 2001

Danny Fanny
Born Rotherfield, Sussex, c.1834 (Hamsey, Sussex, 1871 census)

Heather Feather
Married Peter McClelland, Keighley, Yorkshire, 1992

Richard Stoat Float
Born np, Devon, c.1821 (East Stonehouse, Devon, 1851 census)

Caroline Toil Foil
Born Sidbury, Devon, c.1816 (Honiton, Devon, 1861 census)

Maude Ford
Born Yeovil, Somerset, 1862

Sand Gand
(Female) Born Kingsbridge, Devon, c.1807 (Chatham, Kent, 1881 census)

Sander Gander
(Female) Born Middlesex, c.1774 (St Mary Whitechapel, London, 1841 census)

Sandy Gandy
Married John Evans, Davenham, Cheshire, 31 October 1814

Hugh Glue
Married Ann White, Chelsea, London, 1804

Norman Gorman
Born Pendleton, Lancashire, c.1884 (Pendleton, 1891 census)

Mary Hairy
Married Helmsley, Yorkshire, 1861

Fred Head
Born Stockbridge, Hampshire, 1865

Rose Hose
Born Retford, Nottinghamshire, c.1871
(Laneham, Nottinghamshire, 1871 census)

Molly Jolly
Born np, 1912; died Oxford 1991

Polly Jolly
Born West Ham, Essex, 1921

Sidney Kidney
Born Milton, Kent, 1906

Amy Lamy
Born np, USA, c.1866 (St Saviour, Jersey, 1891 Channel Islands census)

Peg Legg
Born Stuntney, Cambridgeshire, c.1900 (Ely, Cambridgeshire, 1901 census)

Hugh Loo
Died South Shields, Durham, 1878

Ronald McDonald
Married Agnes Cameron, Dunblane, Perthshire, 20 April 1689

Thigh McKay
Born np, Scotland, c.1806 (Brighthelmston (Brighton), 1841 census)

Peter Meter
Born np, Aberdeenshire, c.1821 (Aberdeen, 1841 Scotland census)

June Moon
Born np, Bedfordshire, c.1801 (Bedford, 1841 census)

William Organ Morgan
Born Medway, Kent, 1858

Eater Neater
Born Islington, London, c.1835 (Dulwich, London, 1871 census)

Kevin Nevin
Born Toxteth Park, Lancashire, 1906

Willy Nilly
Married Johan [sic] Crosman, Plympton St Mary, Devon, 26 September 1648

Bob Nob
Born Leeds, Yorkshire, c.1866 (Leeds, 1871 census)

Enoch Nock
Born Wolverhampton, Staffordshire, 1841

Percy Nursey
Born Lambeth, London, 1871

Jane Pain
Baptized Perranzabuloe, Cornwall, 29 October 1682

Hatty Patty
Born Chelsea, London, c.1830 (Islington, London, 1851 census)

Henny Penny
(Male) Born Llanasa, Flintshire, c.1839 (Llanasa, 1901 Wales census)

Berry Perry
(Female) Born Fowey, Cornwall, c.1851 (Fowey, 1871 census)

Louisa Pizza
Born Blything, Suffolk, 1839

Dick Prick
Baptized Barrow, Suffolk, 1 July 1544

Hugh Pugh
Born Llanfihangel-y-Pennant, Merionethshire, 24 February 1826

Ice Rice
(Male) Born St Pancras, London, c.1860 (St Pancras, 1861 census)

Mary Scary
Born Docking, Norfolk, 1843

Dan Scran
Born Chailey, Sussex, c.1851 (St Pancras, London, 1901 census)

Herbert Sherbert
Born Tottenham, London, c.1880 (Stoke Newington, London, 1891 census)

Dick Sick
Married Margaret Bennett, Kirkham, Lancashire, 1 February 1562

Nellie Smellie
Born St Pancras, London, 1897

John Long Song
Born Oldham, Lancashire, c.1825 (Whitley, Derbyshire, 1871 census)

Ray Spray
Born np, Sussex, c.1895 (Lewisham, London, 1901 census)

I. Spy
(Male) Born Tillicoultry, Clackmannanshire, c.1805
(Row, Dumbarton, 1861 Scotland census)

Jack Tack
Born Portsmouth, Hampshire, 1906

Rash Tash
Born np, Germany, c.1871 (St Mary Whitechapel, London, 1871 census)

Jane Vane
Baptized Stanhope, Durham, 29 August 1653

Dick Vick
Born Alverstoke, Hampshire, 1843

Jim Vim
Born np, Sussex, c.1824 (Brighthelmston (Brighton), Sussex, 1841 census)

Sam Yam
Born Leeds, Yorkshire, 1900

HORRIFIC HONORIFICS

*Although these sound like a titled lot, their grandiloquent
first names are those with which they were born.*

Emperor Adrian
Born St James, Clerkenwell Green,
London, 7 May 1809

Reverend James Ball
Born Doncaster, Yorkshire, 1878

Lord Baron
Born Haslingden, Lancashire, 1842

Marquis Baron
Born Burnley, Lancashire, 1880

Saint Bugg
Died Bourne, Lincolnshire, 1840

King Solomon Coe
Born Caxton, Cambridgeshire, 1893

King Cole
Born Wortley, Yorkshire, 1883

William The Second Davy
Born Romford, Essex, 1890

James Lord Drivel

Born Gildersome, Yorkshire, c.1848 (Leeds, Yorkshire, 1871 census)

Duke Dyke

Born St Thomas, Devon, 1849

Sir Dusty Entwistle

Born Bury, Lancashire, c.1877 (Bury, 1881 census)

Bishop Fanny

Born Lutterworth, Leicestershire, 1844

Doctor Septimus Forrest

Born Preston, Lancashire, c.1834 (Blackburn, Lancashire, 1851 census)

Seventh sons were believed to possess special powers, and were sometimes given the name 'Doctor', especially in Lancashire.

King George

Baptized St Martin-in-the-Fields, London, 27 May 1724

Princess Gladys Glastonbury

Born Keynsham, Somerset, 1902

Viscount Heavican

Born Bury, Lancashire, 1890 (Bury, 1891 census)

Surgeon Kershaw

Born Basford, Nottinghamshire, 1860

King Lear

Born Kington Magna, Dorset, c.1898 (Kington Magna, 1901 census)

Czarina Podmore

Born Burslem, Staffordshire, c.1842 (Burslem, 1891 census)

Queen Prince

Died Chester, Cheshire, 1894

Marquis Marquis F. Puschart

Married St Saviour, London, 1892

Sirjohn Robinson

Baptized Old Church, St Pancras, London, 22 March 1796

Pope Smyrk
Married Brighton, East Sussex, 1907

Baron Tool
Married Scarborough, Yorkshire, 1855

Percy King Tutt
Born Highworth, Wiltshire, 1893
He was not named after King Tutankhamun, whose tomb was not discovered until 1922.

Queen Victoria
Born np, c.1840 (Edmonton, Middlesex, 1851 census)

General Washington
Born Halifax, Yorkshire, 1842

Prince Charles Whales
Born Mitford, Norfolk, 1899

King Wong
Married Liverpool, Lancashire, 1934
The film King Kong *had been released the previous year.*

Cardinal Woolsey
Born Croydon, Surrey, 1844

Lady Godiva A. Wright
Born Brixton, Devon, c.1849 (Plymouth, Devon, 1891 census)

◆

THE HUMAN GAZETTEER

Percy Stonehenge W. Ansell
Born St Olave, Southwark, London, 1874

Albania Ash
Born Penzance, Cornwall, 1900

Ann Gibraltar Billing
Born Liverpool, Lancashire, 1846

Armenia Binks
Born Westminster, London, 1869

Mont Blanc
Born np, c.1806; died Huddersfield, Yorkshire, 1881

Henry Barbados Bright
Married Lambeth, London, 1846

Argentina Bull
Born St Pancras, London, 1876

Tunis Butterfly
Baptized Wombourn, Staffordshire, 25 June 1686

Windsor Castle
Born Radford, Nottinghamshire, 1876

William Himalaya Chapman
Born Birmingham, Warwickshire, 1888

Burma Christmas
(Female) Born Hounslow, Middlesex, c.1843 (Brighton, Sussex, 1871 census)

Siberia Constable
Born Swansea, Glamorgan, 1838

Hampton Court
Born Wandsworth, London, 1868

Anglo America Craven
Born Keighley, Yorkshire, 1852

John Brent Cross
Died Clifton, Gloucestershire, 1845

Phila Delphia
Born np, Cornwall, 1840 (Buryan, Penwith, Cornwall, 1841 census)

Sarah Desert
Baptized St Leonard, Shoreditch, London, 1 April 1804

Tiny England
Born Chorlton, Lancashire, 1888
Not to be confused with Little Britain.

May Fair
Born Nantwich, Cheshire, 1880
The cockney pronunciation of 'Mayfair', one of London's smartest areas, gave rise to the title of the musical My Fair Lady.

Florida Fleetwood
Baptized Barkway, Hertfordshire, 1 November 1597

Robert Scunthorpe Free
Born Wisbech, Cambridgeshire, 1906

Arctic Franklin Gray
Born Barton-upon-Irwell, Lancashire, 1891
His name commemorates British Arctic explorer John Franklin, whose expedition was trapped in ice and perished in 1847.

Doris Instance Greenland
Born Pembroke, 1907

Atlas Hilton
(Male) Born Oldham, Lancashire, 1875

Australia Hilton
Married Barton-upon-Irwell, Lancashire, 1850

Ida Hoe
Born Chorlton, Lancashire, 1878

Phillip Ines
Born np, c.1821
(St Paul, Covent Garden, London, 1841 census)

River Jordan
Born Stoke-on-Trent, Staffordshire, 1860

Dover Mongolia R. T. Jose
Born Redruth, Cornwall, 1903

Edwin Singapore Keen
Married East Stonehouse, Devon, 1889

Mary Land
Baptized Taynton, Gloucestershire, 2 February 1599

Luther Denmark Longbottom
(Male) Born Silsden, Yorkshire, c.1848 (Silsden, 1881 census)

Iris Korea Ludlow
Born Dartford, Kent, 1904

Flushing Meadows
(Male) Born Shoreditch, London, 1878

Handel Moscow
Born Wakefield, Yorkshire, c.1857
(Sandal Magna, Yorkshire, 1901 census)

Ben Nevis
Born np, France, c.1845 (St Mary in the Castle, Hastings, Sussex, 1871 census)

Inconstant Hastings Ogle
Born Newcastle upon Tyne, Northumberland, 1852

Cold Pacific
(Female) Born Middlesex, c.1832 (Bow, London, 1881 census)

Tasmania Palfrey
Married Newport, Monmouthshire, 1882

Hyde Park
Died Kensington, London, 1864

Iceland Parrott
Born North Aylesford, Kent, 1872

Robert Hong Kong Phillips
Died Medway, Kent, 1846

Philadelphia Plenty
Baptized St Sepulchre, London, 11 May 1819

William Brazil Pratt
Born St Marylebone, London, 1847

Sweden Rich
(Male) Married Holborn, London, 1845

Heath Roe
(Male) Born Nottingham, c.1836 (Nottingham, 1841 census)

Lebanon Senior
Born Pontefract, Yorkshire, 1862

Indiana Sevil
Married Sherborne, Dorset, 1853

Minnie Sowter
Born Mansfield, Nottinghamshire, 1893

Ethiopia Maud Stemp
Born Guildford, Surrey, 1871

Tennie C. Street
(Female) Born np, Hampshire, c.1894
(Bournemouth, Hampshire, 1901 census)

Windermere Bigot Stringwell
Born np, c.1854; died Chorlton, Lancashire, 1881

Germany Swan
Married Whitechapel, London, 1888

Curly Tennessee
Born Shalford, Essex, c.1887
(West Ham, Essex, 1891 census)

James Afghanistan Tomblin
Born Leigh, Lancashire, 1880

Nan Tucket
Baptized Upton Pyne, Devon, 21 November 1790

Venice Waters
Married Barnet, Hertfordshire, 1850

Isla White
Born London, c.1846
(Aveley, Essex, 1851 census)

Holly Wood
Born Faversham, Kent, 1901

A Boy Named Sue

Although relatively rare, there are a number of examples of children who, for one reason or another (often the obsequiousness of a parent), ended up with a transgender name.

Male

Queen Arthur
Born Dumfries, c.1861
(Preston, Lancashire, 1891 census)

Deborah Brown
Son of Richard and Rebecca Brown,
born np, Worcestershire, c.1889
(Brierley Hill, Staffordshire, 1891 census)

Fanny Duckhouse
Son of Samuel Duckhouse, born Bloxwich,
Staffordshire, c.1896
(Wolverhampton, 1901 census)

Lord Anne Hamilton
Son of the 4th Duke of Hamilton, born 12 October 1709
Anne was named after his godmother, Queen Anne.

Caroline Robert Herbert
Son of Thomas Herbert, 8th Earl of Pembroke, born 28 September 1751
Caroline was the godson of Queen Caroline.

Sir Frederick Anne Hervey
Born np, 18 June 1783; died 20 September 1824

Sue Yates
Son of Thomas Yates, born Huddersfield, Yorkshire, c.1847
(Salford, Lancashire, 1871 census)

Female

Nigel E. Bebb
Daughter of Ann Bebb, born Little Hereford, Herefordshire, c.1897
(Little Hereford, 1901 census)

Dorothy Tony Blair
Born Altrincham, Cheshire, 1889

Noah Brittain
Daughter of Albert and Emely [sic] Brittain,
born Patricroft, Lancashire, c.1895 (Eccles, Lancashire, 1901 census)
*A female Noah has biblical authority: Noah was one of the
daughters of Zelophehad, Numbers 36:11.*

Jude Dustman
Married Michael Fox, Old Church, St Pancras, London, 29 September 1828

Reginald Partridge
Born Odell, Bedfordshire, c.1885 (Odell, 1891 census)

Frederick Ann Payne
Daughter of Thomas and Mary Ann Payne, born Liverpool, Lancashire, c.1856
(West Derby, Lancashire, 1871 census)

Douglas Sheffield
Daughter of Sir John Sheffield, born Milgrave, Lincolnshire c.1612

Philip Speke
Daughter of George Speke, born np, c.1663

Percy Steak
Married Michael Warrant, St Nicholas, Great Yarmouth,
Norfolk, 23 February 1796

Lawrence Anna Yawn
Born Chertsey, Surrey, 1901 (Chertsey, 1901 census)

MADE FOR EACH OTHER

◆

Just as the phenomenon of nominative determinism seems to compel people to work in professions appropriate to their names, so there is a kind of marital determinism that leads people with apt (or otherwise) surnames to end up together:

Aston–Martin

Karen N. Aston married Jonathan R. Martin, York, 1997
One of six Aston–Martin marriages in the period 1987–2002.

Axe–Killer

William Axe married Mary Killer, Ashbourne, Derbyshire, 1914

Batty–Ball

Fred Batty married Clara J. Ball, Ashton-under-Lyne, Lancashire, 1915

Beach–Ball

John Beach married Jane Ball, St Pancras, London, 16 August 1825

Bell–Bottoms

William S. Bell married Barbara A. Bottoms, Chester-le-Street, Durham, 1912

Bird–Nest

John Bird married Margaret Nest, Hopton Wafers, Shropshire, 6 May 1810

Bull–Bush

Frederick C. Bull married Emma E. Bush, Shoreditch, London, 1915

Butt–Payne

Bernard F. Butt married Elizabeth S. Payne, Wandsworth, London, 1915

Cannon–Ball

Ann Cannon married John Ball, St Saviour, Southwark, London, 1830

Carr–Park

David H. Carr married Ethel F. Park, Barrow-in-Furness, Cumbria, 1913

Cock–Ball

Matthew Cock married Phylis H. M. Ball, Farnham, Hampshire, 1924

Cock–Roach

Hannah Cock married Thomas Roach, Burnley, Yorkshire, 1912

Crapp–Beer

Beatrice E. Crapp married William G. Beer, Devonport, Devon, 1920

Day–Light

Elizabeth M. Day married Albert F. Light, Edmonton, Middlesex, 1919

Dick–Holder

Lynette S. Dick married Martin Holder, Northampton, 1997

Fish–Pye

Elizabeth Fish married Charles Pye, Bolton, Manchester, 1927

Flower–Power

Carl E. V. Flower married Rebecca B. J. Power, Dudley, West Midlands, 1996

Fucks–Allott

George Fucks married Alice Allott, Thurmaston, Leicestershire, 1764

Goody–Goody

Jill E. Goody married David D. Goody, Halifax, Yorkshire, 1986

Hand–Baggs

William G. Hand married Mildred Baggs, Wimborne, Dorset, 1925

Handy–Cappe

William Handy married Anne Cappe, Butlers Marston,
Warwickshire, 26 October 1803

Hard–Cocks

Keith A. Hard married Jennifer A. Cocks, Surrey, 1989

Hare–Brain

Deborah K. Hare married Ian M. Brain, Halifax, Yorkshire, 1988

Holmes–Watson

Abraham Holmes married Mary E. Watson, Keighley, Yorkshire, 1915
One of seven Holmes–Watson marriages 1912–15.

Hunny–Bear

Hugh Hunny married Susanna Bear, St Endellion, Cornwall, 11 February 1701

James–Bond
John James married Margaret Bond, Chesterfield, Derbyshire, 1913

King–Kong
Jeremy B. King married Rosalyn L. Kong, Sodbury, Gloucestershire, 1989

Large–Butt
Lottie L. Large married Francis H. Butt, Cirencester, Gloucestershire, 1913

Lea–King
Annie Lea married George King, Birkenhead, Cheshire, 1915

Little–Cock
Maud Little married William J. Cock, St Columb, Cornwall, 1925

May–Pole
Deborah May married Keith Pole, Pontefract, Yorkshire, August 2005

Money–Penny
Ernest J. Money married Annie S. Penny, Chorlton, Lancashire, 1922

Morris–Dance
Nora M. Morris married Francis D. Dance, Basford, Nottinghamshire, 1919

Needle–Cotton
Gary J. W. Needle married Samantha L. Cotton, Rochdale, Lancashire, 2002

Pain–Arsley
Robert Pain married Eleanor Arsley, Codsall, Staffordshire, 2 August 1778

Quack–Quack
Margaret E. Quack married Harold H. K. Quack, Liverpool, Lancashire, 1913

Quick–Lay
Paul R. Quick married Sara E. Lay, Cambridge, 1989

Ring–Bell
Elizabeth M. Ring married Matthew D. Bell, Todmorden, Yorkshire, 1997

Rollings–Stone
Andrea Rollings married Stephen J. Stone, St Austell, Cornwall, 1991

Sargeant–Major
Edwin Sargeant married Catherine R. Major, Brentford, Middlesex, 1912

Sargent–Pepper

Charles Sargent married Lucy Pepper, Aston, Warwickshire, 1916

Shave–Bush

John Shave married Fiona V. Bush, Bournemouth, Hampshire, 1985

Shepherd–Pye

Mark A. Shepherd married Astrid R. Pye, Canterbury, 1993

Sherlock–Holmes

John Sherlock married Florence Holmes, Wolstanton, Staffordshire, 1921

Snow–Mann

Florence M. Snow married Conrad A. Mann, Tendring, Essex, 1919

Street–Walker

Florence Street married Frederick Walker, Wolverhampton, Staffordshire, 1913

Summers–Day

George C. Summers married Rosetta Day, Colchester, Essex, 1918

Sun–Tan

Jian H. Sun married Koi E. Tan, Lewes, East Sussex, 2003

Wall–Flower

George Wall married Sarah Flower, Langar Cum Barnston,
Nottinghamshire, 11 October 1714

Wang–King

Yuan Y. Wang married John G. King, Kensington & Chelsea, London, 1997

Warren–Peace

Alison Warren married Andrew J. Peace, Chichester, West Sussex, 2000

Whyte–Pants

Joyce Whyte married Rogar [sic] Pants, Allhallows London Wall, 7 October 1652

Wolf–Fox

George Wolf married Elizabeth Fox, Humberstone,
Leicestershire, 30 November 1773

Wright–Wong

Billy D. Wright married Vanessa J. Wong, Tunbridge Wells, Kent, 1988

TECHNO BABEL

◆

Windows Aldridge
Born Staines, Middlesex, c.1848 (Staines, 1861 census)

Elizabeth Backup
Married South Leith, Midlothian, 11 November 1708

Sarah Blog Baker
Married East Stonehouse, Devon, 1839

Wiki Baldwin
(Male) Born np, Middlesex, c.1839 (Holborn, London, 1841 census)

James Fax Bee
Born Fosdyke Fen, Lincolnshire, c.1835 (Boston, Lincolnshire, 1851 census)

Samson Blog
Born Whitechapel, London, 1893

William Broadband
Baptized South Leith, Midlothian, 4 October 1660

Cy Burnett
Born Newport, Monmouthshire, 1900

Elizabeth Byte
Married Robert Whittle, Standish, Lancashire, 1 August 1586

Mary Cordless
Born np, c.1817; died Manchester, Lancashire, 1874

Telegraph Dick
Born np, c.1844; died Bishop Auckland, Durham, 1877

Mary Ann Elizabeth Diskette
Born Plymouth, Devon, 1837

Nancy M. S. Dos
Born np, 1914; died South Warwickshire, 2001

Henry Ebay
Born Southwark, London, c.1861 (Lambeth, London, 1901 census)

Temperantia Google
Baptized Aldborough, Norfolk, 13 August 1598

William Hardisk
Died Knaresborough, Yorkshire, 1851

Jane Java
Born Whitechapel, London, 1893

Minnie Macro
Baptized Bolney, Sussex, 30 June 1895

E. Mail
Born Malmesbury, Wiltshire, 1855

Ann Mobile
Baptized Deddington, Oxfordshire, 21 March 1730

Priscilla Monitor
Died St Marylebone, London, 1840

Ann Ode
Born West Derby, Lancashire, 1846

Cath Ode
Born Wigan, Lancashire, 1898

Lincoln Phone
Baptized Melksham, Wiltshire, 18 February 1803

Elizabeth Pixel
Married William Harford, Kinver, Staffordshire, 19 July 1695

I. Pod
(Male) Baptized Whatfield, Suffolk, 20 May 1638

Philip Radar
Born Stepney, London, 1888

Anna Robot
Born np, Germany c.1821 (St George Hanover Square, London, 1851 census)
*The word 'robot' was invented by Czech writer Karel Capek in
his play R.U.R. (Rossum's Universal Robots) (1920), which
was translated into English in 1928.*

Marmaduke Router
Married Elizabeth Worborn, Copgrove, Yorkshire, 26 November 1723

Alys Skype
Baptized St James Garlickhythe, London, 15 May 1560

William Spam
Baptized St Bride's Fleet Street, London, 10 June 1607

Minnie Satellite Spry
Born Sheppey, Kent, 1883

Thomas Text
Born Bourne, Lincolnshire, 1887

Video Thompson
(Female) Born Montevideo, Uruguay, c.1872
(Liverpool, Lancashire, 1881 census)

T. Vee
(Male) Born Boston, Lincolnshire, c.1804
(Skirbeck, Lincolnshire, 1851 census)

Thomas Quark Vernon
Born West Derby, Lancashire, 1901

Whiro Wiki
Born np, c.1896; died Chertsey, Surrey, 1918

Chapter Nine

THE SAGA CONTINUES

The following is a selection of unusual surnames and given names recorded in birth, marriage and death registers in recent years. As with the preceding entries, they are all true, but details have been omitted to preserve their anonymity – though how anonymous can you be if you are called Lollipop or Frisbee?

Delta Molybdenum Abbott

Tina Ager

Ryan Air

X. Rae Alberts

Desiree Skylark Alder

Precious Dollars M. Allsopp

Nonita B. Aspirin

Chris P. Bacon

Jenna Crystal Ball

Leanne Crystal J. Ball

Queen Goddess C. C. Davis-Ferdant Bartley

Ferrari Porsche Beard

Unique Keanu S. Bee

Luxury Lupin Bell

Eva Bendova

Mercedes Bent

Mercedes Bentley

Daisee Treacle Berridge

Brandon Bigone

Grace Tallulah Bigun

Anal M. Bile

Brandon Bin-Matt

Charlie Love Bird

Huckleberry Banjo Bladwell

Tick H. Bong

Amelia Delicious Bosomworth

Emily Jordan Bosomworth

Jedidah A. Breakfast

Calamity Therese Brent

Koala E. Broadfoot

Chromium Brown

Harry Fabulous Brown

Perry Alpachino Brown

Umbra' Moon N. Buntman

Hope Masie Burns

Aaron Lamborghini M. Burris

Shaun Bush

Anus Asif Butt

Arslan Butt

Sphinx Charnley

Bamboo Cheeseman

Austin Chicken

Georgina Crystal Clear

Francesca Coconut Coby

Juliet Cock

Phlegon J. Cocksedge

Dylan Oxford United Collins

Hobbit J. Coward

Frontera Porsche Ford-Nolcini Cray

Ebenezer Hedgehog T. Cringebottom

Lex Luther Crumb

Icicle Star Crumplin

Possible Dadson Dadson

Savannah Marijuana S. Daly

Nemesis Dark

Sunny Day

Katrina Demeanour

Ben Photon Denton

Attila F. Dervish

Poppy Bizarre S. Devereux

Bubacar Junior Diallo-Brookes

Sigourney May Gay Dibble

Anita Dick

Cairo Devontae A. Digital

Lynne C. Doyle

Ruby Slippers Doyle

Epiphany Dring

Piers Morgan Driver

Philip Efuk

Sundance Starmoon S. Elgar

Alchemist-Jinade Leon D. Ellick

Pepsi Chantel Elliott

Atilla Albatros [sic] Emin

Bianca Marie England

Celestial Tranquillity-Te Ericsson-Zenith

Good Evans

Stephen Desire A. Fanny

U. First

Scooter J. Foody

Chanelle Paris France

Princess Diana Frempong

Fiona Friend

Czar David Frost

Amber Fudge

Deborah Fuxall

Ellie Gant

Kraken James Gardiner

Buster Beowulf Ratcliffe Van Der Geest

Caprice Porsche Geisha

Tucker Capability Gibbs

Elizabeth Ecstacy Girling

Ocean Tsunami Golden

Ruby Eskimo Grey

Cool Rembrandt Bontrop Gringhuis

Spike Lion James Hagan – *the brother of:*

Tex Tiger Alice Hagan

Solomon Magick Hamman-Smith

Solomon Wolff Hammer

Laurel Olivia Hardy

Finn Vast Harrigan

Paris Harris

Zirconia-Sapphire Estella B. P. Havisham-Hooper

Zeus He He

Buick Wildcat Hearmon

Popeye Spike Heffernan

Heidi Heidt

Khadence Heritage

Porsche Carrera Hobday

Pelican River Hogg

Abba Blue Hood

Wendy House

William Incredible S. Hudghton

Phil Mike Hunt

Tequilla Sunrise M. Huntley

Albert Einstein Huynh

Tanya Hyde

Flint Inker

Rapunzel Hannah Inskip

Lyron Android Johnson

Indiana Jones

Babegirl Nicole Ruth Jones

Harry Houdini Junior

Mojo Marmalade M. M. Kenward

Ewan Kerr

Quorum Scorpion B. Kevan

Shay King

Precious Kinky

Brittany Merin Knickerbocker

Jedi Key-Ras-Tafari S. Knight

Maserati Lam

Lorraine Popoola Leak

Chandler Lear

Ivor Bigboy Lee

Zsi Zsi A. Le Scrooge

Joshua Luscious R. Levavasseur

Raphaella Bobcat J. Lewis

Ami Summer Loving

Alchemy Arcadia K. Lucas

Amanda Lynn

Sally Mander

Abbi Calamity Mansbridge

Treacle Tesni Manwaring

Sal Monella

Trudy Moody

Fay Mousley

Rowan Chaos T. Myles-Wildgoose

Reality Iceline L. Nash

Orapin Nonthing

Gladys Ofuka

Goodluck Brick Ogbogbo

Jennifer Caitlain O'nions

Radar Oo

Twinkle Patel

Hatty Pattie

Drew Peacock

Emmaline Purple X. Pegrum-Haram

Harvey Blue Peters

Jack Stingray Petley

Casey Pancake Pickup

Atlanta Ocean C. Pink

Jowell Dwayne Piper

Coco Pope

Cheree Pye

Tarzan Elvis Quennell

Dawn Raid

Lollipop Mae Richardson

Slayhne El Nasty Robinson

Romeo Casanova Romaeo (*brother to Venus Valentine, Angel Aphrodite, Isis Ise, Achilles Spartacus Mars and Caesar Augustus Constantine Romaeo*)

Vicky Ruff-Cock

Gonad Saghir

Frisbee C. C. Sheffield

Ray Sing

Pollyanna Sparkle M. Smallpeice [*sic*]

Cezanne Smith

Glorious Smith

Lolita Bambi Smith

Porsche Carrera Smith

Stumpy Smith

Yawn H. H. Smith

Junior Snook

Zenier Snowball Snowball

Dinah Soare

Salmon Ella Rachel Spielmen

Chevallier Sinbad W. Squirrell

Coursamy Suckalingum

Lew Swires

Confetti Ngounou Tabe

Yumi Takeshita

Keia Yellow Thrower

Platinum Che'yrael Townsend
Anas Turki
Gabriella Truffle Turner
Jago Pirate Turner
Alyse Geranique Turnipseed
Matilda Jean Footprint Tustin
Phoenix Claw Unicorn
Valour Vespasian Vanglaive
Porsche Mercedes Wallis
Jasmine May Wee
Auk Welch
Doctor Who
Brian Junior O. Willybiro
Jemima Atomic Wilson
Ocean Storm Wise
Fidel Castro Woodcraft
Quasimodo W. T. Yeung
Trinity Star Zammit
Harry Zona

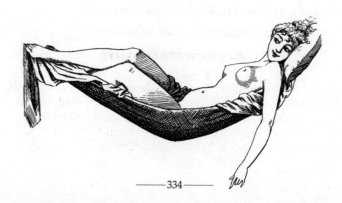

FURTHER READING

Although the subject of unusual British names is mentioned in passing in numerous general books on names, this is the first book devoted to the subject. There is therefore no bibliography as such, but I would like to pay tribute to some nineteenth-century writers who observed the phenomenon of odd names, notably:

In an uncharacteristic display of humour for an official publication, the *Sixteenth Annual Report of the Registrar-General of Births, Deaths, and Marriages in England* (London: HMSO, 1856) included 'A list of peculiar surnames in England and Wales, selected from the Indexes of Births registered in the Quarter ending 31st March 1851, and of Deaths registered in the corresponding Quarter of 1853.'

Names that form themes (food, animals, musical instruments and so on) were identified and listed by the Lewes antiquarian Mark Antony Lower in his magisterial *Patronymica Britannica: A Dictionary of the Family Names of the United Kingdom* (Lewes: G. P. Bacon, 1860) and by Christopher Legge Lordan of Romsey in his *Of Certain English Surnames and their Occasional Odd Phases When Seen in Groups* (London: Houlston & Sons, 1874).

In 1892, Allen Batchelor, a Guildford hairdresser and umbrella-maker, published a poster featuring *An Alphabetical List of Over 2200 Curious Surnames of Her Majesty's Subjects,* 'especially adapted for education in all places where the working classes assemble, such as Coffee and Dining Rooms, Institutions, Inns, Public Houses, Solicitors' and other Offices, Political Clubs, and especially at Railway Stations'. (It's good to know that Victorian plebs could be educated as they waited for their trains.)

Charles Wareing Bardsley, *Curiosities of Puritan Nomenclature* (London: Chatto & Windus, 1897) is an exhaustive survey of all those Praise-god and Fly-fornication names.

ACKNOWLEDGEMENTS

Warm thanks to my family, Caroline, Alexander and Nicholas Ash, Felicity and Julian Page, my agent John Saddler, Val Hudson and Lorraine Jerram at Headline, who have all encouraged me in the project – despite my endlessly presenting them with yet another strange name and asking, 'What do you think of this?' To their names, I should like to add those of Helen Bickley, Nicholas Clee, Paul Dickson, Robert Easton, Matt Evenden, Cassie and Rory Fairhead, Nicolette Jones, Robin Marlow, Virginia Nicholson, Allison Pearson, Sandy Pratt, Barry Simner, Augusta Skidelsky and Howard Spencer.

Thanks are also due to Gerry Toop and the staff of the National Archives and Family Record Centre and the many county record offices and their dedicated archivists and researchers – especially those with senses of humour*. They include: Bedfordshire – James Collett-White; Cambridgeshire – Gill Shapland; Cheshire – Caroline Picco; Cumbria – David Bowcock; Devon – Renée Jackaman; Dorset – A. Munro; Gloucestershire – Pauline Nash; Herefordshire – John Harnden; Hertfordshire – Bonnie West; Isle of Wight – Richard Smout; Lancashire – John Benson; Lincolnshire – Mike Rogers; Norfolk – Claire Bolster; Northamptonshire – Eleanor Winyard; Nottinghamshire – William Bell; Pembrokeshire – Nikki Bosworth; Shropshire – Alison Healey; Somerset – Liz Grant; Suffolk – Dave Feakes; West Sussex – Richard Childs.

The Cornwall Record Office deserves special mention for its inspirational 'Silly Names List', compiled by archivist Renée Jackaman (now at the Devon Record Office). Although this has since been removed from the CRO website, I am grateful to Renée for granting permission for it to appear on mine – see: www.RussellAsh.com/CornwallSillyNames

And finally, all the volunteers who have valiantly (and sometimes imaginatively) transcribed often almost indecipherable records.

Some failed to get the joke: I was assured that no one in the Isle of Man has ever had a silly name – so Arsey Cubbin, Rob Fuck and Easter Loony are clearly considered commonplace thereabouts.
**Fanny End, died Reading, Berkshire, 1865*